SCAFFOLDING THE LANGUAGE OF POWER

SCAFFOLDING THE LANGUAGE OF POWER

An Apprenticeship in Writing at the Doctoral Level

Kathryn Strom

Editorial design and graphic content by Sheldon McV

To Ana Maria,
My academic mom.

I can never truly express my appreciation
for your mentoring and wisdom
(and, of course, all your editing help).

Acknowledgements

Deleuze and Guattari (1987, p. 1) say that a book is not "subject or object." It is not just a book, in and of itself, nor is it attributable to an author—it is an assemblage of human and nonhuman, discursive and material elements. This one is no exception. I would never have been able to complete this book were it not for many people, ideas, and spaces.

I am so, so grateful for the teaching and mentorship of Ana Maria Villegas and Tamara Lucas. Tamara, thank you for being the first to introduce me to the idea of systemic functional linguistics and embedding writing supports in doctoral courses. Ana Maria, not only have I learned so much about the "moves" of academic writing from you, but you have generously continued to mentor me, year after year, paper after paper. I cannot adequately express how much it means that you made time to read every chapter of this book—sometimes twice—and provide constructive, affirmative feedback. Quite simply, this book would not have been possible without you.

I also owe a debt of gratitude to my colleagues, Kathryn Hayes and Mari Gray, who, over the last decade, spent an enormous amount of time discussing the elements and tasks of doctoral level writing and how to teach it in affirmative, highly supportive ways. I am so fortunate to work with such brilliant, kind humans.

I was also lucky enough to have several of my EdD students (now EdD graduates!) read chapters of this book and offer suggestions and encouragement. A huge thanks to Sarah Ansari, Ari Dolid, Jennifer Edens, and Winnie Kwofie. I also send a heart-felt thank you to friends who happened to be doctoral students while I was writing this and volunteered to serve as beta readers: Dee Lagomarsino, Charlotte Marshall, and Adrienne Kitchin.

Finally, a big hug and kiss to the most important people in my life: my mom, Jeanne Sellers, who is forever my most enthusiastic supporter and always knows the right thing to say, whether advice or encouragement; and my husband, Mike Strom, who is good at all the things I'm not and took care of them without complaint (mostly) this past year so I could get this book finally finished. I love you!

About This Book

This book represents almost a decade of my own thinking about scaffolding doctoral writing in affirmative and pragmatic ways. Many of the activities and examples are drawn from lessons I embedded in my courses in the Educational Leadership for Social Justice EdD program at California State University, East Bay. I wrote it with the average EdD student in mind, but PhD students in most humanities or social sciences disciplines, if they are conducting empirical studies, will also benefit from this book; as will those in any discipline conducting qualitative research.

The first chapter in this book provides a general introduction to writing at the doctoral level and explains the theoretical, linguistic, and pedagogical ideas that inform the book. The second and third chapters provide an orientation to six of the central "rules" of academic writing at the doctoral level. Each of the subsequent chapters (four through nine) takes on a major task of the dissertation (problem statement, literature review, theoretical framework, methodology, findings, and discussion). Although all chapters beyond the first have opportunities to practice what you are learning, the "dissertation" chapters (chapter four through nine) offer a carefully sequenced path with activities that build on each other to help you construct the actual pieces of your dissertation.

Because my approach to writing as scaffolding is relatively novel, I often rely on excerpts from my own work to deconstruct and illustrate ideas and demonstrate skills. Because you will see so much of it, let me give a bit of an introduction to my research. I use a range of complex theoretical perspectives to examine how teachers translate their pedagogical learning into classroom instructional practice. By "complex perspectives," I refer to a set of theories that generally take a complex systems perspective that sees the world and everything in it as connected, interdependent, and constantly changing; and see reality as "emergent" as something that is created by the system as a whole (rather than by single individuals). Applied to teaching, this means that teachers are part of classroom and larger school systems, and she interacts with lots of things, including humans (students, other teachers, parents), materialities (physical spaces, textbooks, computers), contextual conditions (local school climate and culture, bell schedules, funding), sociopolitical conditions (demographics, income levels, district policies) and so on. All of these factors collectively shape or influence how she translates her learning into practice.

In addition to examples from my published writing and dissertation, I also feature lots of examples (especially in the later chapters) from my own doctoral students—with their blessing, of course. I hope that you enjoy seeing some of the "behind the scenes" work that goes into writing an actual doctoral dissertation, courtesy of several of our graduates.

I'd like you to keep a few things in mind as you begin this book. One, if you read the chapters straight through, it will likely be overwhelming. Many of the chapters contain an entire semester's worth (or more) of content and exercises. As such, they are not meant to be read in one sitting. Instead, try to complete just one numbered chapter section at a time. Then, step away and do some reading/

thinking before you move on to the next portion of the chapter.

Second, learning is always more powerful when it involves others. If you are not using this book as part of a class, try to recruit another doctoral student as a partner to discuss the examples and exercises throughout this book. That also goes for dissertation writing more generally: although the dissertation is (typically) an individually written product, you do not have to do it in isolation. You can and should form writing partnerships and groups for support along the way.

Finally, I want to emphasize that there are many legitimate ways to approach doctoral-level writing. This book presents one particular view—one that my EdD students have found helpful as they complete our fast-paced three-year doctoral program. But it is not *the way* (*in my best Mandalorian voice*). It is *a way.* As I will discuss further in the first chapter, there is no such thing as "the" way to write (or use language). Because we speak from where we are (or write from where we are, as the case may be), writing is not neutral nor one-size-fits all. The writing approach in this book is informed by my positionalities and multiple other dimensions, including my qualitative methodological orientation, critical-complex perspectives of the world, ideas about writing-as-scaffolding, and overall pragmatic approach.

You also bring a whole constellation of identities, experiences, beliefs, and intentions that will shape your writing. You can and should treat the ideas in this book as a minimum, and work with them, make them your own, to find a form of expression that feels authentic to you.

Happy writing!

Table of Contents

1

Introduction: A Three-Pronged Approach to Writing at the Doctoral Level

Contents

Introduction

Think back to your K-12 (or primary/secondary) education.

Do you remember your teacher, another adult, a peer, or maybe even you yourself, ever referring to a "proper" or "correct" way to speak or write?

Consider that for a moment.

What does it mean to speak properly or correctly? Who would you be speaking like? Who would you *not* be speaking like?

What are the characteristics of this "proper" or "correct" language? What does it sound and look like?

And who decided what is proper or correct—and what isn't—to begin with?

Now, think about the language you used at home with your family or in your community when growing up. How alike or different was it from "proper" English? How did that similarity or difference make you feel? If the language you used at home was different, can you recall specific moments when that difference became apparent? What was the impact of that, emotionally or academically?

One of the foundational ideas in this book is that there is no such thing as "proper" language or "proper" English. Although language and literacy are often presented in a black-and-white, right-or-wrong fashion, in reality, no *inherently* correct way to speak or write exists. Language is simply a system of communication that operates by rules, and those rules change over time. No rule-based system of communication has more intrinsic value over another.

But this does not mean that language is neutral. Although no form of language is inherently more correct than another, there *are* types of speaking and writing that are more socially and culturally valued. We have to be careful not to confuse *sociocultural value* with *inherent superiority.* In other words, just because a particular form of language is valued above others in a particular society does not mean it is better. It simply means that groups with social power have successfully imposed their own mode of speaking and writing on all others (and used their power to label it superior). Because of this imposition, even though particular oral or written literacies are not inherently more correct than other forms, they tend to have a major impact on students' academic trajectories and self-image.

So, just how is it that the way of speaking and writing of the socially dominant group came to be regarded as the most socially valued? To answer this question requires an understanding that *language is bound up with power.* Those socially valued forms of language are almost always the cultural expressions of the power group (which in the western world, is usually white, male, cis-hetero people).

Accordingly, the language we use in school is considered "proper" not because it is inherently better than other linguistic forms, but because those who are in power make and enforce the rules of social institutions (including schools). Therefore, some scholars have called academic language (i.e., the type of language that is deemed "proper" or "correct" in schools, which is the English spoken by middle-class/affluent white people) *the language of power.*

This book takes on academic writing at the doctoral level, or the language of power in academia, as a specific genre of writing. My goal is to provide a pragmatic, hands-on guide to help you learn about the specific tasks of this genre and, ultimately, build out the chapters of your dissertation. The ideas and activities in the book were developed from my own teaching over the last decade and have all been piloted by my own doctoral students (some of whom you will get to meet when I use examples from their dissertations in later chapters).

In this chapter, I describe the three theoretical strands that inform the approach I take to doctoral-level writing in this book. The first strand is *critical theory,* a central aspect of which is the culture of power. From this perspective, education, as a social institution, reproduces social inequities. A critical theory vantage point sheds light on language as a lever of institutional power that keeps the academy (and its valued knowledge and practices) white and male. This first strand reflects my belief that writing at the doctoral level is, at its heart, a social justice endeavor.

The second strand highlights key ideas from systemic functional linguistics, which offers a pragmatic set of tools for learning doctoral-level writing while simultaneously making visible the "rules" of the language of power. The third strand builds on central ideas in sociocultural theories of learning, which provides support for apprenticing into doctoral-level patterns of writing, as I offer in this book. The two latter strands offer specific, supportive methods to carry out a social justice agenda of helping learners of diverse backgrounds to succeed in their doctoral studies. These kinds of supports not only can diversify the population of educational leaders and scholars, but also the very knowledges produced by research.

1.1 A Critical Approach to Doctoral-Level Literacy: Social Justice and The Language of Power

According to dominant western worldviews, our reality is considered neutral and objective. The conditions of the world just *are.* If teachers with this dominant perspective were to be asked "Why is 'proper' English considered proper?" they would probably respond with a variation of, "Because that's just the way it is."

In a neutral, objective world, individuals are more or less assumed to have complete agency and free will to choose what they do. By extension, we could say that because individuals can choose to do as they wish, they are fully responsible for their circumstances.

In the United States, this idea is supported by a *meritocratic* understanding of educational and life outcomes: those who work hard in school will gain knowledge and skills which will pave the way for prosperous careers and a high quality of life. Conversely, using this way of thinking, we could reason that inequities like living in poverty are consequences that stem from individual students who make a personal choice not to work hard. That is, inequities are the fault of the individuals who experience them. To solve the problem, we can conclude, the affected individuals need to "pull themselves up by their own bootstraps," as the saying goes.

Critical perspectives in education present an alternative to this dominant perspective. Drawing largely from ideas promoted by Karl Marx and then extended by the group of theorists known as the Frankfurt school of critical theory (Giroux, 2009), critical theory takes the starting point that the world is not neutral or objective, nor does it operate by means of individual human agency. It is *political* and *composed of systems* that are actively shaped by people as well as history, culture, and social relationships.

All these human and nonhuman factors work together in particular ways to create power imbalances between groups of people (that is, they create dominant and subordinate social groups). This premise–that reality is both political and systemic–helps us arrive at one of the basic assertions of critical theory: that inequalities are not just a given, nor are they the result of individual choices, as the widely accepted meritocratic ideology might suggest. Instead, inequalities are created and maintained through *social reproduction*, or the systemic processes by which the dominant group (i.e., white, cis-het, able-bodied, academic English-speaking men) manipulate social institutions or systems to maintain power (Bourdieu, 1973).

Social Reproduction

Our education system, including schools and universities, plays a central role in social reproduction. For example, much of the U.S. operates on a geographically-determined public schooling system in which students are assigned to specific schools based on their zip code. Depending on where they live (and the corresponding income level), students may have very different educational experiences.

Students living in higher-income neighborhoods (which tend to be populated by a mostly white, native English-speaking population) attend schools that are funded at higher levels and have access to more expansive resources, fully-credentialed teachers, lower teacher and leadership attrition rates, safer campuses with newer equipment, more honors and AP classes, more electives, more comprehensive special education services and college counseling, and so on. The parents of students in these schools tend to have professional or "white collar" jobs with flexible hours, allowing a greater level of engagement at and with their child's school (because many parent engagement opportunities require daytime availability).

In contrast, schools in lower-income areas–which also tend to serve more students of color and multilingual learners–are typically funded at lower rates, and are more likely to have more inexperienced or underprepared teachers, higher attrition rates for teachers and leaders, fewer resources and services, fewer AP/honors classes, and campuses with older or temporary buildings and equipment. Parents are less likely to be engaged at their children's schools because their hourly-wages or "blue collar" jobs give them little time flexibility; and they themselves often experience language and cultural barriers and/or have undocumented immigration status.

These contrasting conditions reinforce and expand social inequities. Students in higher income areas have access to educational conditions that, broadly speaking, open opportunities to college and professional careers, helping them maintain their class status of origin. Meanwhile, students in lower-income areas are subject to inferior conditions that serve as barriers for post-secondary education and higher-paying careers. Working in tandem with other socio-economic and cultural-historic factors, these conditions help reproduce cycles of generational poverty.

However, zip codes–and their impact on school funding, or lack thereof–are just one mechanism of social reproduction.

Another is language.

Let's look more closely at how modes of literacy function as mechanisms of social reproduction.

Language as Social Reproduction

While the type of literacy doctoral students need to successfully complete their doctorates can be considered its own ***genre*** (more on this in a bit), it builds on the foundation of general academic language (that is, the language that tends to be valued in educational settings, beginning with primary school). Because academic language more closely matches the literacy patterns of the white middle or affluent classes, children belonging to this sociocultural group arrive at school *already socialized* into these patterns.

This prior socialization does not automatically ensure their success, of course. But because the language of school is built on linguistic patterns they already are familiar with, these students do have a tangible advantage over youth from non-dominant groups (Delpit, 1988/2006). And, as privileged classes move through K-12 schooling and into college and graduate school, these patterns of success become magnified as they build on the linguistic foundation they already possess. This trend is amplified further by white middle class/affluent students' access to higher quality schooling and other economic and sociopolitical advantages that accumulate exponentially over time (Ladson-Billings, 2006).

The impact of academic literacy is not limited to academic outcomes, however. Bound up with this academic dimension of language, yet often overlooked, is its impact on student identity and self-confidence. Whether we realize it or not, language is an important part of one's identity, and learners who have their home and communal patterns of speaking, reading, and writing validated throughout their schooling are more apt to develop an affirming relation to academic language (and by extension to school in general). Conversely, learners from minoritized backgrounds who are told over time, explicitly or implicitly, that the linguistic resources they bring from their homes and communities are not valued in school are at high risk of internalizing feelings of inferiority, which can affect their academic confidence.

Every year, I see the damaging effects of this institutionalized language discrimination on students manifest as writing paralysis, impostor syndrome, and intense frustration with instructor feedback. Without question, learning doctoral-level literacies is a difficult endeavor for all students, even those from mainstream backgrounds. But for students from historically marginalized groups, the struggle with academic writing is often accompanied by acute emotional and mental anguish as well.

Although competency in writing at the doctoral level is absolutely crucial to successfully completing the dissertation (a prerequisite for obtaining a doctoral degree), most doctoral programs fail to focus on explicit writing instruction. Because writing at a doctoral level is necessary for success, but not specifically taught, the skills involved become part of the "hidden curriculum" (Jackson, 1968, cited in Giroux & Penna, 1979) of doctoral education.

Because white middle class/affluent students tend to enter their doctoral programs with access to the language of schooling (an important foundation for doctoral-level literacies), many are able to bridge into the necessary skills. However, for those who experience discomfort with these culturally-specific language patterns, language at the doctoral level becomes an exclusionary mechanism—one of the above-mentioned levers that keeps people from non-dominant groups (e.g., Black and Indigenous people of color) from achieving their doctorates. This, in turn, keeps positions of power where doctorates are often needed, like superintendencies, white and mostly male.

Doctoral-level language also works as one of the gatekeeping devices that perpetuates inequities in academia (Lillis & Tuck, 2016). Universities have historically generated most research (i.e., knowledge)—and because our positionalities shape our ways of knowing (Haraway, 1988), the knowledge that has been produced over time, and today informs practice and policy, reflects that of a mainly white and male perspective (Braidotti, 2013). Put another way: doctoral level language functions as an institutionalized lever of power that perpetuates white/male knowledge and ways of being as "proper," and as such upholds white heteropatriarchal supremacy in every aspect of our school system and larger society.

Lisa Delpit (1988/2006) offers a concept to help us understand how these inequity-maintaining mechanisms operate at the classroom level. She refers to this idea as ***the culture of power.***

According to Delpit, classroom activity is mediated by power relations, and those power relations operate according to rules established by the dominant culture (white middle class/affluent people). If you know the rules, you have access to power, and if you do not know or are only vaguely familiar with them, you are denied access. The culture of power systemically advantages white people (although they are often not aware they are benefitting) and excludes Black and Indigenous people of color (BIPOC) from quality educational experiences and the life outcomes attached to those.

A major aspect of the culture of power is language. Accordingly, those students who come from mainstream white backgrounds are more likely to already have at least a starting place for developing the language of power (i.e., the language of schooling) that likely will benefit them, as described earlier in this section. However, Delpit also argues that, if you do not know the rules of the culture of power, they can be explicitly taught—and that goes for the rules of the language of power too. This taught knowledge can help students access and mobilize power.

This idea applies to the language of power not only in elementary and secondary school, but also at the doctoral level. In the next section, I introduce a toolbox for learning the rules of the language of power in academia, which I derived from ***systemic functional linguistics.***

1.2 A Pragmatic Approach to Doctoral Level Literacy: Systemic Functional Linguistics

Building on Delpit's suggestion for increasing access to the culture of power, the aim of this book is to help make visible the rules of the language of power at the doctoral level and explicitly teach them to readers.

To do this, I draw on ideas from ***systemic functional linguistics (SFL),*** which I suggest is a pragmatic way to approach learning about doctoral level literacy. At first, some of the ideas I discuss below may be dense or somewhat difficult to understand. However, I will be coming back to these ideas over and over again throughout the subsequent chapters of this book and will help you unpack them as well as put them into action in your own writing.

SFL (Derewianka, 2012; Halliday, & Hasan, 1985) is concerned with the ways language works differently across contexts. More specifically, it focuses on the choices we make when we use language to communicate in different situations. This idea reflects the fundamental SFL belief that language doesn't really come to life until you put it to work in a particular context. This is because language and context interact and shape each other. You make choices—whether consciously or not—with your language based on where you are, who you are talking to (and your relationship with them), what you are trying to accomplish, and so on.

For example, the language choices you make when you speak to the director of your doctoral program likely differ from patterns of speech you use when you talk to your best friends. Not only do you (most likely) have a different relationship and history with your best friends as you do with the director, but your reasons for communicating with them are probably very different. In the same way, the language patterns in a book of poetry look different from those in a chemistry textbook—because the communicative purposes are different.

Language forms that correspond to a specific communicative context (like a poetry or chemistry book) are referred to as ***genres.*** Australian education researcher Beverly Derewianka (2012) describes genres as "dynamic, evolving ways of doing things through language" (p. 133). Genres are generally defined by their communicative purposes and draw on particular patterns of language to achieve those purposes. The types of writing mentioned above—poetry and academic science text—are two different examples of genres.

In this book, we will consider doctoral-level writing—or writing that works toward your dissertation and/or academic publication—to be a particular genre.

The Rules of the Language of Power

Just like the genres described above, doctoral-level writing has specific linguistic patterns (that is, language features).

Over the past several years, I identified several language features that seem to cut across all doctoral-level writing. I synthesized these into a six-point framework (see Figure 1.1). We can think of these features as the rules of the language of power. If you have read academic articles, you likely already are familiar with some, if not all, of these. Although we discuss the framework further in chapter two, alongside corresponding exercises, I offer a brief overview below as a general introduction to begin familiarizing you with these "rules" of the language of power at the doctoral level.

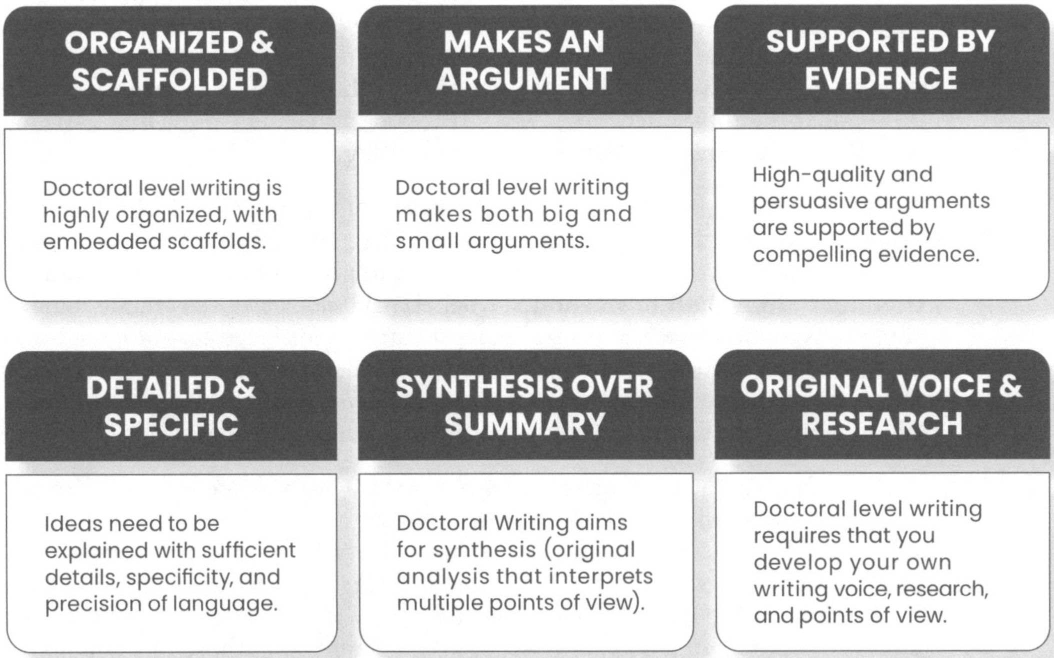

ORGANIZED & SCAFFOLDED	MAKES AN ARGUMENT	SUPPORTED BY EVIDENCE
Doctoral level writing is highly organized, with embedded scaffolds.	Doctoral level writing makes both big and small arguments.	High-quality and persuasive arguments are supported by compelling evidence.

DETAILED & SPECIFIC	SYNTHESIS OVER SUMMARY	ORIGINAL VOICE & RESEARCH
Ideas need to be explained with sufficient details, specificity, and precision of language.	Doctoral Writing aims for synthesis (original analysis that interprets multiple points of view).	Doctoral level writing requires that you develop your own writing voice, research, and points of view.

Figure 1.1: The Rules of the Language of Power

First, academic writing at the doctoral level is *highly organized and has embedded cues or scaffolds for the reader to follow along.* This is evident in academic papers, which generally include introductions that serve as road maps both at the beginning of the paper and in each major section. These introductory comments clearly identify the main argument or major claims and points that will be discussed. Paragraphs also have clear topic sentences that articulate the key idea of the paragraph, and the sentences that follow build in a logical sequence. Transitions and connector words (e.g., "For example," "in contrast," "First...second...last") are used to create flow and coherence, and headings are used judiciously to "chunk" content into manageable sections.

Academic writing at the doctoral level also *makes an argument.* There are multiple kinds of arguments you will make in your dissertation. For example, there's an argument regarding a problem that needs to be solved; an argument drawn from literature regarding the need for particular research; an argument that a particular theoretical framework is appropriate for the study at hand and offers promise for increased understanding of the topic investigated. Arguments are typically laid out in the introduction to a dissertation chapter or section, and then unpacked within that chapter/section with smaller claims or assertions that connect to the main argument in some way.

Further, high quality and persuasive arguments are *supported by evidence.* Compelling evidence can come in many different forms, including examples from peer-reviewed research, statistics from entities like the National Center for Education Statistics (NCES), reports from research organizations like the Pew Center, and even vignettes from your own practice.

Another characteristic of doctoral-level academic writing is the use of *detailed and specific language.* You will need to communicate a set of complex ideas to a reader who likely does not have the same background that you do. As such, those ideas need to be well-defined and explained. In addition, you will need to provide sufficient details for the reader to judge the importance and veracity of the argument made through examples, illustrations, and descriptions of evidence. Avoid the use of vague language–for example, words like "stuff" or "things," or rather than "did the study," use the more precise phrase "conducted the study".

Synthesizing across multiple sources, rather than summarizing, is another key feature of academic writing at the doctoral level. Summarizing is a recap of key ideas from a single source. In contrast, synthesizing refers to discussion of an idea that integrates multiple sources and/or points of view. A critical difference here is that a summary typically does not offer anything original, while a synthesis provides an interpretation or evaluation that does.

This more complex writing approach supports the fifth element, *the development of an original voice and research.* At the doctoral level, writing is a creative exercise. That is, YOU are creating something new, drawing or building on what already exists. Along the way, you will develop your own writing voice to communicate these original points of view and begin to build your research agenda.

Subgenres of Writing at the Doctoral Level

Within the genre of doctoral-level writing, there are different communicative purposes. Many of them correspond to the different chapters of the dissertation, which also align to the structure of a standard empirical research paper in the field of education. Therefore, I propose that the chapters of the dissertation (and major sections of a standard empirical manuscript) can be divided into multiple ***subgenres*** (e.g., the problem statement, theoretical framework, literature review, and so on). Each of these subgenres have an overall purpose and specific goals corresponding to a set of linguistic practices and patterns (while also incorporating the general academic writing framework elements outlined above). The dissertation subgenres and corresponding purposes are summarized in the figure below. Again, these ideas may be conceptually dense at first, but I will be unpacking these ideas further in each of the chapters to come.

SUBGENRE	PURPOSES
PROBLEM & PURPOSE STATEMENT	▪ Articulates and describes problem to be addressed and its background ▪ Provides a rationale for the study ▪ Outlines purposes/goals ▪ Names potential contributions of the study
LITERATURE REVIEW	▪ Synthesizes previous research, evaluates state of knowledge ▪ States gap in literature
THEORETICAL FRAMEWORK	▪ Discusses main theory(ies) or concepts ▪ Provides rationale for using them
METHODOLOGY	▪ Defines/describes methodological approach and components of research design ▪ Establishes trustworthiness
FINDINGS	▪ Describes the outcomes of the analysis with evidence
DISCUSSION/ RECOMMENDATIONS	▪ Analyzes the findings in light of research, theory, policy, and/or practice ▪ Offers recommendations for specific educational partners ▪ Concludes the dissertation

Figure 1.2: Subgenres of the dissertation

The first chapter of your dissertation, typically referred to as the ***problem and purpose statement***, has several purposes relating to offering a context and frame for the overall study. These include articulating and describing the problem driving the study; providing a rationale that shows the significance and urgency of addressing that problem, as well as demonstrating that there is a need to conduct the study (i.e., showing that a "gap" in literature exists); outlining the purpose/goals of the study; and outlining the possible contributions of the study.

The second dissertation chapter contains two different subgenres. The first is the ***literature review,*** which has several aims: synthesizing an extant body of (typically empirical) research to map out the current state of knowledge regarding a particular topic (i.e., *reviewing the literature*); identifying a research gap (or multiple gaps) from your review or mapping; and describing how the study will address this research gap.

Another subgenre typically found in chapter two of the dissertation is the ***conceptual or theoretical framework***. The purposes of this section include describing the theory, theories, or set of concepts that inform the study; providing a rationale for why you will use this particular theory, theories, or set of concepts in the study; and indicating how the framework will be used throughout the study.

The third dissertation chapter, ***methodology,*** is more technical than the preceding chapters. Its purpose is to outline the methodology/methods of the study in a concise yet detailed way to allow for transparency and trustworthiness. As such, the methodology section articulates and describes in detail the methodology of the study and the different components of the research design, including the participants, context/setting, instruments/data sources, data collection procedures, and analysis. This chapter also offers evidence for measures of quality (i.e., trustworthiness and positionality descriptions).

The fourth chapter of your dissertation includes the ***findings.*** The findings, also known as the "results" chapter, describe the outcomes of the analysis in ways that are understandable to the reader and offer sufficient evidence to support the analysis. The findings also "answer" your research questions (I put that in quotes because typically there's not one answer).

The final chapter of the dissertation includes the ***discussion*** and ***recommendations***. The discussion analyzes the study findings in light of current contexts, extant research, theoretical framework, policy, and practice, while the recommendations draw on the findings to suggest actions for specific educational partners or groups. The discussion chapter also ends with a conclusion that summarizes big ideas and contributions of the dissertation as a whole.

To achieve the specific purposes of each of these subgenres, you'll use language in particular ways (i.e., linguistic moves, which are also part of the "rules" of the language of power). In the chapters of this book dedicated to subgenres, I make these moves clear, and provide ***scaffolding*** in the form of examples and exercises intended to help you generate and edit text to build out the pieces of your dissertation. Scaffolding is at the core of the third theoretical strand that informs my overall approach to doctoral-level writing, so in the next section, I elaborate on that concept.

1.3 A Supported Approach to Doctoral Level Literacy: Sociocultural Theory and Learning

Readers who are educators likely have likely come across the notion of scaffolding in relationship to learning, even if they have not studied it closely. For others who are not familiar, take a moment to think about a time when you have seen a large building under construction (or a photo of one). You may have noticed a structure around the building that almost looks like a cage. That is scaffolding.

Scaffolding holds the building in place and supports it as construction work is completed (see Figure 1.3 for a visual). And, as the work on the building progresses, the scaffolding moves accordingly—so at each step, the scaffolding is in a different place and/or configuration, supporting the building and crew through that particular phase.

Scaffolding as a pedagogical method works similarly: It is a temporary and targeted support that helps people move forward in their learning and changes in nature as learners become more autonomous and skilled (Walqui & van Lier, 2012). In this book, I use scaffolding as a pedagogical method to support you, the reader, to learn and practice modes of doctoral-level literacy (and hopefully help you build out the pieces of your dissertation). I also use scaffolding as a supportive approach to writing itself, which I discuss in detail in the next chapter.

Figure 1.3: Scaffolding surrounding a building in New York City (Citylimits, 2021)

Scaffolding, as it relates to the learning process, has theoretical roots in the sociocultural theory of learning, which is generally credited to Russian psychologist Lev Vygotsky (1978). Coined as a concept by Jerome Bruner (Wood et al., 1976), scaffolding has been taken up and expanded by other sociocultural theorists in education like Leo van Lier (1996), Barbara Rogoff (1994), and Roland Tharp and Robert Gallimore (1991). Sociocultural theory is an understanding of learning that holds the following principles (Walqui & van Lier, 2012):

- Learning is social and occurs through active participation.
- Learning is mediated principally by language, but also by artifacts, both physical (e.g., texts, materials) and symbolic (e.g., cultural norms).
- Learning can be observed through changes in activity over time (e.g., enacting more autonomy).
- Learning occurs first on the interpersonal plane (social construction), followed by intrapersonal accommodation (schema building).

- Learning occurs ahead of development in the "zone of proximal development" (ZPD), or the space between what students can do or grasp by themselves and what they cannot do or understand autonomously.

Learning in the ZPD happens with the support of an expert other, peer, internal self-talk, or other supportive mediating device—that is, with the help of scaffolds. In relation to learning, the term "scaffold" refers to a support that is dynamic, responsive to situated student developmental needs, and can potentially encompass a range of things both material and discursive. For example, a scaffold may take the form of a guiding question the teacher asks, or it could be a partner discussion. It might be a graphic organizer, a metacognitive reflection, a set of sentence stems, or a modeled think-aloud.

Accordingly, there are multiple types of scaffolds you will see in this book:

- *Warm-ups:* These introductory questions and reflective prompts focus you on the goals of the chapter and bridge into the content.
- *Free-writes and text generation:* These initial-thinking exercises ask you to freely generate ideas/text that you will later be able to pull from or work with to move toward the goals of the chapter.
- *Graphic organizers:* These tools help you identify specific elements of the genre or subgenre, generate related text, and organize your ideas as a pre-writing step to formally writing your sections.
- *Metacognitive and metalinguistic supports:* These supports ask you to explicitly reflect on your ideas and/or linguistic choices and how they meet the goals of the genre or subgenre. They may be free-standing or embedded in graphic organizers.
- *Modeling:* These supports offer insight into the process of constructing specific types of writing and appear mostly in the form of examples with annotations or descriptions that unpack the thinking and choices behind them.

Generally, the most effective scaffolds involve structures that are modified on the spot during learning activities, as the teacher gauges where students are in terms of their ZPD (that is, what they already have learned, what they are on the cusp of understanding, and what might push them into the "zone of frustration"). These are the instances in which a structure (such as a graphic organizer) meets the process (the teacher evaluating student thinking and providing in-the-moment assistance with the organizer). However, in a book such as this, it is only possible to provide the structure; you (or an instructor using this book) will have to add the process. Thus, in the chapters that follow, the activities, exercises, and tools provided may not fit your specific needs at that time. As such, I invite you to see them as flexible, and modify them to meet your own developmental trajectory.

Summary of this Book

Altogether, I aim for this book to provide an affirmative apprenticeship into doctoral-level writing. I begin from an assets-based perspective that you, the reader, bring a tremendous amount of knowledge and resources to your doctoral journey. Each chapter provides activities that purposefully build upon each other to offer a supported path toward being able to participate in an academic writing community (and by that, I mean both your doctoral program, as well as the larger community of academic writers across the globe).

The second and third chapter of the book delve further into the general rules of the genre of writing at the doctoral level, building on the 6-point framework summarized in this chapter. In these chapters, each point of the framework will be discussed alongside exemplars and exercises. In chapters four through nine, I discuss each of the subgenres of writing at the doctoral level (i.e., the major tasks of the dissertation), as outlined above and shown in Figure 1.2. In each, I begin with a warm-up that focuses you on one or more of the major aims of the specific subgenre addressed in that chapter. I also provide explicit discussion of purposes and linguistic moves of the subgenre, then model and unpack examples demonstrating those moves. Throughout, I offer interactive and carefully designed exercises that move you toward autonomy. These exercises will support you to build out the majority of your dissertation.

2

The Rules: Writing as a Pedagogical Act

Contents

Introduction

This chapter begins your apprenticeship into the *language of power*, a framework I introduced in chapter one to describe the kind of writing that tends to characterize doctoral-level texts. I start with the rules by which the language of power operates—a deliberate move to make a form of "hidden curriculum" (that is, how to be successful with doctoral-level writing) more transparent. In this chapter, after a brief introduction to the whole framework, I focus on the first rule—organization and scaffolding as a method of reader support. I dedicate substantial space to this strategy for two reasons: One, careful organization and scaffolding will directly contribute to your success by helping your committee members more readily understand and follow the major ideas of your dissertation; and two, taking a pedagogical approach to writing through scaffolding can disrupt the historically exclusionary nature of academic writing by making it more accessible.

2.1 Rules of the Language of Power

WARM UP

What is one type of writing you really excel at? (Personal narrative? Texting or emailing? Grant writing? Poetry? Songwriting? etc.) What is the purpose (or purposes) of that type of writing (what does it seek to do or achieve)?

- Imagine a really high-quality version of whatever writing type you identified. What makes it high-quality? For example, what makes a really great poem, or email to parents, or grant narrative? Write out those characteristics of quality.
- Think about those quality markers that you just identified. How do those relate back to the purpose? How does the writer use them to help meet the goals of that type of writing?

In the warm-up exercise, you identified a *genre* of writing, its purpose(s), and the features of the genre that help meet that purpose. These features can be thought about in terms of linguistic moves. Every genre of writing has these specific patterns of language use that work to accomplish that particular genre's goals. I do this activity in my classes to introduce the idea of genre, genre purpose, and patterns of language (i.e., linguistic features) of that genre. In the example box at the top of the next page are some of the answers my students have come up with.

- Letter to parents/professional emails: The purpose is to provide important information in an accessible way; requires clear, concise language, clear objectives. Are more procedural, no need for a clear or defined writer's voice.
- Giving student feedback: The purpose is to provide technical mentoring and emotional support. One characteristic of quality feedback is the sandwich method of 'positive, improvement, positive.'
- Writing curriculum: The purpose is to create materials for instruction aligned to standards. Quality curriculum includes clear language that sets out goals, procedures, and foresees possible questions the teacher might have when implementing.
- Personal narrative: The purpose is to share personal experiences that readers can connect with. Quality personal narratives discuss meaningful experiences and include rich sensory details that help the reader visualize what is happening.

Let's think about the purpose and linguistic features of a letter or email to parents. The main purpose of the letter, typically, is to convey important information to parents about something involving their child. To achieve that purpose, the letter needs to present that information in a way that is specific, clear, and understandable. The author then needs to make linguistic choices that help them achieve this purpose. They can do so with two strategies: first, the author needs to be purposeful about the details they use, including only the most important information so parents can easily see what they need to know on a skim. And second, they need to use accessible language that parents from a variety of educational backgrounds can easily comprehend. These, then, become some of the key language patterns that help achieve the purpose of that genre of writing. In other words, these are some of the "rules" of successful writing in that genre (even if you haven't always necessarily thought of them that way).

The genre of academic writing at the doctoral level, along with its subgenres, is no different. It operates via specific purposes, and there are identifiable features that help you successfully meet those purposes. These are what I refer to as the "rules" of academic writing at the doctoral level, which I introduced in the first chapter. Based on my own systemic functional linguistics (SFL) analysis of academic writing at the doctoral level over the last decade, I identified the most commonly-occurring rules and synthesized them into a framework which encompasses six core features: it is (1) *highly organized and scaffolded* to help support the reader to understand the key ideas; (2) *makes an argument*, and that (3) argument is *supported by sourced, credible evidence*; (4) uses *detailed, specific, and sophisticated language*; (5) aims for *synthesis*, rather than summary; and (6) develops an *original voice and research/agenda*. These rules are summarized below in Figure 2.1.

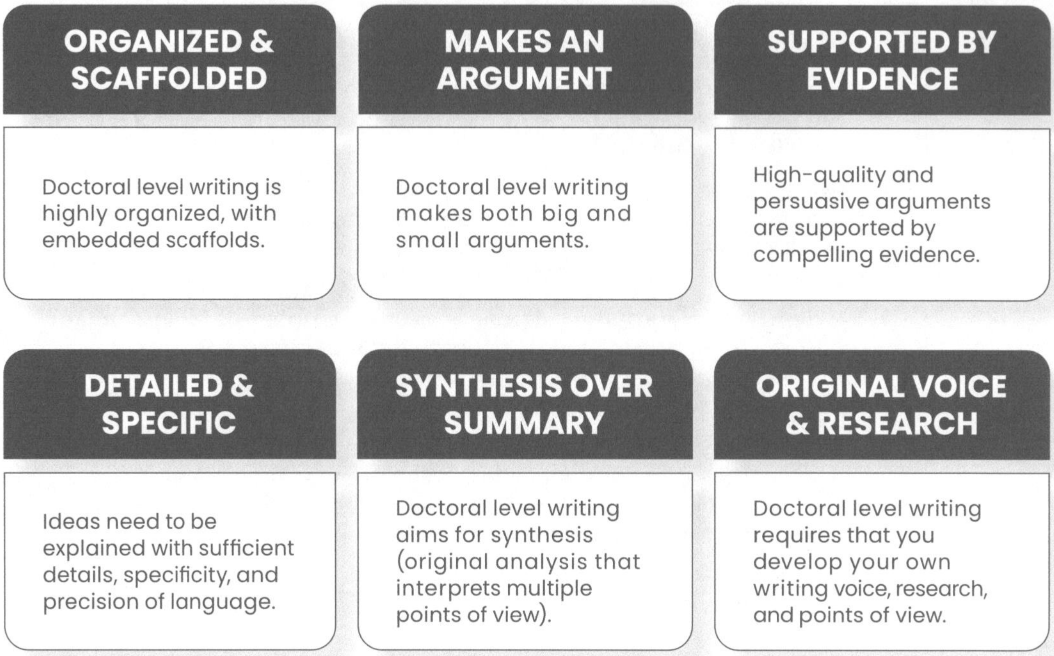

ORGANIZED & SCAFFOLDED	MAKES AN ARGUMENT	SUPPORTED BY EVIDENCE
Doctoral level writing is highly organized, with embedded scaffolds.	Doctoral level writing makes both big and small arguments.	High-quality and persuasive arguments are supported by compelling evidence.

DETAILED & SPECIFIC	SYNTHESIS OVER SUMMARY	ORIGINAL VOICE & RESEARCH
Ideas need to be explained with sufficient details, specificity, and precision of language.	Doctoral level writing aims for synthesis (original analysis that interprets multiple points of view).	Doctoral level writing requires that you develop your own writing voice, research, and points of view.

Figure 2.1: The Rules of the Language of Power at the Doctoral Level

2.2 Organization and Scaffolding

One of the central features of academic writing at the doctoral level is its high level of organization–that is, it is structured so that the purpose of each part is clear and those parts clearly make a whole.

Organization is one way that we can support our readers to understand what tends to be highly specialized content. In other words, careful and purposeful organization is one very important form of scaffolding. In this section, I offer multiple strategies for organizing your writing, as well as other methods for supporting your readers' understanding, such as signal words and idea connectors.

Before we get into some different types of organization and scaffolding strategies, let me introduce my scaffolding approach to writing. In the last chapter, I initially acquainted you with the idea of scaffolding–a temporary support that helps a learner stretch beyond their current level of capability to develop a new understanding or skill. While scaffolding (as an educational concept) is usually understood in relation to pedagogy, or the act of teaching, it can also be applied to writing.

When we read academic texts, our job as readers is to process the information in a way that allows us to understand the key ideas and follow the writer's argument or line of thinking. However, as you probably know by now, academic texts have a well-deserved reputation for being difficult to decipher. In my opinion, it does not have to be that way—we *can* make our academic work more accessible.

But it will require taking a stance that, as authors, we are not just responsible for getting content on the page; we also need to support our audience to understand that content. In other words, we have the duty to scaffold our ideas for our readers. And, for doctoral students, a scaffolding approach comes with a bonus: you can use it to help your instructors and committee members understand the main ideas of your work, which will help you enormously throughout your doctoral journey.

There are multiple levels at which you must support your reader's understanding. At the macro-level, scaffolding involves organizing the paper, dissertation chapter, or (entire) dissertation. Each chapter of your dissertation or your individual papers will also be further organized into sections, constituting a meso-level. Some of these may also be broken down into sub-sections or even smaller pieces intended to help your reader identify the major ideas contained in the larger paper/chapter (this move is referred to as "chunking").

At the micro-level, quality paragraphs are also carefully organized and can be purposefully scaffolded to help your reader follow your argument using elements like topic sentences and connecting transitions.

I have identified five main organization and scaffolding moves, summarized in the figure below, to be discussed in-depth in this section. As you will see, some of the features are more appropriate for one particular paper or dissertation chapter level (macro, meso, or micro), while others may be used at two or more of these levels.

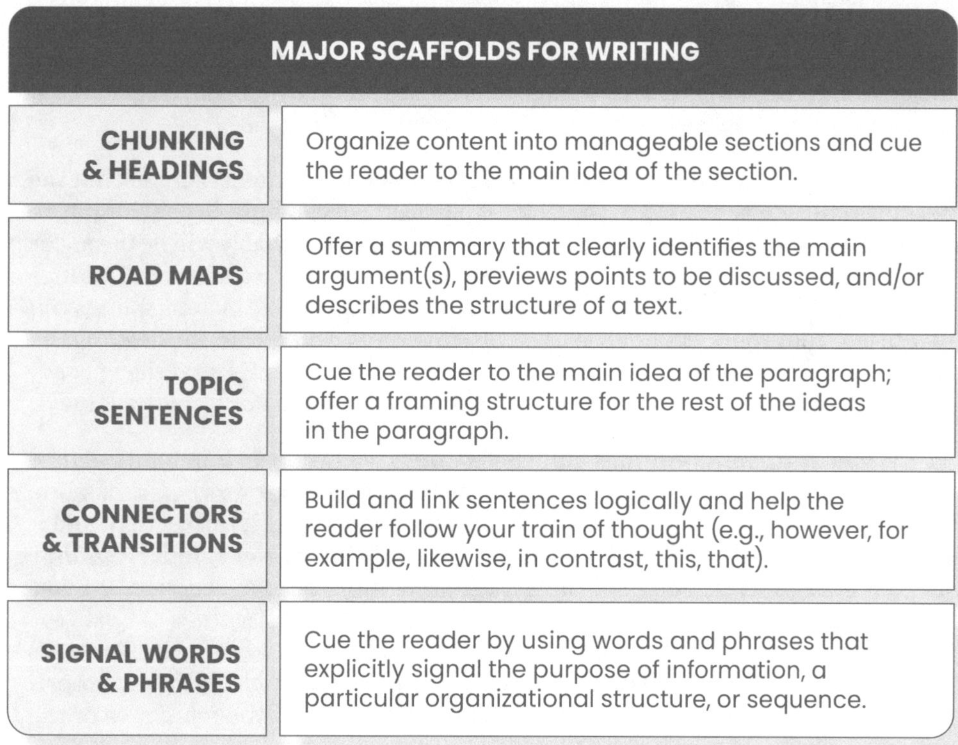

MAJOR SCAFFOLDS FOR WRITING	
CHUNKING & HEADINGS	Organize content into manageable sections and cue the reader to the main idea of the section.
ROAD MAPS	Offer a summary that clearly identifies the main argument(s), previews points to be discussed, and/or describes the structure of a text.
TOPIC SENTENCES	Cue the reader to the main idea of the paragraph; offer a framing structure for the rest of the ideas in the paragraph.
CONNECTORS & TRANSITIONS	Build and link sentences logically and help the reader follow your train of thought (e.g., however, for example, likewise, in contrast, this, that).
SIGNAL WORDS & PHRASES	Cue the reader by using words and phrases that explicitly signal the purpose of information, a particular organizational structure, or sequence.

Figure 2.2: Major scaffolds for writing

2.3 Headings and Chunking

The most basic and foundational organizational strategy is to ***chunk*** content into key ideas. This strategy will be used both at the paper and section levels. Beyond the actual chunking of the text, this scaffold also involves 1) identifying the units of meaning that need to be chunked, and 2) crafting ***headings*** that cue the reader to the main idea of the "chunk."

As much as possible, the major sections of your dissertation chapters and/or papers should be decided in advance via outlines and other pre-writing tools. These are essential to help you organize your thinking in a logical manner from the start (and there are examples of these tools throughout this book). However, it is not uncommon to make decisions to further chunk out a section or subsection during the editing process. You may realize (or get feedback) that the section contains many dense ideas and would benefit from identifying up front what the main ideas are.

In many areas of the dissertation, the major headings are dictated or shaped by the purpose of the chapter. For example, in the first chapter of the dissertation, the "Level 1" headings (i.e., the primary headings, according to APA) are often set by the doctoral program and/or field convention. In the program in which I teach, for instance, we require students to use the following common Level 1 headings for their first chapter: *Problem of Practice, Background of the Problem, Rationale, Purpose Statement.* However, within these sections, individual students have to judge whether the ideas might need to be signaled more clearly, and therefore chunked into subheadings (which are not dictated). For example, most students identify three or four big ideas for their background of the problem. If the ideas include more than a couple of paragraphs of text, they will most likely need to chunk them into subheadings.

Other chapters of your dissertation may not have the content dictated, but the headings still will be shaped by the chapter purpose. For example, in your literature review (typically in chapter two), your first-level headings probably will be the major themes that arose from your analysis of the studies you reviewed. In your findings chapter (typically chapter four), your headings will likely be the major findings you identified from your data analysis. In both instances, you create the headings as signposts to communicate the major outcomes of your analysis (and then probably chunk further into smaller ideas, but that will depend on your methodology).

As you draft your headings and subheadings, you want to aim for a balance of *brevity, identification,* and *support* for the reader. In other words, the heading needs to be brief, it needs to clearly identify the main topic of the section, and it needs to do so with enough detail that it scaffolds the reader's understanding. Let's go back to the example of the background of the problem section. If I was providing background to help my reader understand the difficulties of first year teaching practice, I would need to chunk my background and contextual factors into subsections and craft subheadings for them. If these subheadings appropriately support the reader, they will be able to get the gist of the main idea of the subsection from reading them.

Take a look at the subheadings below, each of which represent a subsection for a background of the problem. Would you be able to figure out the main idea(s) of each subsection from these headings?

- Pedagogy
- Support
- Neoliberalism

As you could probably tell, there is not enough detail provided in these headings for the reader to understand the gist of these sections. To better support reader understanding, I might expand the headings as follows:

- Complexities of Enacting Participatory Pedagogies
- Inconsistent Mentoring and Leadership Support
- Pressures of Neoliberal Accountability Measures

While I would certainly expand on each of these in the connected text, the subsection headings should provide a clue regarding what my key assertion is for each of the sections of my background statement. For the factors above, the assertions are as follows: 1) actually putting participatory pedagogies into action in the classroom is complex for most new teachers; 2) new teachers typically receive inconsistent mentoring and induction support, which hinders them in continuing to develop participatory practices; 3) teachers experience pressure associated with standardized testing and evaluation movements that try to link teacher performance to student test scores, which tends to reinforce traditional teaching.

Your headings should also be designed in a way that scaffolds in both micro- and macro- directions. In terms of the micro-level, the heading should cue the reader as to the main idea that the section or subsection will contain, as noted above. However, it should also work in tandem with the other headings in the larger chunk to make a logical, coherent whole–i.e., the macro-level. To double check that your heading supports understanding at both levels, articulate the relationships between each of the headings and subheadings, and then describe how the ideas, together, form a unit. You can do this as a free-write exercise or discuss it out loud with a critical friend (and, of course, reciprocate for them).

To provide an illustration of this alignment: In the last example, I described the complexity of pedagogical struggles of first year teachers in more detail (subsection one) then offered two additional contributors to that pedagogical struggle (subsections two and three). Together, these helped to explain the reasons for the problem (i.e., that first year teachers tend to revert to traditional pedagogies even when prepared to enact progressive and transgressive pedagogies).

In some instances (like in the literature review and findings chapter), you will want to think of your headings, in aggregate, as an organizational schema–that is, as one communicative structure that tells a coherent story. I will discuss this idea in greater detail in chapters five (the literature review)and eight (the findings).

ACTIVITY 1. CHUNKING AND CREATING HEADINGS	
Read the example section. If you were to chunk these ideas into subsections and label them, how would you do so? Use brackets to mark each section and write the headings out to the left side at the approximate place each section would start.	
	Complexity theories, also referred to as complexity science or complexity thinking, refer to a set of explanatory frameworks that focus on the spontaneous emergence of phenomena out of what might seem to be chaos. As there is not one agreed-upon complexity perspective, the summary we provide is consistent with conceptual and empirical work utilizing complexity science in the field of social science research (e.g., Butz, 1997; Byrne, 1998; Clarke & Collins, 2007; Davis & Sumara, 1997; Davis & Sumara, 2006; Mason, 2008). According to this interpretation, human activity (such as teaching/learning), occurs at the edge of chaos (Butz, 1997; Waldrop, 1992) which introduces conditions to which the system must collectively adapt and grow. Existing in at "the edge of chaos" means that the state of complex systems offers enough disequilibrium to spur growth and learning, but not enough to precipitate a plunge into total disorder (Butz, 1997; Waldrop, 1992). The edge of chaos concept is analogous to Piaget's (1954) notion of cognitive dissonance: a state in which enough conflict must occur to produce change (or learning). A certain amount of disequilibrium must be present to be considered a living system (Morrison, 2008), as it is a vital part of the process by which systems let go of their present shapes to reorganize into forms that are better suited to survival in their current environments (Clarke & Collins, 2007). In the case of beginning teachers, much of their first-year teaching is characterized by major dissonance of one kind or another, not the least of which often entails a misalignment between the ideals espoused by their teacher preparation programs and the realities of schools (Huberman, 1989; Veenman, 1984). However, for new teachers to continue to learn and grow on the edge of chaos and ultimately survive their first year of teaching, the disequilibrium they experience must not

ACTIVITY 1. CHUNKING AND CREATING HEADINGS (CON'T)	
	be too severe. To ensure personal survival under these conditions, the teacher may change schools or leave the profession entirely. Systems interacting on the edge of chaos are nested—that is, they are simultaneously an autonomous system, a system of systems, and embedded in a larger system (Davis & Sumara, 1997, 2006). Because of their nestedness—both arising from and being part of other complex systems while being a system in and of itself—their boundaries tend to be fluid and overlapping (Davis & Sumara, 2006). As we discuss in the findings section, nested within beginning teaching are: the first-year teacher system (the micro-level, including the teacher's preservice learning; her beliefs about self, students, teaching, and learning; and her personal qualities, background, and needs); the classroom system (the meso level, including the teacher, the students, available resources, and the physical environment); the school system (the macro level, including the administrators, teachers, mentors, parents, school culture, school structures, the level of difficulty of the novice's teaching assignment, and accessibility of professional support resulting from school-university partnerships); and larger educational systems (the super-macro level, including the district and broader policy landscape).

2.4 Road Maps

Think back to the last time you took a road trip or drove to an unfamiliar part of your city/geographic region. What did you do to prepare, to make sure you knew how to get to your destination?

Most likely, before embarking on your journey, you used some sort of navigational device or app—a GPS, or maybe Google Maps or Waze—to help you conceptualize the journey ahead and provide directions along the way. The writing scaffold version of a road map operates in much the same way by supporting readers of your writing on their journey through your paper or dissertation. It keeps them from getting lost (structurally and conceptually, anyway).

Road maps typically communicate the main ideas you will be discussing in a paper or dissertation chapter (or in a section of one). Sometimes, the road map may also communicate the organizational structure of a chapter or paper. This type of scaffold helps to focus the reader on the key topics or argument you will make, anticipate the way you are organizing those ideas, and/or build initial background information or schema for the content to be addressed.

You will likely include multiple road maps at different levels in your paper/chapter. First, the introduction to a paper or chapter should *always* include a road map to give your reader an overall sense of the ideas and structure. In addition, at the beginning of lengthy sections of your paper or chapter, provide some type of road map, even if it is a short one. For a shorter section (one without subheadings), and at the paragraph level, you can use a mini-road map that doubles as a topic sentence (I discuss this further in the next section).

When you write a road map for a section with subheadings, the statement should preview the main topics that you've chunked the section into. Importantly, make sure these previews match the subheadings. You don't have to use the exact same words, but make sure the language maps onto them, and introduce them in the same order—otherwise, you may miscue your reader, who can end up lost. You might also want to foreshadow (or even just state explicitly) any big "ahas" that you want the reader to walk away with from the section.

For example, a road map of a "background of the problem" section that explores issues contributing to the cultural gap between teachers and students might begin as follows:

> The cultural gap between teachers and students is a multi-faceted issue with roots in school desegregation and the mass firing of Black teachers. There are also multiple modern barriers that continue to keep the teaching force relatively white. These include educational and financial disparities that prevent a healthy pipeline of students of color to teacher preparation programs; and the disproportionate impact of neoliberal school defunding

The introduction above is structured in a way that not only introduces the main topics you will be discussing, but also prepares your reader to anticipate that there will likely be two main sections (and the way those will be structured). You are letting them know that the first section will discuss where the problem came from (when schools were desegregated in the 1950s and 1960s, a huge number of Black teachers were fired) and the second will explain why the issue persists (educational barriers, economics, and neoliberal defunding of schools where Black teachers work).

Remember that your road maps are a way to explicitly support your reader and prepare them for what is coming. Sometimes when I'm trying to decide what to put in my road maps, I like to imagine I'm having a conversation with my reader, and what I might want to say. In this case: "Ok, get ready: I'm about to talk to you about two different things. First, we are going to talk about school desegregation and how that resulted in a huge loss of Black teachers. Then, we are going to talk about a few different reasons why our teaching force is still mostly white."

2.5 Topic Sentences

At the paragraph level, ***topic sentences*** provide an important scaffold by cuing readers to the main idea of the paragraph. You can think of them as a mini-road map. Importantly, the topic sentence should clearly relate to every sentence of the paragraph—and you should be able to articulate what that relationship is. If you can't, delete the sentence or move it to another paragraph where it is connected to the topic sentence.

Let's look at an example. The following paragraph comes from a chapter written by Lucas and Villegas (2011, p. 57-58) regarding linguistically responsive instruction. The topic sentence appears in bold.

> **Language is the medium through which the norms and values of a cultural group are passed on from one generation to the next and are expressed.** The language each of us speaks is therefore deeply entwined with our sense of identity and our affiliations with social and cultural groups (Valdés, Bunch, Snow, & Lee, 2005). This connection is evident, for example, when two speakers of Spanish or another language shift to their common mother tongue, even though both are fluent in English. It is also evident when speakers of "standard" English transition into their childhood dialects when they interact with family members. Language is also the primary medium through which we construct our personal identities in interaction with people in our lives as children. Lisa Delpit (1998) has powerfully described this dimension of language in discussing Ebonics: "I can be neither for Ebonics nor against Ebonics any more than I can be for or against air. It exists. It is the language . . . many of our African-American children . . . heard as their mothers nursed them and changed their diapers and played peek-a- boo with them. It is the language through which they first encountered love, nurturance, and joy."

The first sentence in the above example tells us what the main topic of the sentence will be: that language is an important mediator of culture, a conduit by which different groups pass on their norms and values. Each sentence that comes after it relates to that point in some way. For example, the second sentence expands on this point by making a connection between language and social/cultural identity; it also focuses the reader on a specific element of culture that will be referenced throughout the paragraph (identity). The two sentences after that illustrates this point by providing two concrete examples.

The following graphic (Figure 2.3) breaks down these relationships, sentence by sentence to show how each either expands on the main idea or illustrates it through evidence and examples. Read through it and examine the explanations for each sentence. Afterwards, go on to Activity 2 and analyze the paragraph in the same way.

TOPIC SENTENCE:
Language is the medium through which the norms and values of a cultural group are passed from one generation to the next and are expressed.

Sentence	Relationship
The language each of us speaks is therefore deeply entwined with our sense of identity and our affiliations with social and cultural groups (Valdéz, Bunch, Snow, & Lee, 2005).	This sentence expands on the main point by making a connection between language and social/cultural identity.
This connection is evident, for example, when two speakers of Spanish or another language shift to their common mother tongue, even though both are fluent in English.	This sentence uses an example to provide evidence supporting the cultural connection between language and identity.
It is also evident when speakers of "standard" English transition into their childhood dialects when they interact with family members.	This sentence provides another example to support the cultural connection between language and identity.
Language is also the primary medium through which we construct our personal identities in interaction with people in our lives as children.	This sentence expands on the idea of the culture-identity-language connection, linking it to childhood interactions.
Lisa Delpit (1998) has powerfully described the dimension of language in discussing Ebonics: "I can be neither for Ebonics nor against Ebonics any more than I can be for or against air. It exists. It is the language... many of our African-American children... heard as their mothers nursed them and changed their diapers and played peek-a-boo with them. It is the language through which they first encountered love, nurturance, and joy."	This sentence provides a quote from a well-regarded expert on culture and education which offers a tangible illustration of the connection between culture, language, identity, and childhood (through the example of Ebonics).

Figure 2.3: Topic sentences and relationships

ACTIVITY 2. TOPIC SENTENCES

a. **Underline the topic sentence in the following paragraph. How does each sentence that follows it relate to it (unpacking the ideas, expanding, illustrating, etc.)?**

Another key critical posthuman concept is distributive agency (Bennett, 2009), a key characteristic of assemblages. This concept suggests people are not autonomous, self-regulating, conscious actors, but instead share agency with all elements of an assemblage, both human and non. Distributive agency decenters the human actor or participant in the assemblage and foregrounds relationality, as well as highlights the role and influence of the non-human (Strom & Viesca, 2021) and the vitality of matter itself (Bennett, 2009). In teaching, distributive agency presents an important counter-argument to the taken-for-granted notion that teaching is a one-way transaction that teachers "do" to students. Instead, teaching is a collective activity that is jointly produced by the collaborative activity of teacher-students-space-content-context plus (Strom, 2015). (Strom & Martin, 2022, p. 3)

b. **Choose a paragraph from your own work to analyze. First, underline the topic sentence. Then, describe how each sentence that follows it relates to it.**

2.6 Transitions and Connectors

Another very important set of scaffolds for your reader falls under the category of what I call ***transitions*** and ***connector words/phrases***. These important elements help create overall cohesion and flow in your writing, linking paragraph to paragraph and idea to idea. They also express the relationships between ideas. For your reader, transitions and connectors are crucial threads that pull your important points through from one sentence to the next, building bridges between ideas that ultimately construct a well-marked path through your dissertation. Below, I discuss different kinds of transitions and connectors and demonstrate how they help support your reader to follow your key ideas.

Basic Transitions

When viewed through a lens of scaffolding, your basic transitions become important cues for your reader to follow the construction of your argument and key ideas. So, choose transitions with your purpose in mind—what you are trying to accomplish with the ideas at hand. Are you indicating that two ideas are linked in terms of cause/effect (*as a result, because, hence, therefore, thus*)? Are you expanding an idea (*also, additionally, moreover, further*)? Are you drawing a contrast between ideas (*in contrast, however, although, despite*) or pointing out commonalities (*likewise, similarly, in the same way*)? Are you offering an illustration (*for example, to illustrate, for instance, e.g.*) or a clarification (*i.e., in other words, that is, to rephrase*)?

Read the following paragraph. What are the purposes of the highlighted transitions? How do you know?

> **Therefore,** the development of teacher subjectivity and teaching practice is not a linear process: **that is,** it is not the end result of completing a teacher preparation program, attaining state licensure, and gaining employment in a school. **Instead,** becoming a teacher is an intra-active process: teacher preparation programs, schools, and policy assemblages work together to produce teacher subjectivity**. For example**, the intra-actions within a kindergarten classroom with the students, the material resources (tables, toys, crayons, paints, scissors), the time (weekdays between the hours of 8:00 a.m.-3:00 p.m.), the discourse (ideas relevant to the content areas of mathematics, literacy, and so on), and spatial engagement (the adult moves about the room as the students work at their tables) intra-act to enable the recognition of the adult in this space and time as "teacher").
> *(Strom & Martin, 2022, p. 3)*

In the above paragraph, I have highlighted four examples of basic transitions. I begin the paragraph with "*therefore,*" letting the reader know that I am offering a conclusion drawn from information I have laid out in the previous paragraph (i.e., teacher subjectivity and learning is not linear). I then use the transition "*that is*" to tell the reader that I am about to provide a clarification (in this case, I am applying the argument in the context of beginning teacher pathways to help the reader understand my point). I start the next sentence with "*instead,*" which indicates that I am going to make a counter-argument to something (in this case, I am contesting the notion of linearity in teacher development). Finally, I offer an example that illustrates and provides support for my point.

Weaving Language and Transitions

Another important use for transitions is to pull ideas through from sentence to sentence, weaving strong threads that support the reader to follow the writer's train of thought. *Strategic repetition* and *pronouns* (words that refer back to something said in a previous sentence) are two important strategies for braiding ideas together across sentences.

Let's return to the previous example from Lucas and Villegas (2011, p. 57-58). Reread it below, this time taking note of the bolded words, which show strategic repetition of language as well as pronouns and related terms. How do they function to pull ideas through from sentence to sentence?

> **Language** is the medium through which the norms and values of a cultural group are passed on from one generation to the next and are expressed. The **language each of us speaks** is therefore deeply entwined with our sense of identity and our affiliations with social and cultural groups

(Valdés, Bunch, Snow, & Lee, 2005). **This connection** is evident, for example, when two speakers of Spanish or another language shift to their **common mother tongue**, even though both are fluent in English. **It is also evident** when speakers of **"standard" English** transition into their childhood **dialects** when they interact with family members**. Language** is also the primary **medium** through which we construct our personal identities in interaction with people in our lives as children. Lisa Delpit (1998) has powerfully described **this dimension of language** in discussing **Ebonics**: "I can be neither for **Ebonics** nor against **Ebonics** any more than I can be for or against air. It exists. It is the **language** . . . many of our African-American children . . . heard as their mothers nursed them and changed their diapers and played peek-a- boo with them. It is the **language** through which they first encountered love, nurturance, and joy."

In the above paragraph, to keep the focus on *language*, the authors use that word strategically and repeatedly in each sentence, alongside synonyms or related terms (*mother tongue, English, dialect, Ebonics*). This kind of strategic repetition with synonym use is one way to ensure that the focus remains on the main topic and threads the main idea from one sentence to the next, thereby creating a supportive structure for your reader.

However, using the same words and phrases over and over can also sound repetitive. To avoid that, another transition strategy to use involves pronouns and referent phrases. Pronouns are single words like *this, that, these, those, they* and *it* which refer back to something said in a previous sentence. Referent phrases usually include both a pronoun and a referent word/phrase (something previously said that brings a key idea forward into the next sentence, creating a clear link). Looking back at the paragraph above, the authors use this strategy multiple times to refer back to an idea, again creating a strong thread that serves as a guide for the reader. For example, in the third sentence, they begin with the referent phrase "*this connection* is evident," which summarizes and refers back to the key point of the previous sentence (that language, identity, and sociocultural affiliation are intertwined). They echo the language-identity-culture link yet again in the beginning of the next sentence with a single pronoun: "*It* is also evident," with *it* referring back to the relation discussed in the previous two sentences.

There is one caveat to keep in mind when including a pronoun in a transitional phrase: Be careful to ensure that the reader has enough context to understand what you are referring back to. In cases where the referent may not be clear, use an additional phrase to support understanding. For instance, in the example above, the authors chose to use the phrase "*this connection*" rather than simply "this," which provides additional context to ensure the reader knows what the authors are talking about. Similarly, in the next sentence, the authors repeat a word (evident) to ensure that the connection is apparent ("*it is also evident*"). When I provide feedback on student papers, one of my most frequent comments is "unclear referent." In your editing/revision stages, make sure that any time you use pronouns, your reader can clearly identify what that pronoun is referring back to.

ACTIVITY 3. TRANSITION ANALYSIS

Pick a paragraph from a paper you have written. In the lefthand column, write each sentence of the paragraph, in order. In the righthand column, analyze your use of transitions and connectors using the following questions:

- What transitions and connectors are you using and why? What are they connecting and signaling?
- How are you using pronouns? Are the referents clear?
- What words or phrases are you using for strategic repetition? What synonyms are you using?

Sentence	Transition/Connector Analysis

2.7 Signal Words and Phrases

Signal words and phrases are closely related to transitions/connectors, and in some cases, overlap with them. These words and phrases deliberately signal to your reader the information you are providing to them.

As I am sure you are aware, academic writing is often dense, containing multiple ideas in a paragraph (and sometimes in a single sentence). You can help your reader navigate this complexity by offering them signposts that point out what they need to pay attention to or that provide organizing frames (such as sequencing words, e.g., *first, second, next*). Using these signal words strategically can also help you ensure that you achieve the purposes/goals of each chapter of your dissertation (see Figure 1.2 in chapter one). For example, in the first chapter of your dissertation, one important goal is to clearly and succinctly state the purpose of your project. To help your reader locate that statement, directly signal them by using the phrase "The purpose of this study is..."

Another way to use signaling is to foreground an organizational statement or phrase, followed by sequencing words. For example, many times, we will need to provide an explanation that is multi-faceted or contains multiple parts. To cue your reader that you will be presenting a multi-part explanation or description, offer a statement prior to beginning that description. To illustrate, when presenting a theoretical framework with a number of principles, such as critical race theory, you might begin the explanation of these tenets with the following organizing sentence: "Critical race theory has five main principles." This phrase then cues the reader to expect five different tenets to be presented. You would then use sequencing words to help your reader follow the enumeration of your points—*first, second*, and so on.

ACTIVITY 4. SIGNALING WORDS AND PHRASES

Read the following example. How is signaling used to help organize the paragraph and provide scaffolding for the reader? Highlight the signaling words and phrases.

Sociocultural theory has five main principles. First, learning is social and occurs through interaction. Second, it is mediated by tools or artifacts such as language, which is why dialogue is so important in the learning process. Third, learning happens first interpersonally, as students talk, and then intra-personally, as they internalize their learning. Fourth, learning occurs in the "zone of proximal development," or the area just beyond what students are capable of doing by themselves, as they receive tailored assistance or "scaffolding" to stretch themselves to grasp the knowledge or skill. Finally, learning can be observed as changes in participation.

Chapter Summary

In this chapter we returned to the rules of the language of power, a framework of six overarching principles that characterize writing at the doctoral level. We focused specifically on the first rule in our framework (doctoral writing is highly organized and scaffolded) and learned about writing as a pedagogical act (i.e., understanding writing not just as putting ideas on a page, but also actively supporting your audience to understand them). We also learned about scaffolding strategies you can use to help your reader follow your lines of thinking, anticipate and comprehend key ideas, and understand the relationships between the ideas you present.

Key concepts and takeaways from this chapter:

- One of the central features of academic writing at the doctoral level is its ***high level of organization***. Papers and dissertations are structured so that the purpose of each part is clear and those parts clearly make a whole.
- ***Scaffolding*** is a pedagogical approach to writing in which the writer uses multiple organizational strategies and other supports that actively help the reader follow the main ideas.
- The first strategy, ***chunking***, means to organize the text by separating the key ideas into sections. This strategy entails 1) identifying the units of meaning that need to be chunked and 2) crafting ***headings*** that cue the reader to the main idea of the "chunk."
- The second strategy, ***road maps***, provide the reader with a statement that lets them know the main ideas that will be discussed and cues them to the structure of the paper, chapter, or section.
- The third strategy, ***topic sentences***, are "mini-road maps" that communicate the main idea of the paragraph.
- The fourth strategy, ***transitions*** and ***connectors***, are words and phrases that create overall cohesion and flow in your writing by providing bridges between ideas, sentences, and paragraphs.
- The final strategy, ***signal words and phrases,*** provide signposts so your reader knows that you are providing specific information.

3

The Rest of the Rules of the Language of Power

Contents

Introduction

This chapter focuses on the other five rules of the language of power that I have identified from my work with doctoral students. I begin with arguments, which are central to the quality of your doctoral work—specifically, that your arguments are well-reasoned. They are also supported by compelling and credible evidence—and there are many kinds of evidence you might choose from. From there, I delve into the use of detailed, specific, precise language in your writing, followed by a section aiming to help you understand the difference between summary and synthesis (as well as practice your synthesizing skills). I conclude with the development of voice and point of view, which I address through a lesson on the use of quotes. Throughout the chapter, I offer exercises to practice these writing skills. Although you can complete them alone, I encourage you to find a partner to discuss them with (learning is always more powerful with others).

3.1 Making a Well-Reasoned Argument

WARM UP

One of the first things you will do as you begin your research is make an argument that there's a problem or issue that needs investigating (the investigation being the study you eventually want to do). Jot down your thoughts on the following: What are the characteristics of a really persuasive argument and why?

Arguments are assertions or claims meant to persuade, which are unpacked with appropriate reasoning and supported by compelling and credible evidence. Throughout your dissertation, part of your role as author is to make arguments in every chapter for specific purposes.

- In writing the *problem statement*, you'll make an argument to persuade the reader that the problem you are laying out for investigation is significant and urgent enough to warrant the study you propose to conduct (for the dissertation proposal phase) or have already conducted (for the oral dissertation defense).
- In *the literature review* section, you'll draw on your analysis of extant literature on the topic of investigation to make a case that the study you will be doing or have done fills a gap in the research literature (and therefore is necessary).
- In your *conceptual framework*, you'll make an argument that the theories, concepts, or other ideas underlying your study are appropriate, purposeful,

and will lead to new or different insights than those already reported in the literature.

- In your *methods section*, you'll need to make an argument that the methodology/approach you have chosen for the study is appropriate to "answer" the guiding questions and achieve its aims.
- In your *findings section*, you'll make an argument regarding the main outcomes of your analysis.
- In the *discussion section*, you'll make an argument regarding the significance of the findings, the ways they relate to theoretical and empirical literature, and how the findings should inform future research, policy, and practice.

Parts of an Argument

There's lots of different argumentation models, but I use the good old standby proposed by rhetorician Toulmin (1958) because of its simplicity and the applicability of its the structure across the dissertation. According to the Toulmin model, an argument has three main parts: ***the claim*** (the actual point you want to make), accompanying ***explanation*** that unpacks the claim (the reasons why that claim is credible/trustworthy, also known as the warrant), and ***evidence*** (data or other forms of support to illustrate or back up your claim and explanation). Below, I focus on the first two parts (I tackle evidence later in this chapter).

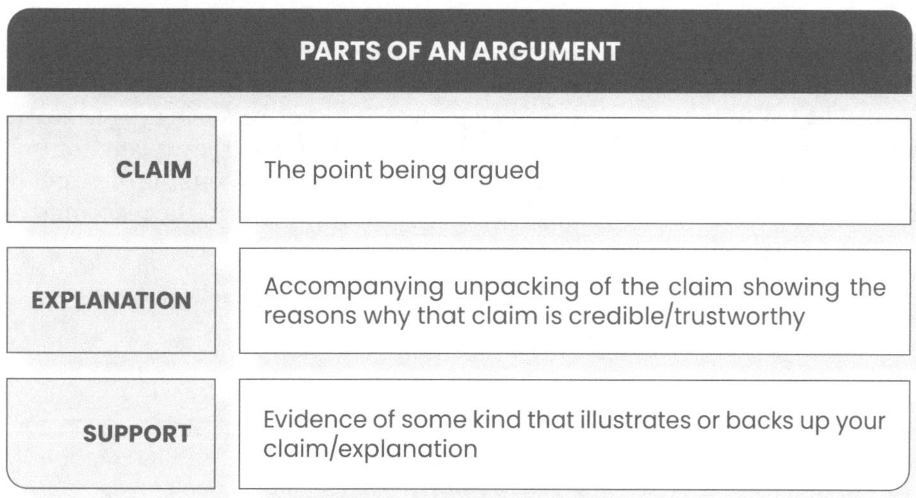

Figure 3.1: Parts of an argument

Claim

A claim is a declarative sentence that lays out the point you are arguing. Basically, it is the idea that you want to persuade your reader to accept for a particular purpose related to your study. Throughout your dissertation, you will be making claims connected to each particular element of the dissertation and its chapters, as noted above. For example, the following are examples of claims from specific parts of a dissertation:

- **Problem statement claim.** The dominant western ontology and epistemology that underlie science education contribute to the perpetuation of deficit perspectives for multilingual youth. *(This claim makes an argument about the partial cause of a problem.)*
- **Theoretical framework claim.** A theoretical framework grounded in complexity perspectives can better account for the non-linear, multi-causal nature of teaching. *(This claim provides a rationale for the theoretical perspective that will be used in the study.)*
- **Methodology claim.** Examining how asset-based pedagogy affects classroom power dynamics requires micro-level analysis of the moment-by-moment unfolding of teacher moves and student interactions. *(This claim provides a rationale for the methodology that has been chosen for a study.)*

Explanation

Although a clear, strong claim is important, it cannot stand on its own. All claims must be unpacked with explanation that provides sound reasoning and which persuades your reader that your claim is credible and trustworthy. For larger claims, the reasoning may be complex and multi-faceted, requiring you to scaffold the reader's understanding by signaling the different parts of the explanation (more on this below), and then discussing those pieces one by one, chunking them out into their own sub-sections as needed. For smaller claims, however, the reasoning may be summarized with just a sentence or two.

Let's take one of the examples above and think through what type of accompanying explanation might be needed.

> The dominant western ontology and epistemology that underlie science education contributes to the perpetuation of deficit perspectives for multilingual youth.

This claim actually has three parts:

- There is such a thing as "dominant western ontology and epistemology";
- That dominant western ontology and epistemology is an important influence of science education; and
- Its influence on science education at least partially perpetuates deficit perspectives for multilingual youth.

To persuade the reader of the veracity of this claim, the sentence requires reasoning for all three of these pieces. In other words, I will need to 1) unpack what I mean by "dominant western ontology and epistemology," 2) explain how those logics inform science education, and 3) show how that influence translates into deficit perspectives in science classrooms. This multi-part explanation might be structured in the following way:

- Eurocentric onto-epistemology, or ways of knowing and being, is characterized by multiple features, such as a linear, dualistic, disconnected, "either/or" worldview that centers and hierarchically positions humans as actors with complete agency, and understands the world as neutral, objective, static, and universal (Braidotti, 2013/2019; Strom & Viesca, 2021).
- Although it is only one way of knowing-being, this Eurocentric onto-epistemology has imposed itself as the *right and only* way—and western science is very much grounded in these values (Bang et al., 2012). Western science presumes separation between the researcher and object of inquiry, assumes that scientific activities are neutral and objective, and sees western scientific conventions like the scientific method to be universal and transcendent of culture—while de-legitimizing non-western science knowledge and practice, such as those from indigenous communities (Medin & Bang, 2014; Kayumova & Strom, 2023).
- In science classrooms, teachers regard western ways of knowing/doing science and being a science person as universal and correct, which delegitimizes the cultural, linguistic, and experiential meaning-making resources of youth from nondominant communities, viewing them from a deficit perspective and framing these youth as lacking the knowledge/skills to be successful in science (Kayumova & Strom, in press).

The first bullet explains what I mean by "Eurocentric onto-epistemology" and introduces its key characteristics. The second bullet delves further into this concept and connects it to western science. This sentence also begins to show how Eurocentric onto-epistemology privileges particular ways of thinking. The final bullet contextualizes the information introduced in the first two bullets to science classrooms, showing the ways that only valuing Eurocentric ontoepistemology fosters deficit perspectives of youth.

Figure 3.2 explains the thinking and logic flow behind each of these bullets.

Eurocentric onto-epistemology, or ways of knowing and being, is characterized by multiple features, such as a linear, dualistic, disconnected, "either/or" worldview that centers and hierarchically positions humans as actors with complete agency, and understands the world as neutral, objective, static, and universal (Braidotti, 2013/2019; Strom & Viesca, 2021).

This first part, which begins to unpack the argument, defines "Eurocentric onto-epistemology, " and introduces some of the major features that later will be connected to deficit perspectives of students.

Although it is only one way of knowing-being, this Eurocentric onto-epistemology has imposed itself as the right and only way-and western science is very much grounded in these values (Bang & Medin, 2012). Western science presumes separation between the researcher and object of inquiry, assumes that scientific activities are neutral and objective, and sees western scientific conventions like the scientific method to be universal and transcendent of culture-while deligitimizing non-western science knowledge and practice, such as those from indigenous communities (Medin & Bang, 2014; Kayumova & Strom, 2023).

In the second part of the exploration, I explain Eurocentric onto-epistemologies' dominance and connect it to western science. I then describe this connection further using the characteristics I mentioned in the first part.

In science classrooms, teachers regard western ways of knowing/doing science and being a science person as universal and correct, which deligitimizes the cultural, linguistic, and experiential meaning-making resources of youth from nondominant communities, viewing them from a deficit perspective and framing these youth as lacking the knowledge/skills to be successful in science (Kayumova & Strom, in press).

In the final part of the explanation, I contexualize Eurocentric onto-epistemology to science classrooms, explaining how this perspective materializes as a deficit view of non-western youth.

Figure 3.2: Deconstructed argument

ACTIVITY 1. ANALYZING CLAIMS AND REASONING

Read the following paragraph from Strom et al. (2018, p. 3).

In the case of first-year teaching, complexity theory— the study of complex, living systems—helps conceptualize novice practices as arising from interactions occurring between the teacher and other elements within a larger network. As such, complexity theory enables an examination of the forces that coalesce on multiple planes to produce first-year teaching practices. This perspective provides an ecological approach to conceptualizing teaching practice that examines phenomena as a whole, rather than merely focusing on their parts (Cochran-Smith, Ell, Ludlow, Grudnoff, & Aitken, 2014).

1. What is the claim the author is making in this excerpt?
2. What reasoning is provided to persuade the reader that this claim is plausible or believable?

In the activity above, the claim is made in the first sentence of the excerpt: I'm arguing that complexity theory is useful because it helps conceptualize beginning teacher practice in a way that accounts for its multi-actor complexity ("*arising from interactions occurring between the teacher and other elements within a larger network*"). I then provide a two-part explanation for why it is useful: one, it can help us understand the factors that "produce" first-year teaching practice; and two, it allows a holistic examination of teaching that accounts for the whole system, rather than a partial one that looks at just a slice.

ACTIVITY 2. ANALYZING ARGUMENTS

Read the following excerpt from Strom and Martin (2023, p. 4).

Teacher practice is also mediated by their beliefs about teaching and learning (e.g., Bergeron, 2008; Starkey, 2010). As an example, in the New Zealand context, Starkey (2010) examined first-year teachers' use of technology and found that their traditional beliefs regarding mathematics learning (i.e., that working out problems with paper and pencil was most effective) interfered with their ability to integrate technology into their lessons. Teachers' backgrounds and experiences also have the potential to impact teaching (e.g., Birrell, 1995; Coffey & Farinde-Wu, 2016; Newman, 2010). Newman (2010), for instance, interviewed beginning teachers in the U.K. who entered the profession after a career change and reported that their previous career experiences influenced the way they approached pedagogy.

1. Identify the two claims made in this paragraph.
2. What reasoning is provided to persuade the reader that these claims are plausible or believable?

3.2 Supporting Arguments with Sourced, Credible Evidence

ACTIVITY 3. WHAT IS EVIDENCE?

Write a reflection on the following.

What is your understanding of evidence? Why is it important in your dissertation? What might be some of the different types of evidence you would draw on to support your arguments or claims?

The third part of a high-quality argument is *evidence*—information you provide your reader that illustrates or provides support for your claim. For every claim you make that does not come from your original research, you must provide evidence of some kind. In this section, I begin with a discussion of some of the most common types of evidence.

Types of Evidence

There are multiple ways to provide evidence to support claims throughout your dissertation. One of the most common is *peer-reviewed empirical publications.* Often considered the gold standard of evidence, this refers to research studies that collect, analyze, and report on original data; have been reviewed by experts in a double-blind process (i.e., both author and reviewer are kept anonymous); and are published in a peer-reviewed or "refereed" journal. However, not all journals that claim to be peer-reviewed are the same—a wide variety of quality exists. At a minimum, make sure that the journal is indexed and considered credible in your field.

An example of a peer reviewed article is my 2015 publication, *Teaching as Assemblage: Negotiating Learning and Practice in the First Year of Teaching.* This article presents a case study examining the way a first-year teacher translated their pre-professional learning into their first-year instruction. Data were collected regarding the teacher's instruction and interactions with students, analyzed, and presented as findings.

Generally, you will draw on peer-reviewed empirical research throughout your entire dissertation. However, there are some areas where the references you use *must* be empirical—for example, in your literature review, the purpose is to offer a synthesis of the state of research in the field, so your support in this section needs to be drawn from studies that collect, analyze, and report on original research. A quick way to tell whether an article is empirical or not is to look for a methods section that describes data sources, collection procedures, and analysis. If it does not have one, it is almost certainly not empirical.

Beyond empirical studies, there are other types of peer-reviewed publications you might draw on in your dissertation. For example, *peer-reviewed conceptual publications* discuss theoretical ideas or offer original conceptual frameworks. These can provide support for claims having to do with theoretical or conceptual understandings in your problem statement, theoretical framework, or discussion. Another type is a *peer-reviewed literature review,* a journal article that offers original syntheses of research on a theme, issue, or problem, and you also might refer to an article like this in multiple areas of your dissertation. Still other peer reviewed publications could include critical essays on a specific topic, historical analyses, policy analyses or commentaries, or discussions of particular practices.

Another source to draw on for evidence could come from *research reports produced by organizations.* This could include research studies conducted by entities such as the Pew Center, the American Educational Research Association (AERA), or the Center for Research on Education Outcomes (CREDO). Research reports such as these can be just as rigorous as studies published in journals—although they are not always peer-reviewed. They also often offer snapshots of data that are particularly useful for framing your proposal. However, before using a report, always make sure that the organization is credible. Also make sure to find out if the organization has specific political agendas and, if they do, consider the ways those may influence reported research findings.

You may also cite *books* as evidence to support your claims. Books are longer publications, often 100-300 pages, and could be empirical, conceptual, historical, policy-focused, and/or practice-related. While many go through some kind of review process, it is often not as rigorous as journal peer review, and therefore they are not considered the same gold standard of evidence as peer-reviewed publications. This is not to say books are not an important resource. For example, many top scholars develop books out of the same projects that they publish in journals about, and books provide the opportunity to go further in depth on these topics than articles do. In addition, although you may cite books throughout your dissertation, one area in which you may reference books for much of your evidence is in your methodology section (most research design references tend to come from texts expounding on certain methodological approaches).

Conference papers and/or presentations are yet another type of evidence that may be used in different places in your dissertation. Although it is preferable to cite a published paper, there may be times where conference papers and/or presentations could be cited, especially when topics are just beginning to be explored. Conferences present an opportunity to learn about the latest research, often as it is in process, so citing conference papers and/or presentations can be a strategy for supplementing discussions of phenomena just beginning to be investigated.

As an example, when I was writing my dissertation proposal, few scholars were making the case for disrupting linear thinking in teacher preparation, at least in those terms. Marilyn Cochran-Smith, a teacher education scholar, presented about that very thing in 2013 at the American Educational Research Association, and until her publication came out a year later, I cited that presentation in my argument for the need for a more complex perspective on teacher development.

Policies, codes, statutes, or court cases are another category of evidence. Especially for those working on projects involving policy analysis, or with some kind of policy element, it will be necessary to describe specific policies, codes, and/or statutes to support your argument. Court cases might also be referenced in policy or legislative discussions, in building context, or describing historical events.

Another type of evidence includes *online sources*, like government websites, organization websites, blogs, or news sites. For instance, many dissertations in my program make use of documents available on the U.S. Department of Education website. Others might reference information found on a certain organization's site: a proposal investigating teacher unions might reference information gained from the National Education Association's website, or a study examining student mental health might include a fact sheet from the National Alliance on Mental Illness (NAMI).

It is also possible to draw on blogs as evidence, but as always, make sure that the author of the blog is credible (and it's even better if they include citations of their sources). Other online sources include news and magazine articles, which might be used to provide evidence for current events (for example, someone writing about COVID-19 might reference a *New York Times* article regarding death tolls).

A final type of evidence (discussed here, anyway—there are certainly more ways to support claims than can be covered in this chapter) encompasses *examples* and *scenarios*. Often, examples are used in conjunction with other references to provide detail, as I will describe further in the next section, and to concretize or contextualize meaning for the reader. Examples can come from history, media, popular culture, practice, and more.

For example, in a recent introduction to a special issue, my co-authors and I drew on the example of the COVID pandemic to illustrate the inadequacies of individualistic, human-centric thinking (the coronavirus is a more-than-human force that does not care about imaginary, human-drawn boundaries). A hypothetical scenario, as long as it is plausible, can serve the same purpose.

This is not an exhaustive list of types of evidence, of course. Can you think of any other types of evidence?

In the chapters to come, I will provide further information on evidence and exercises specific to use of evidence in each specific chapter.

ACTIVITY 4. EXPLORING EVIDENCE

- **Make a list of the top 10-15 peer-reviewed journals that will be relevant for your topic.**
- **Find examples of empirical, conceptual, and lit review articles. What language and text features tell you what kind of article it is?**
- **Make a list of professional organizations or entities in your field or that are relevant to your topic. Look up their websites to see if they might have reports or data that might be useful to you.**
- **Make a list of the top scholars in your field. Using your school library website or Google scholar, search to see if they have books that may be relevant to your topic.**

3.3 Using Detailed, Specific, Precise Language

Another characteristic of academic writing at the doctoral level: it is detailed and elaborated, while also using specific and precise language.

To adequately develop arguments and effectively explain and support them requires writing with enough detail that your reader can enter into and follow your thinking. Writing with a heightened attention to detail is an important scaffold for your reader because it helps them build schema—that is, it supports your reader to learn the necessary information to understand your argument (and determine its plausibility and/or applicability to their own work). And, given that you will have specialized and contextual knowledge that your reader likely will not, it's really important to avoid assumptions about what they know.

However, you also want to strike a balance between providing *enough* detail for your reader to understand what you are writing about, while also being concise enough that they do not get lost in the details. The keys to achieving this balance is regular practice and external feedback (so another person can cue you to places where you need more elaboration).

To further aid readers of your work, the language you use should be specific and precise, rather than general and vague. This will help you more accurately convey your meaning and leave less room for confusion or misinterpretation.

Let's analyze a few examples.

Sentence 1: New teachers often abandon their pre-service learning and adopt traditional practices.

Sentence 2: New teachers often abandon the student-centered and equity-minded practices learned in their preservice programs and adopt instead transmission-oriented, technicist teaching practices.

The two sentences above are drawn from a problem statement setting out the "problem of enactment": that is, that teachers are typically taught more equitable, interactive pedagogies in their teacher preparation programs, but they have a lot of difficulty putting those ideas into practice.

In the first sentence, there are embedded assumptions that the reader knows what the dominant pedagogies taught in preservice teacher preparation programs are; and what is meant by traditional methods (is the author talking about traditional pedagogical methods? Or are they referencing more traditional classroom management practices?).

The second sentence addresses these issues by adding further detail and specificity: The author provides information so that the reader understands that they are specifically talking about what preservice teachers are taught in their programs about student-centered and equity-based pedagogical practices; and that by "*practice*," they are specifically referring to the dominant pedagogical model of transmission teaching. By adding the detail of "*technicist*," the author also makes it clear that part of their argument contains a critique about this pedagogical model.

Here is another example of vague language and how it could be made more specific:

> **Sentence 1:** This study examines the ways that three new teachers negotiated their preservice learning in their new settings.
>
> **Sentence 2:** This qualitative multiple case study examines the ways that three first-year high school science teachers negotiated their preservice learning with human and contextual elements in their new classroom settings.

The first sentence above offers a purpose statement for a research study. However, very little detail is provided: "*new*" could encompass the first three to five years of teaching, and we know nothing about the teachers beyond that "new" status. It also lacks detail regarding the phenomenon under study (the ways they negotiated their preservice learning in their new settings).

The second sentence clears up this vagueness: readers learn that the teachers are in their first year, and that they are high school science teachers. Further, readers gain clarity about the focus of study—the ways that these three science teachers negotiated what they learned in their preservice programs *with respect to students as well as other contextual elements, at the classroom level.* This provides more of a focus (i.e., looking at students and context) as well as bounds the study in a different way than just "*settings*", which could simultaneously refer to the classroom, school, and district.

Let's take a third example, one drawn from the conceptual framework of a research study:

> **Sentence 1:** Teaching arises from joint activity of multiple human actors and nonhuman elements.
>
> **Sentence 2:** From a rhizomatic perspective, teaching arises from joint activity of multiple human actors (e.g., teachers, students, colleagues, administrators) and nonhuman elements (e.g., content, physical space, school cultures, bell schedules).

The first sentence above aims to communicate a different take on the phenomenon of teaching: rather than seeing teaching as something the teacher does to students (i.e., a linear transaction controlled by the teacher), it presents it as something that is collectively produced by a whole host of factors, both human and nonhuman. However, this idea presents a very different way of thinking about teaching (and one that is fairly abstract, at that), so it might be difficult for readers to understand with clarity. To make the idea more concrete, a bit of detail in the form of brief examples would help. Therefore, the second sentence offers elaboration in parentheses in terms of what we mean by "*human actors*" and "*nonhuman elements*." It also specifies that those ideas come from a particular theoretical perspective, rhizomatics.

Now, let's take a behind-the-scenes look at what a real-life revision process might look like. In their recent dissertation (a self-study of their culturally responsive teacher educator pedagogy), one of my EdD students, a teacher educator, wrote about how they found one of their doctoral assignments to be so powerful that they decided to incorporate it into a preservice teacher preparation course they were currently teaching (Potts, 2024). To explain why they found the assignment to be a high-impact learning opportunity, the student wrote, "The Stepping Stones assignment from EDLD 710 forced me to really think about the important moments from my different educational experiences, and then my professional ones, which really allowed me to see the growth trajectory from where I had started to where I was at that moment."

As a professor in the EdD program who was very familiar with the key assessments from the courses, I already knew the specifics of this assignment. However, the average reader would not have this specialized information. To make it accessible, my student needed to add sufficient details to provide readers of their writing with enough background information to understand their explanation of the "Stepping Stones" assignment.

In addition to this revision, I pointed out that my student had included a detail that was not absolutely necessary for understanding the key point she was making (the course number). I also provided feedback about the last part of the sentence, which communicated that this assignment allowed the student to see their own growth in the program. This information was an important part of the explanation regarding their decision to incorporate the Stepping Stones assignment into their TESOL course, but it could be streamlined for redundancy. This edit would also help strike a balance, given the additional details that needed to be added to help the reader understand the context.

I worked with my student to add background information about the assignment and more clearly describe its purpose. However, with the additions, the sentence became unwieldy. To increase readability, I suggested that we split the original sentence into two. The final sentence read: "*One of my first doctoral courses featured an assessment, 'Stepping Stones,' an auto-biographical essay that required students to reflect on their educational journeys and describe the key moments, or stepping stones, along the way. Analyzing the important moments from my different educational and professional experiences made apparent to me my growth trajectory as an educator.*"

Let's examine these edits more closely.

Figure 3.3: Annotated example of a revision for specificity

First, we added some details to provide context, explaining that this assignment came in the one of the first courses the student took as they began the doctoral program. We also added specificity to the description of the assignment and its purpose, explaining that it is autobiographical in nature and asks students to engage in reflection about the pathway that brought them to their current positions as educators. Along their "pathway," students identify a series of moments, which the instructor calls "Stepping Stones," that were important in their development and analyze them. Notice that the brief explanation of Stepping Stones is embedded and set off with commas as a rephrasing ("key moments, or stepping stones"). This is a strategy you can use throughout your writing to offer the reader quick definitions or elaborations without breaking up the current logic sequence.

However, these additional details, in combination with the student author's contextualization to their own experience from the original, made the sentence too complex (and long). Although the details and specificity about the assignment itself are important, the final part of the sentence makes it clear how the assignment impacted the student, which was the "so what" of the paragraph. A long sentence would not only be hard for a reader to follow, but it also might obscure this "so what." So we moved the contextualization into a new sentence, beginning with a more precise substitution for "*forced me to really think about.*" Instead, we used the word "*analyzing*," which points to a more concrete cognitive activity. The rest of the sentence filters out unnecessary language to help the reader zero in on the "so what", thereby striking a balance between the newly added details and a concise explanation.

ACTIVITY 5. DETAILS AND SPECIFICITY

Examine the first example, then the revision. Then, compare the two versions using the questions that follow.

Example: Elements in the classroom environment affect teachers' practices. For instance, Brashier and Norris (2008) found participants changed their practices based on how students behaved.

Elaborated example: Within the classroom environment, the teacher must attend to her students, and their diverse needs and dynamics as a class, with each of these elements recursively influencing her practices. For instance, in a study of 25 teachers' enactment of developmentally appropriate practice, Brashier and Norris (2008) found that to maintain order in their classrooms, participants tended to reduce—but not necessarily abandon—the use of learning centers and play they had learned in their preservice preparation programs. (Strom, 2015, p. 323)

- What was elaborated in the revision?
- What additional details and nuances were added?
- How is understanding of classroom complexity supported?

ACTIVITY 6. REVISING FOR DETAILS AND SPECIFICITY

Choose an assignment you have completed from a doctoral class. Use the following questions to assess your writing in terms of details and specificity.

- Find and evaluate an example where you use specific, precise language.
- Find and evaluate an example where you provide a high level of detail.
- Identify an example where you use vague language and determine what words or phrases you could use that are more specific and precise.
- Identify an example where you think you might need more detail. If you were someone without background knowledge on this topic, would you be able to access all the ideas? Are there any terms that need brief definitions or examples, or ideas that could use some elaboration? Edit accordingly.

3.4 Striving for Synthesis Over Summary

In your dissertation proposal, you will draw on a range of empirical, theoretical, and methodological literature to describe a research problem and its background, offer a review of the relevant literature, articulate a theoretical framework, and outline your research design. Because doctoral-level writing offers an original contribution—which I elaborate on in the final section of this chapter—this writing should aim to *synthesize* sources, rather than summarize them (with the exception of specific examples from your literature review, which I will discuss in detail in chapter five).

Summary refers to a recap of an individual source without interpretation, whereas synthesis entails a discussion across multiple sources that includes interpretation and/or shaping of information for a specific purpose. In a synthesis, you might see an articulation of key ideas or themes that cut across these sources, discussion of how the sources relate to or build on each other, or discussion of ways that the sources together create holistic understanding. For example, the excerpt below (Strom, Margolis, & Polat, 2019, p. 2) provides a critical evaluation of the way that "teacher dispositions" have been defined, comparing and contrasting multiple sources with original analysis.

> One tension evident in various definitions of teacher dispositions is the extent to which they reside either in the attributes or the actions of the individual teacher. For example, NCATE (2001) defines dispositions as the former:
>
> > The values, commitments, and professional ethics that influence behaviors towards students, families, colleagues, and communities and affect student learning, motivation, development, as well as the educator's own professional growth. Dispositions are guided by beliefs and attitudes related to values such as caring, fairness, honesty, responsibility, and social justice. (NCATE, 2001, p. 30)
>
> Language like "values," "beliefs," and "attitudes" locates dispositions primarily within the psyche of the teacher while phrases like "are guided by" imply causal relationships with other cognitive traits, an approach that only diminishes the possibility of a sound operational definition of the term. Similarly, Damon (2007) defines dispositions as "... a trait or characteristic that is embedded in temperament and disposes a person toward certain choices" (p. 376). The linking of the word "trait" with "dispose" places dispositions somewhere within the teacher's internal world.
>
> On the other hand, others have promoted a more action-centered definition of teacher dispositions. For example, Villegas (2007) argues that dispositions are "tendencies" for particular behaviors, but they are made concrete in the behavior itself.

From the authors' analysis of literature that addresses the ways that dispositions are defined, they developed a synthesis of that literature, which makes an original argument about ways that those definitions are in conflict: "*One tension evident in various definitions of teacher dispositions is the extent to which they reside either in the attributes or the actions of the individual teacher.*" The authors then provided an example of a definition of teacher dispositions as attributes from NCATE (formerly the main teacher preparation program accreditation agency in the US), interpreted the quote with respect to their argument, and then offered a critique ("*an approach that only diminishes the possibility of a sound operational definition of the term*"). They provided a second example of a definition of disposition as an individual teacher attribute before moving on to provide contrasting examples that show the second part of their initial interpretation (a definition of disposition as orientation-realized-in-action).

What differentiates this excerpt from a summary is the addition of original argument, the interpretation and critique, and analysis across multiple sources (the authors are discussing their identification of two main trends in the body of literature defining the fraught concept of dispositions, and the handful of studies described here are examples drawn from that larger body of literature).

We will discuss synthesis in further detail in later chapters (especially chapter five), but for now I will add just one more example to demonstrate how synthesis might be used for a specific purpose. Take a look at the example below and consider the following questions. How is the author synthesizing literature to paint a broader picture? What do you think her purpose might be? After you come up with your own answers, compare to my analysis below.

> It is little wonder that many believe educational leadership itself is in a crisis. Some relate the crisis to a lack of qualified candidates for superintendencies (Esparo & Rader, 2001) or school principalships (Chirichello, 2001; Malone & Caddell, 2000). Others believe that the crisis has occurred as a result of naïve, conservative, and traditional leadership responses to increasingly complex, challenging, and postmodern educational contexts (Maxcy, 1994). Giroux (1992) associates difficulties of educational leadership with crises of democratic government. Still others are concerned about the lack of leadership offered by school boards themselves (van Alfen, 1993) or about the propensity of educators to adopt a series of reforms in rapid succession (Fullan, 2003), failing to empower either teachers or administrators. (*Shields, 2010, p. 110*)

In the paragraph above, Shields (2010) presents a synthesis across multiple studies, each of which offer a different explanation for a crisis of educational leadership. Her synthesis of these explanations accomplishes two purposes: one, it substantiates her claim that "*many believe educational leadership itself is in a crisis.*" It also vividly paints a picture for readers, showing that the educational leadership crisis is multi-faceted, encompassing multiple levels of leadership and policy.

The tasks of summarizing sources from individual ideas and synthesizing across these ideas are important skills for successfully completing a dissertation proposal. In the next activity, I offer four quotes about qualitative research from different authors and provide an opportunity to practice these skills. First, summarize them in your own words. Then use those summaries to construct a synthesis definition that integrates insights from the multiple sources.

ACTIVITY 7.1. SUMMARIZING AND SYNTHESIZING IDEAS FROM MULTIPLE SOURCES

Summarize the key ideas from each of the definitions of "qualitative research" in your own words.

1. Qualitative research is generally characterized by inductive approaches to knowledge building aimed at generating meaning (Leavy, 2014). Researchers use this approach to explore; to robustly investigate and learn about social phenomenon; to unpack the meanings people ascribe to activities, situations, events, or artifacts; or to build a depth of understanding about some dimension of social life (Leavy, 2014). The values underlying qualitative research include the importance of people's subjective experiences and meaning-making processes and acquiring a depth of understanding (i.e., detailed information from a small sample). Qualitative research is generally appropriate when your primary purpose is to explore, describe, or explain. *(Leavy, 2017, p. 9)*
2. Qualitative research is a situated Part that locates the observer in the world. It consists of a set of interpretive, material practices that make the world visible. These practices transform the world. They turn the world into a series of representations, including field notes, interviews, conversations, photographs, recordings, and memos to the self. At this level, qualitative research involves an interpretive, naturalistic approach to the world. This means that qualitative researchers study things in their natural settings, attempting to make sense of, or interpret, phenomena in terms of the meanings people bring to them. *(Denzin & Lincoln, 2005, p. 3)*
3. Basically, qualitative researchers are interested in understanding the meaning people have constructed, that is, how people make sense of their world and the experiences they have in the world.... The following four characteristics are identified by most as key to understanding the nature of qualitative research: the focus is on process, understanding, and meaning; the researcher is the primary instrument of data collection and analysis; the process is inductive; and the product is richly descriptive. (*Merriam, 2009, p. 13-14*)
4. Qualitative research is an umbrella term for a wide variety of approaches to and methods for the study of natural social life. The information or data collected and analyzed is primarily (but not exclusively) nonquantitative in character, consisting of textual materials such as interview transcripts, fieldnotes, and documents, and/or visual materials such as artifacts, photographs, video recordings, and Internet sites, that document human experiences about others and/or one's self in social action and reflexive states. The goals of qualitative research

ACTIVITY 7.1. SUMMARIZING AND SYNTHESIZING IDEAS FROM MULTIPLE SOURCES (CONT.)

are also multiple, depending on the purpose of the particular project. Outcomes are most often composed of essential representations and presentations of salient findings from the analytic synthesis of data and can include: documentation of cultural observations, new insights and understandings about individual and social complexity, evaluation of the effectiveness of programs or policies, artistic renderings of human meanings, and/or the critique of existing social orders and the initiation of social justice. (*Saldaña, 2011, p. 3-4*)

ACTIVITY 7.2. SUMMARIZING AND SYNTHESIZING IDEAS FROM MULTIPLE SOURCES

Use your notes from the exercise above to create a single definition of 1-3 sentences that synthesizes across the four sources. Use your own words.

3.5 Developing Original Voice and Research

Doctoral-level academic writing for research differs from the majority of other types of academic writing from the bachelor's and master's level in its emphasis on *original contribution*. For example, you will make a case for conducting original research by assessing, evaluating, and synthesizing the contributions of others to show a need for the research; and you will present and discuss the outcomes of that original research, its significance, and its contributions to the field. The arguments for the study and its significance will illustrate your specific point of view and agenda as a researcher, and even though you may be drawing on others' work in much of the written dissertation, your academic voice should shine through.

The best way to develop that academic voice is to *practice, practice, practice*! Throughout the book, I will be providing exercises and activities where you will be able to do that while crafting your original arguments and shaping your point of view. Therefore, in this final section, I will focus on one particular area related to the development of an academic voice where I often see students experience difficulties: the use of direct quotes.

In doctoral-level writing (and beyond), a good quote can be a very powerful writing tool. However, if you overuse quotes, it will not only obscure your own emerging writer voice but also could send a message to the reader that you have not adequately read, interpreted, and synthesized the literature for yourself. So, when using a quote, be selective and make sure that it is accompanied by your own analysis. Below, I discuss when and how you can use quotations in academic writing for research as you develop your original voice.

When to Use Quotes: Impact or Aesthetics

You may want to use a direct quote when the original words of the author you are citing are *so eloquent* or *so powerful* that you feel it necessary to include exact phrasing. For instance, in much of my research I write about rhizomatics, a non-linear theory of thought/social activity. I often explain that this paradigm is about fluid connection and expansion rather than static binaries. However, I also use a particular quote alongside my own explanation that captures a beautiful turn of phrase from Deleuze and Guattari (1987) that made a major impact on my own thinking: "While the tree imposes the verb 'to be,' the fabric of the rhizome is 'and...and...and" (p. 25).

As part of my responsibility in using this quote, however, I have to recognize that many of my readers may not have read the text from which this quote comes—*A Thousand Plateaus*—or any work on rhizomatics, for that matter. It is up to me, then, to interpret Deleuze and Guattari's words for my reader to scaffold their understanding of this quote. Thus, if I were to use this quote in a conceptual framework that introduced rhizomatics, I would need to both introduce the quote and tell them what I think it means. In the paragraph below, examine the ways that I support my reader's understanding. How does the text that comes before the quote connect directly to it? How does the interpretation after the quote help them understand what it means (and why I'm using it here)?

> Rhizomatics is a non-linear theory of thought and social activity based on the rhizome (Deleuze & Guattari, 1987; Strom, 2015), which, scientifically speaking, is a tubular plant that grows unpredictably in all directions. As a philosophical concept, the rhizome shifts attention away from static "either/or" binaries to complex "both/and" ways of seeing the world. **As Deleuze and Guattari note,** "While the tree imposes the verb 'to be,' the fabric of the rhizome is 'and...and... and" (p. 25). In other words, while traditional Western "tree" thinking produces a linear perspective of fixed *being*, a rhizomatic paradigm sees the world in ever-expanding multiples that are constantly changing, or *becoming*, as new connections are forged.

When to Use Quotes: Emphasis, Illustration, and Evidence

Other purposes for direct quotes include emphasizing or illustrating a point and providing evidence/support for your statements.

For example, in the next excerpt, Valencia, Martin, Place, and Grossman (2009, p. 304) make a point that multiple actors impact student teachers' work and learning, and then use a quote from a literature review on the learning of novice teachers to emphasize their assertion.

> Student teachers' work is done in complex settings where an array of people with varied histories, understandings, beliefs, and perspectives on instruction and curriculum interact. **As Wideen, Mayer-Smith, and Moon (1998) suggested,** "What we learn from studying the process of learning to teach depends on whose voices are being heard" (p. 156).

Below is a second example from the literature review referenced in the above excerpt. In it, Wideen, Mayer-Smith, and Moon (1998, p. 160) use a quote to support their critique that most teacher preparation programs take a reductive, process-product view of teacher learning rather than a complex, ecological one.

> As we indicated in the opening section of this review, programs of teacher education have traditionally been based on the view that learning to teach is a process of acquiring knowledge about teaching (Carter, 1990). An implicit notion of integration lies behind this positivistic tradition in which the university provides the theory, skills, and knowledge; the school provides the field setting where such knowledge is applied and practiced; and the beginning teacher provides the individual effort that integrates it all (Britzman, 1991). Feiman-Nemser and Buchmann (1989) **describe such programs in this way:**
>
> > The typical programs of teacher preparation as an additive process that largely bypasses person and setting. None of these models illuminates the role of prior beliefs of preconceptions in teacher learning. Nor do they take into account the influence of program features, settings, and people as they interact over time. (p. 368)
>
> Virtually all the studies we reviewed were conducted within the theory and practice setting of this traditional model of teacher education.

How to Use Quotes: Introducing and Contextualizing

When you use a quote in academic writing, you have to make sure that the quote is clearly connected to a point you are making, and your readers understand its meaning and significance. It is your job as the researcher/writer to introduce the quote and interpret it for your readers to show them why it is important/meaningful in the context of your topic/argument. As such, you should never, ever leave a "naked" quote for your readers to interpret themselves. Moreover, in the vast majority of instances, you'll want to provide an introduction to the quote, which serves as a connector. (If you look at the previous examples, the introductions to each quote have been bolded to highlight them).

In the example below, McDonald (2005, p. 420) discusses Ladson-Billings' use of critical race theory.

> **For example, Ladson-Billings (1999a) used critical race theory to illustrate how individuals and programs more explicitly challenge prospective teachers to address issues of race and inequality.** <u>She suggested that Cochran-Smith's work at Boston College challenges teachers to more directly explore how race and racism inform their views and practices by supporting them to develop five different perspectives that are critical to addressing issues of race and language diversity:</u> "reconsidering personal knowledge and experience, locating teaching with the culture of the school and the community, analyzing children's learning opportunities, understanding children's understanding, and constructing reconstructionist pedagogy" (p. 229).

With the bolded text, she introduces and contextualizes the quote; with the underlined text, she tells the reader what the quoted text is about.

ACTIVITY 8. ANALYZING QUOTE USAGE

Read the following excerpt from Zeichner (2010, p. 1546) and analyze his quote usage. Then, answer the questions that follow.

The solution to the teacher quality problem according to some is to deregulate teacher education and open the gates to individuals who have not completed a teacher education program prior to certification (e.g., Hess, 2009; Walsh, 2004) rather than to improve the conditions in public schools that are driving teachers out. Andrew Rosen, president of Kaplan College, which is part of one of the major for-profit teacher education companies to enter the U.S. teacher education market in recent years, stated the following in an online conversation about teacher education that clearly illustrates this stance: "Teaching is less lucrative and is rife with work environment issues that many deem not to be worthy of investment. By reducing the barriers for bright-minded professionals, we can increase the population of qualified candidates" (Rosen, 2003).

1. What is Zeichner's purpose in using this quote from Rosen's work? (What does this quote DO for him?)
2. How does Zeichner introduce the quote?
3. What words does Zeichner use to let the reader know why the quote is being used?

ACTIVITY 9. DEVELOPING VOICE THROUGH QUOTE USAGE

Select a paper you wrote for one of your past doctoral classes and find a passage from it that contains a direct quote. Then, use the prompts below to evaluate and edit the passage.

- Analyze your use of the quote. What is the purpose of the quote in the selected passage? Is the purpose of the quote clear to your reader? Is it introduced and explained?
- If you answered "no" to any of the questions above, edit the passage.
- Explain what edits you made and why.

Quote Used	Analysis/Explanation

Conclusion

This chapter presented the rest of the "rules of the language of power," or the major characteristics of doctoral level writing. We discussed the following key ideas:

- ***Making a well-reasoned argument*** is one of the most critical skills to learn for your dissertation (because you will be making arguments in every single chapter). Arguments have three main parts. The first is *the claim* (the actual point you want to make), followed by accompanying *explanation* or reasons why that claim is credible. The third part is *support,* or evidence of some kind.
- ***Supporting arguments with credible evidence*** is essential for illustrating or backing up your claims/explanations for your arguments. There are multiple types of evidence that you can use to support your arguments in compelling ways, such as peer-reviewed articles, books, websites, and even descriptions of personal experience.
- ***Using detailed, specific, precise language*** is crucial to make sure that you accurately convey your meaning and support readers to enter into and follow your thinking.
- ***Striving for synthesis over summary*** means, rather than recapping ideas from a single source, providing an original interpretation or evaluation by discussing ideas across multiple sources.
- ***Developing original voice and research*** is a distinguishing feature of doctoral-level writing. This chapter focused specifically on quote usage as an important part of voice development, exploring how to use quotes purposefully alongside your own interpretation and analysis.

The Problem Statement

Contents

4.1 Introduction

I entered my doctoral program after the end of my third year at a school in in southern California where 100% of the youth qualified for free lunch (a proxy for poverty). For a multitude of reasons, including tough working conditions, burnout, and feelings of failure, a mass exodus of teachers occurred each year. Leaders then spent the summer scrambling to find enough teachers to start the year fully staffed. At times, vacancies were not filled until well into the year—if at all—which, as you can imagine, harmed an already vulnerable student population. I wondered what could be done about this "revolving door" of teachers—if there was a way to prepare teachers specifically for the challenges of working in contexts like ours. This became the initial problem that framed my emerging dissertation project.

In this chapter, I offer guidance for writing the problem (or issue) statement, which is typically chapter one of your dissertation proposal (and later, your full dissertation). The problem statement does exactly what it sounds like: it states a problem or issue that serves as the impetus for your research. However, naming the problem is just the start—you'll need to thoroughly explain that problem, where it came from, and what its impacts are. You will then present your proposed study and describe how it will address (or begin to address) that problem. I discuss each of these dimensions in the sections that follow, with activities that will help you draft out sections of your own problem statement.

4.1 Purposes of the Problem Statement

WARM UP

What do you want to study, and why? What is the underlying problem or issue that your study responds to? Why is it a problem, and how do you know?

Your eventual dissertation will involve an inquiry driven by a problem or issue of significance. The specific research study you propose and carry out aims to address that problem—or, at least, to generate knowledge that could help in solving it. That problem or issue is laid out in the first section of your dissertation proposal, which later becomes your chapter one of your dissertation.

This first chapter of your dissertation—sometimes known as the "problem statement" or "issue statement"—has several purposes, which will correspond to particular elements that will make up the structure of this chapter. (These elements are denoted in the following sentences with italics.) First, you will clearly and concisely articulate and define the problem. You will accomplish this in an introductory paragraph or two, which I refer to as the ***problem summary***. Second, you will delve more deeply into the problem to describe where it came from, its contributing factors, and/or why the problem persists in the ***background of the problem*** section. Next you need to convince the reader that the problem warrants study with a ***rationale.*** This rationale shows the problem's significance and urgency, as well as demonstrates that it would fill a gap in research literature. Then, this initial chapter of your dissertation concludes with a statement of ***purpose*** that lays out your goals for the study and briefly outlines the proposed study, including the ***research questions*** (this last section provides a "roadmap" for the rest of your proposal/dissertation). See Figure 4.1, below, for details on these purposes and elements. Each of these will be unpacked in the sections that follow.

PURPOSES OF THE PROBLEM STATEMENT	
CLEARLY DESCRIBE THE PROBLEM	Articulates a specific issue or problem that is driving the study (or that the study seeks to address) with enough context to understand what the problem is and why it is a problem.
SKETCH THE PROBLEM BACKGROUND	Situates the problem in a particular context and describes what factors (historical, political, sociocultural, etc) gave rise to the problem; and/or why it persists.
PROVIDE A COMPELLING RATIONALE	Makes an argument for the necessity of attending to this issue by 1) showing the reader the problem is urgent/significant; and 2) demonstrating a corresponding gap in research.
DEFINE KEY CONCEPTS	Defines ideas/concepts that are central to the study.
PROVIDE OVERVIEW OF STUDY	Identifies the specific purposes(s) of the study and states research questions; briefly summarizes research design, theoretical framework, and any important characteristics of the study.

Figure 4.1: Purposes of the problem statement

4.2 First Steps: Exploratory Reading and Writing

To meet the purposes of the problem statement (namely, adequately describing the problem driving your study and make a convincing case that it is, indeed, a problem that is worth investigating) you will need to provide evidence from credible sources. This evidence will support your assertions, help you illustrate the scope of the issue, and demonstrate your broad familiarity with key research in the area of your topic.

To accomplish that means you need to do some substantial reading and writing on the issue or problem.

I recommend that you begin by searching and reading articles and reports that discuss the problem you are interested in addressing. At this point, however, it not vital that the articles you read are about exactly what you want to study. A good thing to keep in mind (and which I'll talk more about in the next section) is that the problem driving the research, and what you actually want to study, are not the same thing. For now, you are focusing on being able to clearly articulate, define, and provide evidence for the problem driving your study. To find that information, you may be reading texts that do not speak to precisely your area of interest in terms of the investigation you want to conduct.

As you read, make sure to keep a chart that documents each text and records information that will be relevant to your goals for the problem statement (describing the problem, showing that it is urgent and significant, and supporting both with compelling evidence). I provide a suggested format in the Activity 1.1.

After every few articles you read, write a synthetic memo. A synthetic memo is a reflection in which you begin to synthesize or integrate the key ideas of the readings *as they pertain to the problem.* In the memo, reflect on how these readings help you understand what exactly the problem is; why/how it's a problem; what evidence you have that it is a problem; and what the background or contributing factors to the problem are. (Notice that these correspond to some of the important purposes from the graphic above.) Your synthetic memos will help you connect studies and flesh out your thinking in ways that will support your writing later.

In your charts, make sure that you include both the full citations, and cite specific articles when you write about them in the memo. I recommend this step because, if you look at the memo a few weeks or months later, you probably won't remember where the information came from. Another important practice: if you use direct quotes, make sure you enclose them in quotation marks and include a page number, so that 1) you know where it came from and 2) you don't accidentally plagiarize later. (Six months after you've written something, you will likely not remember that you pulled it directly from the article. So, you could read it and think "wow, what a great sentence I wrote there. Let me stick that in my problem statement." Then, without meaning to, you could end up with plagiarism in your work.)

ACTIVITY 1.1. PROBLEM STATEMENT CHARTS AND REFLECTIVE MEMOS				
Create a citation chart for each text you read to develop your problem statement. Make notes on the relevance of the reading to the problem you are articulating. Suggested format for the chart:				
Citation	**What is the problem?**	**Where does the problem come from? Why does it persist?**	**What evidence shows the significance and urgency of the problem?**	**Quotes and Notes**

ACTIVITY 1.2 REFLECTIVE MEMOS
Every 3-5 articles you read, write a reflective memo that explores the following prompts in light of your reading: 1. What is the problem? 2. Where did the problem come from, or why does it persist? 3. How do I know it is a problem (what evidence is there)?

4.3 The Problem Summary

Your problem summary is the very first thing you will write, and should make up the first paragraph(s) of your problem statement (typically, the first chapter of your dissertation). The problem summary introduces your overall problem statement and provides an overview of the problem driving your study. These paragraphs offer a very important overall framing for your first chapter.

The problem summary also has with multiple purposes. In the first few sentences, you need to clearly *name the problem* that will be driving your study. You will also need to *provide enough details* to help your reader understand the problem, who it affects, and why/how it's a problem (but you do not want to go too far in depth yet, because you will unpack key ideas in the sections that follow). You will also *set the context*, which helps place your issue within the larger landscape of your field or profession. Of course, with all of this, you also need to *provide evidence.* And finally, for most projects, the overarching problem has many dimensions, so you will need to *locate the entrypoint,* or narrow in on the specific aspect of the issue that your study will address. Figure 4.2 summarizes these purposes, and I unpack each of them in turn in the sections that follow.

PURPOSES OF THE PROBLEM SUMMARY	
NAME THE PROBLEM	Clearly and concisely articulate a specific problem that will be driving the study.
PROVIDE DETAILS	Provide adequate details so the reader understands the what, who, why, and how of the problem.
SET THE CONTEXT	Frame the problem and situate it within the larger context of educational issues relevant for your study.
PROVIDE EVIDENCE	Draw on key literature/current research to frame the problem and provide compelling evidence that supports claims.
LOCATE THE ENTRYPOINT	Locate the problem within a particular aspect of the overarching issue, and/or offer a specific entrypoint foreshadowing the study focus.

Figure 4.2: Purposes of the problem summary

Name the Problem

As described above, the problem summary provides an overview of the central problem or issue and serves as the introduction to this first chapter. This requires clearly naming the problem that drives your study. And as I mentioned before, the problem is not *what you want to study.* These are two different things, although they are related. Typically, the problem you are naming is a situation or condition that is resulting in harm, or an issue that needs to be addressed to improve something, which the study you are proposing will help to address (or begin to address) in some way.

Below, I present several examples of clear problem "namings." Examine them. As you read, think about the following questions: what kinds of data or other evidence could you provide that would demonstrate the existence of these problems? What kinds of data or evidence could illustrate the significance and urgency of these issues?

- Large disparities in achievement levels exist between student racial/ethnic groups.
- Students of color are disproportionately identified for special education.
- Low-income students of color are less likely to have access to honors and AP courses than white students.
- The teacher workforce does not represent the student population in terms of diversity.
- Multilingual learners are not reclassified into general education at appropriate rates.

Let's take one of the above examples and flesh it out along the dimensions of *what, who, why,* and *how* as we talk through the rest of the purposes and goals of the problem summary.

Example Problem: The teacher workforce does not represent the student population in terms of racial/ethnic diversity.

This sentence clearly and concisely states the problem, but the reader needs a little more information to understand what that entails. What exactly does it mean that the teaching force doesn't represent the student population? And why is that a problem? To answer these, add context.

Set the Context

Let me apologize, because I am introducing the element of *context* out of order. It is important first *for you* to name the problem—because without that, you cannot draft out any of the other elements. However, I don't start the problem summary with a sentence that articulates the problem my study responds to. Instead, I like to provide some kind of overarching context to set the stage in the first sentence or two—for example, I can begin by describing a current condition that shows that the problem is a significant one. In this way, the *setting the context* portion of the problem summary is both an introduction and a "hook." It should effectively and naturally segue into "naming" the problem, *and* it should be compelling enough to grab your reader's attention and keep them going. So, think carefully about your strategy for presenting this initial information.

One common strategy is to use statistics (see example below), which can paint a vivid picture (just be careful, because statistics are often misused or tell a very incomplete picture). Or, you might begin with a hard-hitting quote. For instance, to set the stage for a problem summary regarding teacher attrition, the text might begin with this quote from Halford (1998, p. 34): "Teaching is the profession that eats its young." I used this quote in my own dissertation—the metaphor paints a horrifyingly vivid picture while driving home the point that our profession does a terrible job supporting teachers as they begin their careers.

Stories are also a very effective way to draw in readers. So, you might consider beginning your problem summary with a powerful example or short narrative related to the issue driving your study. To illustrate, if I were introducing the issue of the under-preparation of pre-service teachers to support MLLs, I might begin with a story like the following:

Alison, a new teacher, has three multilingual learners (MLLs) in her seventh-grade social studies classroom. All three are failing the class and are at risk of retention. She asked the other teachers in her department for help, but they were unhelpful—a few even told her that it is her responsibility to teach social studies, not language. She has talked to the ESL teacher a few times, but he focuses on the linguistic basics, not supporting language-learners as they learn content. She doesn't know what to do to support them, and often wishes that her teacher education program had offered more than just a one-unit module for teaching MLL students.

I can then transition into a statement of the problem, picking up on the last sentence of the story and citing research that shows the lack of initial teacher preparation for supporting the success of MLLs in general education classrooms.

Let's work through the context for the example problem posed above—*"The teacher workforce does not represent the student population in terms of diversity."* In adding context, I would describe the current conditions in school that make this a problem. I also would need to provide some additional detail in terms of what I mean by "diversity" (which is often code for Black and Brown and/or multilingual students).

To do that, I might add the following information:

- Over the last three decades, the student population in the United States has become markedly more diverse.
- The teacher population has remained about 80% white and monolingual.

Provide Details

In addition to context and a clear statement of the problem, we also need to add *just enough* details that the reader can understand, on a foundational level, the what, who, why, and how of the problem. That is, *what* the problem is, *who* it affects, *why* it's a problem, and *how* we know that. In addition, because the lack of teacher diversity in terms of race/ethnicity is already a well-documented issue, we might also add some details here qualifying why the problem persists. Again, we are still going to be relatively brief—we will go deeper into what, who, why, and how as we build out the problem background and rationale.

The information below directly names students of color, along with teachers of color, as affected populations (the *who*). It also spells out three reasons the retention of teachers of color is an important topic (the *why*).

- Students of color receive multiple benefits from teachers of color.
- Teachers can serve as cultural brokers for students with similar backgrounds.
- It is essential for students of color to see people who look like them in positions of authority.
- Teachers of color are more likely to work in high-needs schools, therefore helping stem teacher shortages.

The next piece of information addresses why the problem persists, despite the field knowing about it.

- While there have been efforts to diversify the teacher workforce, structural barriers have impeded progress. These include entrance tests, which are seen by some scholars as biased against populations of color, and financial requirements of student teaching, which place a major burden on many preservice students of color.
- In addition, Black and Brown teachers, who are mostly employed low-funded and high demanding schools, leave the field at higher rates than their white counterparts, who are mostly employed in higher funded, suburban schools.

Support with Evidence

Alongside these details, we need to show evidence that the problem exists—in other words, we need to indicate to our reader *how* we know it's a problem. This could include statistics or qualitative evidence from research, reports, or non-partisan organizations. The following evidence supports claims made so far in this example summary.

Student diversity: According to a 2019 NCES report regarding public school student demographics, in the last two decades the number of white students has increased by 1%. Meanwhile, the number of Black students has increased 18%, the number of Asian students 73%, and the Hispanic population by 64%. In 2018, for the first time, white students comprised a minority (47%) of all public-school students in the United States (NCES, 2021).

Teacher lack of diversity: 80% of teachers are white (NCES, 2020).

Efforts to diversify: Multiple states have policies, programs, and incentives aimed at recruiting and retaining more teachers of color (Villegas, Strom, & Lucas, 2012).

Barriers: Prospective teachers of color face multiple barriers First, they tend to face higher debt burdens than their white counterparts; second, they experience more difficulty completing their degrees due to several factors, including taking fewer classes due to work and family responsibilities, being underprepared by their high schools, and feeling alienated by the lack of diversity and cultural connection; and 3) they experience disproportionate licensure exam failure rate likely due to bias (Carver-Thomas & Darling-Hammond, 2017).

Attrition: Teachers of color leave the field at a rate that is 24% higher than white teachers (Ingersoll & May, 2011); they are also more likely to experience challenging work conditions, and are disproportionately affected by school closures (Carver-Thomas & Darling-Hammond, 2017).

Student benefits: Villegas & Irvine (2010) conducted an exhaustive review of studies examining the impact of teachers of color on students of color, finding evidence that 1) they serve as role models for all students; 2) they positively affect achievement of students of color because they can serve as cultural brokers; and 3) they are more likely to work in high-needs, high poverty areas, thus helping to solve teacher shortages.

The example below puts together all the pieces of the problem summary to illustrate how they might be edited together as a cohesive whole.

Example Problem Summary

Over the last three decades, the student population in the United States has become markedly more racially/ethnically diverse. According to a 2019 NCES report regarding public school student demographics, in the last twenty years the number of white students has increased by 1%, while the number of Black students has risen 18%, Asian students 73%, and Latinx students 64%. In 2018, for the first time, white students comprised a minority (47%) of all public-school students in the United States (NCES, 2021).

Our changing student population creates an imperative for our teacher workforce to reflect their diversity. Villegas and Irvine (2010) conducted an exhaustive review of studies examining the impact of teachers of color on students of color, finding evidence that 1) they serve as role models for all students; 2) they positively affect achievement of students of color because they can serve as cultural brokers; and 3) they are more likely to work in high-needs, high poverty areas, thus helping to solve teacher shortages. Yet, despite efforts to diversify the teacher workforce, such as the adoption of state policies aimed at recruiting and retaining more teachers of color (Villegas, Strom, & Lucas, 2012), the teacher population remains about 80% white and English monolingual (NCES, 2018).

Teachers of color face many barriers both prior to entering the classroom and afterward. They are less likely to complete their degrees due to financial struggles and lower-quality educational preparation, and disproportionately fail licensure exams, likely due to bias (Thomas &

Darling-Hammond, 2017). Moreover, once in the classroom, they are more likely to experience challenging work conditions (Sutter, Darling-Hammond, & Carver-Thomas, 2016) and are overrepresented in school closures (Carver-Thomas & Darling-Hammond, 2017). It is no wonder that they are 24% more likely to leave the profession than white teachers (Ingersoll & May, 2011).

Locating the Entry Point

Often, the first problem you identify may be too big, or have too many dimensions to it, to feasibly respond to in one study. For example, many students I have worked with are concerned about disparities in academic success between students of color and white students—sometimes called the "achievement gap," or the "education debt" in social justice terms (Ladson-Billings, 2006). However, this problem is quite complex and encompasses many layers or dimensions.

For example, part of the problem has to do with funding disparities. Students of color and multilingual learners are more likely to attend under-resourced schools with more inexperienced and/or underprepared teachers, which contributes to achievement disparities. Then there are issues with educational access: students of color are disproportionately tracked into remedial and special education classes and are more likely to receive disciplinary actions that take them away from the classroom.

However, we could also locate the problem with teachers and teaching. For one, educators often bring deficit perspectives of students of color. Relatedly, dominant pedagogies are normed on white ways of knowing and being that invalidate and devalue the resources of students of color. Research has shown that both of these issues negatively affect achievement for marginalized groups. Then there are the tests themselves, which many researchers argue are biased. For example, studies have shown that test questions often contain culturally-specific terms that unfairly penalize students from non-dominant cultures.

As you can see, the issue of achievement disparities is enormous and multi-faceted. A project on this topic that can be completed by a single researcher in a reasonable amount of time requires zooming in on a specific dimension.

Most other problems in the social sciences are similar—after all, social issues are complex and multi-dimensional—so you will need to narrow down or focus in on the particular "slice" of the problem you will be focusing on. I like to to think of this is the "entry point" to the problem. With this addition of a specific entry point, or a narrowed focus on the issue you identified, your problem summary begins to take the shape of a funnel: starting with the broad context of an issue, articulating an overarching issue/problem relating to that broad context, and then narrowing down to an aspect of that issue/problem that will lead you into the focus of the study you are going to propose (see Figure 4.3 on the next page).

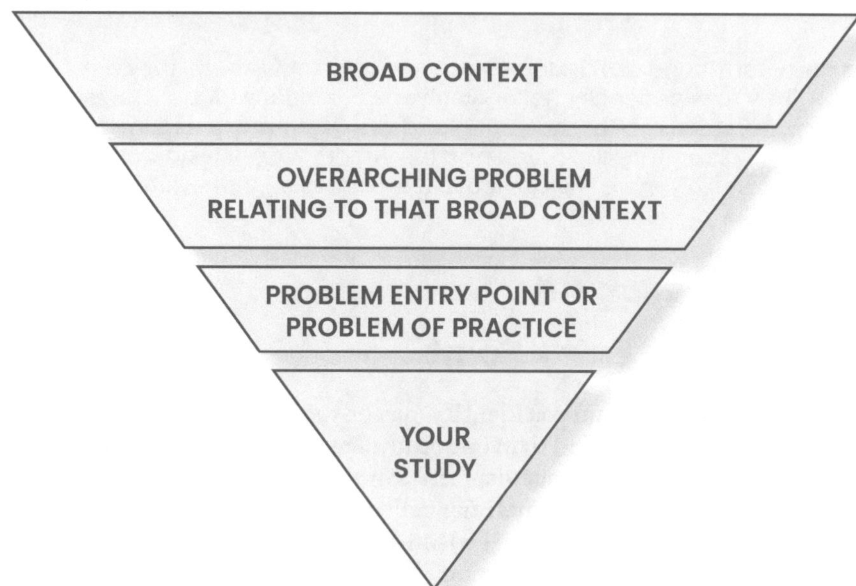

Figure 4.3: Problem summary funnel

In some programs, and particularly those focused on the more practice- oriented EdD degree, the entry point is referred to as the "problem of practice." For this type of entry point, "locating" means articulating how the overarching problem matters in a particular practice setting.

Your professional context will likely make a difference in terms of where you locate the problem: for example, take the problem of preparing teachers to support multilingual learners. Someone working in an initial teacher preparation program would probably locate the problem in pre-professional preparation that helps teachers develop related knowledge and skills around second language acquisition. However, someone involved in a K-12 school setting will likely locate the problem with in-service learning opportunities addressing pedagogies for multilingual learners (like professional development workshops) that can support practicing teachers already in classrooms.

If you aren't sure of your entry point or problem of practice, one strategy is to conduct an inventory of the *need*, your *interest*, your *access*, and the *feasibility* of studying a particular topic.

- *Need:* First and foremost, do we *need* a study on this topic? To answer this question, doing some thinking about the social justice rationale and the literature rationale can help. In terms of the social justice rationale: can you make an argument, based on concrete evidence, that the topic you want to study can shed light on or help address a significant and urgent problem? Regarding the literature rationale: do plenty of studies already exist on this topic? For example, if there are already 500 studies regarding a specific phenomenon, there would be no immediate reason for you to conduct another.

- *Interest:* What area of the problem are you most interested in and passionate about? You will be writing about this topic for an extended period of time, so make sure that it is something that will keep your interest and enthusiasm alive through the more tedious dissertation phases.
- *Access:* What dimensions of the problem are you most well-positioned to research? For example, imagine you are a classroom teacher who wants to study ways to support quality pedagogy in science classrooms. There are many places you could locate this study. However, you will probably have more access to other teachers for interviews and observations than district leaders, which could be a factor to take under consideration when deciding what aspect of the problem you would like to investigate.
- *Feasibility:* In terms of practicality, can you research the topic you want to, given your access to participants and settings, time to complete the study, resources, and so on? For example, if you were interested in whether teaching from an assets-based perspective made a difference in terms of standardized test scores, you'd have to think about the amount of time that would take. If you are in a PhD program and plan to take a few years to conduct your study, then yes, it is probably feasible to study assets-based teaching in certain classrooms and then obtain the scores of the students in those classrooms the next year. However, if you are in a three-year EdD program, you typically have one year to complete the entire dissertation. That gives you about 2 months for data collection. That means that it probably would not be feasible to examine students' change in achievement on standardized tests.

The example below provides two additional examples of "funneling" or "narrowing" your topic or identifying your entry point to the issue.

Example 1: Science Equity and Multilingual Learners

- **Overarching problem:** Inequities in science for youth of color
- **Narrowed problem:** Patterns of exclusion in participation and belonging for Black and Brown youth in science education classrooms
- **Even more narrowed problem:** Patterns of exclusion in participation and belonging for Black and Brown multilingual learners in science education classrooms

Example 2: Translating First-Year Teaching Practices

- **Overarching problem:** Dominant methods of teaching continue to approximate transmission teaching, which contributes to inequities for marginalized youth.
- **Entry point:** First-year teachers struggle to translate their learning about socioculturally-based pedagogy into their first-year practices and often revert to transmission-based methods.

ACTIVITY 2. ELEMENTS OF THE PROBLEM SUMMARY ORGANIZER

Bullet out your thoughts about each element below.

1. Name the Problem: Clearly and concisely articulate a specific problem related to educational equity that will be driving the study.
2. Provide Details: Provide adequate details so the reader understands the what, who, why, and how of the problem.
3. Set the Context: Frame/situate the problem within the larger context of current educational issues.
4. Support with Evidence: Draw on key literature/current research to frame the problem and provide compelling evidence that supports claims.
5. Locate the Entry Point: Locate the problem within a particular aspect/dimension of the overarching issue, and/or offer a specific entry point that foreshadows the study purpose/focus.

4.4 The Problem Background

ACTIVITY 3: FREE WRITE

Off the top of your head, what pieces of information does your reader need to understand the problem driving your study, where that problem came from, and why it persists? Challenge yourself to write at least three ideas down.

Once you have established the problem in brief, the next step is to provide a background of the problem, which gives the reader additional context so they can understand what created the problem and why it persists (even, perhaps, despite efforts to address it). In this section, authors typically will identify contributing factors and start fleshing out the argument regarding the significance of the problem, which will support the need for the study.

The background of the problem draws on foundational and current literature to explain the conditions, factors, patterns, and/or events that have contributed to the creation, maintenance, and/or expansion of the problem. This discussion may involve the issue's historical factors, political dimensions, sociocultural aspects, and so on. This section also provides more detail about the current context of the problem, explaining what is going on *right now* that is amplifying the current issue in some way or making it particularly urgent to address. The problem background often foreshadows the key points and arguments that will be made in the literature review; and may also briefly introduce key concepts so the ideas are accessible to a range of readers.

Problem Background Versus the Lit Review

In my classes, students often express confusion between the problem statement background and the literature review (which typically comes in chapter two of the dissertation). The problem statement background and the literature review should align and may also contain some of the same points. However, there is a major difference in terms of their purposes, which in turn affects the way they will be written.

The main purpose of the problem background is to help support the reader's general understanding of the problem. This is accomplished by exploring the question, *why does this problem exist and persist?* Accordingly, the statements you will make in this section are geared toward bigger picture comprehension of the issue—they should focus on articulating macro-patterns from literature (which may be historical, conceptual, practical, or empirical). And, because part of the purpose here is introducing and framing information, researchers tend to foreground big ideas (rather than individual researchers and studies).

In contrast, the purpose of the literature review is to analyze, critically evaluate, and synthesize research literature on your topic. The major question the literature review answers is *what do we know—and not know—from empirical literature about [your phenomenon of study]?* To answer this question, you typically will provide a thematic review of the major findings and evidence from specific studies that have been conducted on the topic of your proposed research. Then, you will use that review to make an argument about a gap in the literature, which becomes part of your argument regarding why your study is necessary (i.e., your rationale). To achieve these goals, statements made in the literature review tend to focus on findings from sets of empirical studies and individual exemplars (for more on this, see chapter five).

As an example, let's say a student is focusing their problem statement on the ways that higher education workplaces perpetuate inequities for people of color. The concept of *microaggressions* (i.e., subtle, normalized instances of oppression) might pop up in both the background statement and the literature review. However, the treatment would be different. In the problem background, the author would likely define microaggressions and provide evidence of their harmful nature in higher education workplaces in broad strokes. The purpose here would be to help the reader understand what microaggressions are and why they are important for the problem at hand—in other words, emphasizing the big idea. In the literature review, however, the focus is on understanding what the evidence does and doesn't say about inequities in higher education. So, in this section the author would more likely discuss specific studies (or sets of studies) investigating microaggressions in higher education and analyze their evidence regarding the relationship between microaggressions and racialized workplace inequities.

Deciding What to Include

To get started with the background, you will want to decide on the kinds of factors and information you will include. Then, you will start to create an outline with that information.

In the next exercise, you will generate text along multiple possible dimensions to help you start to decide the main ideas or topics to discuss in this section. This includes the roots of the issue, or factors that help explain where the problem came from; current context, or information that explains why the issue is being exacerbated (or is making it particularly urgent to solve); any important policies, programs, or concepts that need to be defined or further discussed to help your reader understand the problem and its significance; and any foreshadowed information, or ideas you may have introduced in the problem summary that need to be unpacked further.

ACTIVITY 4. BACKGROUND IDEA GENERATION

Use the questions below to jot down important topics or ideas to include in your problem background section. Some of these may overlap.

1. Roots: Where did the problem come from? What created it?
2. Current Context: What is happening in education right now that is making the problem especially urgent to solve?
3. Policies, Programs, or Concepts: Are there any important policies, programs, or concepts that need to be discussed?
4. Foreshadowed Information: What information did you introduce in the problem summary that you need to explain in more detail?

Another way to consider what you'd like to include in your problem statement background is to think through what might be relevant about different dimensions of the problem, including its *historical, political, sociocultural, and institutional/ organizational* facets (see Figure 4.4). Do you need to discuss anything about the history of the issue for your reader to be able to understand where it came from and/ or why it persists? Are there policies or political movements that have impacted or exacerbated it? What about sociocultural facets, like cultural norms or social practices? Do organizational or institutional factors play a role?

These are some of the major dimensions, but depending on the problem, there may be additional dimensions of the problem to explore. There also could be *economic, pedagogical,* or *philosophical* factors that could help explain the problem, just to name a few possibilities. What other potential dimensions can you think of beyond these?

DIMENSIONS OF THE PROBLEM	
HISTORICAL	Is there historical information, such as important events, movements, or trends, that might be important for your reader to know? For example, if your problem had to do with the overrepresentation of Black students in special education, you would likely need to include discussion of the Eugenics movement.
POLITICAL	Are there policies/legislation, court cases, or political movements relevant to your problem? For example, a problem statement identifying achievement disparities for multilingual learners might discuss policies like Prop 227 in California, which prohibited languages other than English for being used in mainstream classrooms for instructional purposes.
SOCIOCULTURAL	Are there any relevant sociocultural contributors to the issue, such as norms and practices? For example, in a problem statement regarding disproportionate discipline for boys of color, a discussion regarding the valuing of white behavioral norms in classrooms is likely important context to provide.
INSTITUTIONAL OR ORGANIZATIONAL	What about factors stemming from the ways institutions or organizations operate? For instance, when considering the problem of high attrition for teachers in high poverty schools, the failure of institutions to provide consistent mentoring or patterns of institutional isolation may be helpful to help the reader understand the problem.

Figure 4.4: Dimensions of the problem

Let's look at some examples to further investigate what might be included in a "background of the problem" section.

First, let's take the following issue, which originates from Richardson (2019): *First generation, low-income college students of color graduate at lower rates than other demographic groups.* In her background section, Richardson provides information regarding four elements contributing to the problem. First, she offers an overview of *historical conditions* that created educational inequities in K-12 schools (such as educational access and funding disparities), which translate into lower quality preparation for this demographic, as well as lower confidence and a more difficult transition to college.

Next, she discusses *sociocultural* factors affecting the population of first-generation, low-income students—for example, they tend to come from nondominant cultures, and high poverty rates often mean they are working and caring for family while going to school. Bound up with these sociocultural factors are *institutional* ones—first generation students tend to experience dissonance with university culture, and often have difficulty navigating university systems and structures. Finally, Richardson describes a *political* dimension, which includes the California Master Plan and the systemic defunding of higher education.

Let's examine a second example problem from my own work (Strom, 2014): *First-year teachers tend to revert to traditional teaching even when they are prepared in more progressive ways.* I discuss factors from three dimensions in the problem background section. First, as important context, I describe a *political* factor, the neoliberal accountability movement. This era ushered in a massive increase in "accountability" by tying high-stakes testing to teacher performance and school sanctions. In turn, the focus on accountability pressured teachers to teach to standardized tests, which narrows curriculum and discourages active forms of learning.

Second, I outline a *sociocultural* factor contributing to the problem —cultural beliefs regarding traditional forms of teaching (i.e., transmission). Teachers tend to have a deeply entrenched "cultural script" that the teacher is an expert who transfers information to students, as well as strongly held beliefs that they need to control their classrooms. Finally, an *organizational* factor that contributes to the perpetuation of transmission-style teaching includes the general lack of support for teachers to continue developing the complex skills for more participatory forms of pedagogy. Teachers aren't "finished" when they graduate and require support from leaders or mentors, but often that support is inconsistent or absent altogether.

ACTIVITY 5. DIMENSIONS OF THE PROBLEM

Jot down or bullet out relevant background information along these common problem dimensions (see Figure 4.4 for details).

1. Historical Dimension
2. Political Dimension
3. Sociocultural Dimension
4. Institutional or Organizational Dimension

Building Out the Background Section

Now, let's start developing the building blocks of your problem background section. Start by reviewing your readings, notes, and reflections to identify the key topics you will include. Then create an outline with these key topics. For each background topic, 1) outline the assertions or claims you are making; 2) decide what relevant details and information are needed; and 3) identify the compelling, scholarly evidence you have that support them. You might notice that this structure looks familiar—that's because it is the three parts of an argument, which we talked about in the last chapter (i.e., *claim, explanation, evidence*). As I mentioned before, you will be making different arguments all throughout your dissertation, and this is one more area where that is the case.

Below, I have provided an example of an outline for one background topic. The outline articulates the topic (corporate education reform) and then lays out the main claim (the current corporate education movement poses a particularly challenging environment for new teachers). Next, I add bullets for the necessary accompanying information or details, which serve as my "explanation"—in the example below, that includes unpacking corporate education reform as a concept. Finally, I include multiple pieces of evidence that demonstrate the negative impact of this particular movement.

Topic: Corporate Educational Reform

Main idea: The era of corporate education reform creates challenging conditions for new teachers to implement their preservice learning.

Details: Definition of corporate education reform.

- "A marriage between neoliberalism and neoconservatism" (Sleeter, 2008, p. 1947)
- Labeled "corporate" because of it is based on market logic and they are financially backed by corporate interests
- Corporate ed reform is looking to privatize public education, increase standardized testing, eliminate teacher protections (like tenure), close low-performing public schools, open charter schools, institute voucher programs for private schools, and standardize curriculum

Evidence of negative impact of these reforms:

- Center on Education Policy, 2006: increased testing narrows curriculum
- Darling Hammond, 2010: increased testing "pushes out" low-performing students
- Civil Rights Project, 2009: charter schools underserve minorities, special needs students, and ELLs
- CREDO, 2009: only 17% of charter schools actually report gains higher than public schools

Now, let's put this information together in a paragraph, along with references and transitions. As you examine the paragraph, notice how the claim, explanation, and evidence are edited together in a cohesive manner. Then identify the ways that the transitions help logically sequence the ideas presented.

Example Problem Background Paragraph

The challenges faced by teachers entering the workforce have always been daunting, but the current era of corporate reform is a particularly trying time to become a teacher. Under what Sleeter (2008) refers to as "a marriage between neoliberalism and neoconservatism" (p. 1947), public education is being threatened from a bi-partisan effort to privatize public education, increase standardized testing, eliminate teacher protections such as tenure, close low-performing schools and open charters in their wake, institute voucher programs for private schools, and standardize curriculum (Karp, 2012; Lipman, 2011).

A multitude of research has surfaced that problematizes these reform moves. Studies have shown, for example, that increased testing narrows curriculum (Center on Education Policy, 2006) and has resulted in the "push-out" of low-performing or "at-risk" students (Darling-Hammond, 2010) rather than increased achievement for all. Others have demonstrated that charter schools underserve minorities, special needs students, and ELLs (Civil Rights Project, 2009), and only 17% of charter schools actually report gains higher than their public counterparts (CREDO, 2009). However, despite the volume of scholarly work decrying what some have termed "corporate education reforms" (Karp, 2012)—due to both the pervasive market logic that undergirds them and the financial backing of their proliferation by corporate interests (Ravitch, 2011)—politicians and educational leaders continue to impose these reforms in schools and districts. *(excerpted from Strom, 2014, p. 5-6)*

ACTIVITY 6. BUILDING OUT THE ELEMENTS OF THE PROBLEM BACKGROUND

In the graphic organizer:

- **Name your main topics/factors/ideas.**
- **Bullet out your key assertions and details.**
- **Add your supporting evidence.**

Then, for each factor, reflect on the connection between the topic/factor/idea and the problem, ensuring you can articulate why each idea you include is essential to help the reader understand where the problem came from and why it persists.

ACTIVITY 6. ELEMENTS OF THE PROBLEM BACKGROUND (CONT.)			
Problem			
Contributing Factor or Idea	**Key Claims/Main Details (bullet)**	**Supporting Evidence to Support Claims**	**Reflect:** ***How does this factor help us understand the problem? Why is it important to know?***

4.5 The Problem Rationale

ACTIVITY 7. FREE WRITE
Free write on the following: ▪ Why does this issue need to be urgently addressed? How do you know? ▪ What specifically do we need to research to be able to address it? How do you know we need to do that particular research?

One of the main tasks of your problem statement is to provide a two-part rationale that makes an argument, supported by evidence, that persuades your reader that your study is warranted. The first part of the argument is the ***practical rationale*** (also known as the impact or social justice rationale), which demonstrates why the issue is one that is both significant and needs to be addressed urgently. The second part of the argument is the ***research rationale***, which establishes that there is a gap in literature and identifies the contributions that the study would likely make. Because we will spend time discussing the research gap in chapter five (the literature review), I dedicate more space here to the first part of the rationale.

PRACTICAL RATIONALE: WHY IS THIS A SIGNIFICANT ISSUE WE NEED TO ADDRESS RIGHT NOW?

Communicates the significance and urgency of the problem by providing a rationale that:

- Clearly articulates why the problem equates to a compelling justice issue, or is otherwise significant
- Clearly communicates the urgency of the issue
- Shows how the problem impacts a particular population, and connects that impact to broader sociocultural, economic, political, ecological, etc. trends/issues

RESEARCH RATIONALE: WHY DO WE NEED TO CONDUCT A RESEARCH STUDY ON THIS ISSUE?

Clearly communicates a gap in the research by:

- Establishing the state of current knowledge on the topic
- Stating what we still need to research to be able to address the problem
- Indicating how this study will address the gap
- Identifying what the potential contributions will be to the field in terms of knowledge/practice/policy

Practical Rationale

The first part of the rationale is the significance, or what I call the *practical rationale*. The purpose of this section is to convince the reader that the issue the author has laid out so far is one that is important enough to warrant a study that will help address it. To accomplish that goal, you will need to clearly articulate why the problem is something we urgently need to solve. I recommend the following three "moves": 1) concretely what show that the short- and long-term impacts of the problem are on the population(s) the problem affects; 2) connect those impacts to larger, or macro-level, issues or patterns; and 3) support those claims with details, examples, and current citations.

To get started, you will want to free-write multiple *impact statements*.

Impact statements can be quantitative or qualitative, but they must be written concretely and be supported with credible references. Typically impact statements are crafted in reference to particular populations (for example, teachers), and should connect micro-level impacts to larger societal outcomes.

Let's take a look at an example problem and sample impact statements that provide a compelling rationale for studying it.

Problem: The thinking that informs research, policy, and practice regarding teacher development is linear, causal, and simplistic. These dominant perspectives consider the teacher to be an autonomous actor who takes her learning from her preservice program, drops it into the classroom fully intact, and has full control of the teaching and learning that occurs.

Impact Statements:

- Dualistic thinking informs the separation of learning and practice activities (Zeichner, 2010).
- Simplistic, linear thinking informs teacher evaluations that attempt to grade teachers based on their students' test scores (Strom, 2015).
- The notion of teachers as autonomous agents is a one-way, transactional view of teaching that supports the banking model (Strom & Martin, 2017).
- New teachers tend to experience "praxis shock" when they have difficulty putting their preservice learning into practice (Smagorinsky et al., 2004).
- Struggles of new teachers contribute to an enormous teacher turnover rate (Ingersoll 2003; Strong & Ingersoll 2011).
- Teacher turnover is worse in high poverty, diverse settings (Simon & Johnson, 2011).

The draft impact statements above offer concrete details regarding the ways that linear, causal thinking about teacher development impacts teachers and schools. These include keeping learning and practice separate, reinforcing ineffective teacher evaluation practices, perpetuating inequitable models of instruction, and amplifying the struggles of new teachers.

The last two impact statements also gesture to larger patterns that could be connected to more macro-level issues of inequity: teacher turnover, or attrition, creates instability; and since it is highest in the poorest and most diverse schools, that means teacher turnover is adding to the educational difficulties faced by our most vulnerable populations.

Now, let's consider the way we might edit these statements together into a paragraph that communicates these multiple impacts in a concise way. In the example that follows, I put these statements into a cohesive paragraph, adding a transition sentence to begin. Read it carefully, examining the ways that I introduce different impacts of the issue and support them with evidence. Then, continue on to Figure 4.5, which identifies the impact claims, their support, and a connection to the larger impact of the problem.

POSSIBLE RATIONALE: These linear perspectives have far-reaching impact. They shape the way we prepare, support, and assess teachers—such as learning and practice activities in preservice education that are kept separate (Zeichner, 2010) and teacher evaluations that attempt to grade teachers based on their students' test scores (Strom, 2015). They also affect students' access to quality teaching and learning, since, for example, teachers are not taught to account for student agency, which makes participatory, interactive teaching difficult (Strom & Martin, 2017). This adds to the "praxis shock" (Smagorinsky et al., 2004) new teachers often face, which in turn contributes to the "revolving door" of teachers that leave the profession in the first few years (Ingersoll 2003; Strong & Ingersoll 2011) that further destabilizes already under-resourced settings (Donald & Johnson, 2011) and feeds into the well-documented patterns of inequality that have historically plagued educational systems.

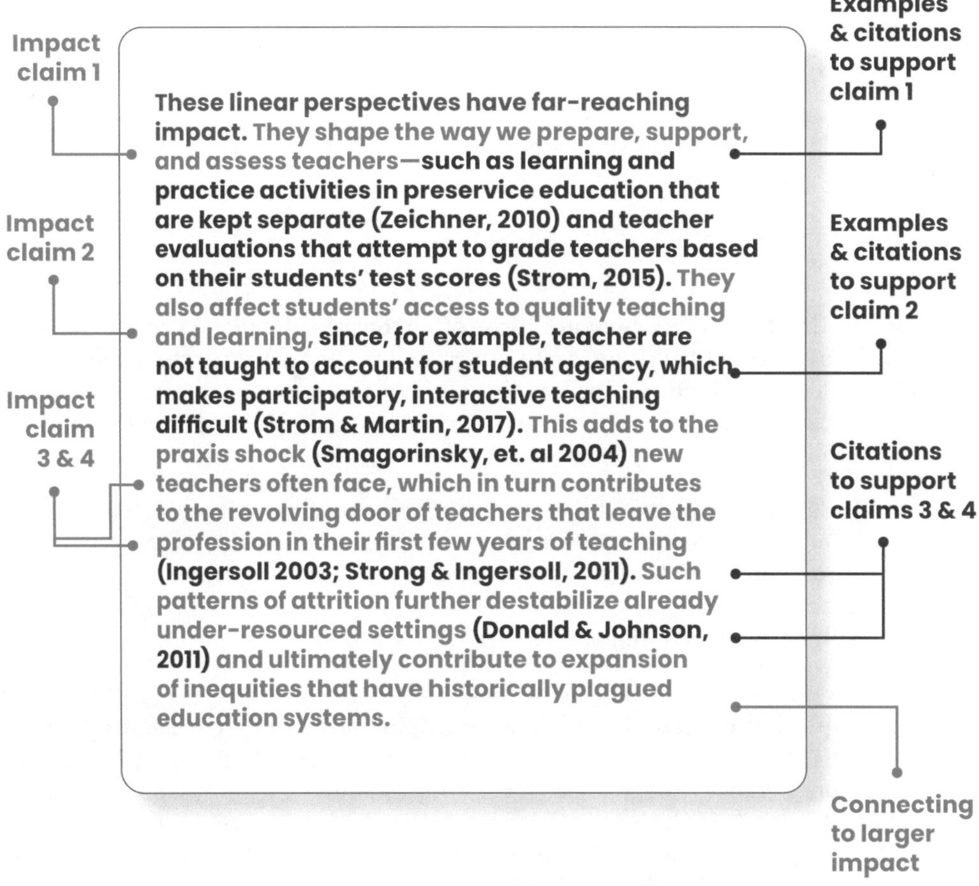

Figure 4.5: Annotated rationale

Let's take a closer look at the annotated version.

Following the initial transition sentence, I begin by offering a high-level impact statement, "*they shape the way we prepare, support, and assess teachers.*" To unpack this a little and provide evidence to support my claims, I offer two concrete examples: the separation of learning and practice activities (that is, the learning about teaching takes place in the university, and the practice of teaching takes place in schools, and these two are often not connected), and teacher evaluation practices that simplistically assume student test scores reflect teacher quality. I then move to an impact statement concerning student access to quality pedagogy, adding details and evidence regarding the ways that linear perspectives interfere with social constructivist teaching methods. I connect this to another impact, the "praxis shock" (i.e., the dissonance that new teachers tend to experience when they have difficulty enacting their preservice learning). With the last several clauses, I connect the teacher and student impacts I've named to the broader issue of teacher attrition. I then link that impact to even more macro-issues of inequality.

ACTIVITY 8. BUILDING OUT THE PRACTICAL RATIONALE.

In the table below, use your reading notes to bullet out information you have on short/long-term impacts and how those relate to larger society issues. Then, from those bullets, draft impact statements to work with and add your supporting evidence for them.

	Bulleted Notes	Impact Claim(s)	Evidence
Short Term Impacts			
Long Term Impacts			
Connection to Larger Societal Issues			

Research Rationale

The second part of your rationale is the research rationale. This part of the statement answers the question, "*Why do we need to conduct a research study on this issue*?"

While the social justice rationale focuses on practical, on-the-ground impact, this section focuses on scholarly contribution. In other words, the research rationale describes what the study will add to the field of research in which you are situated. This section closely corresponds to your gap in literature, which emerges from your literature review. Therefore, this part of the rationale likely will only be a few sentences, since you will be discussing the gap in research in more depth in that section of your dissertation.

The research rationale summarizes previous work, identifies a gap in research, and articulates how your study will address that gap. It should follow the following general formula:

- Researchers have studied *[part of the problem].*
- However, we still do not know enough about *[the gap].*
- Therefore, I will *[summarize how the study will address the gap].*

First, establish the state of current knowledge on the topic. This statement corresponds both to the "funnel" you've been developing, as well as your review of literature. For example, in a study on how first-year teachers construct their practices, I might summarize what we know about that research with the following: *Researchers who have examined first-year teaching practices have identified many factors from multiple system levels that influence first-year teachers' instruction. These include teacher-level factors (e.g., the teacher's background, beliefs about teaching and students, and confidence levels); classroom-level factors (e.g.,student diversity, student agency, class size, classroom dynamics, material space), school-level factors (e.g., colleagues, leadership, resources, school culture) and larger systems (e.g.,testing, mandated curriculum, policy).*

Second, state the gap that your study will address. It should directly build on or logically connect to the summary you have just provided. Continuing with the example offered above, I might transition to the summary of the gap with the following: *However, these researchers have largely studied these factors in isolation or by taking a "slice" of the teaching system. Few studies consider the ways that factors at all educational system levels interact to collectively generate first-year teaching practices.*

Finally, move into how your study will address (or begin to address) the gap you just outlined. This description should directly map on to your statement of the gap. Again, continuing with this example, I might offer: *Therefore, to provide a more complex and holistic portrait of the enactment of first-year teaching practices, this study will examine the ways elements at the teacher, classroom, school, and district/policy levels interact to jointly produce teaching.*

ACTIVITY 9. DIMENSIONS OF THE PROBLEM

Jot down notes answering each question to the best of your ability.

Note: you will need to complete at least a draft of your literature review prior to completing this section. If you are not there yet, skip for now and come back after completing chapter five. Alternately, you can complete this based on what reading you've already done, and then come back and revise once you've completed your lit review and formally articulated the gap.

1. What do we know about the issue from the research?
2. What do we NOT know (the gap in the research)?
3. How will your project address this gap.

4.6 The Purpose Statement

ACTIVITY 10. FREE WRITE

Free write on the following:

- What are your objectives for this project?
- What will the project do for the field?

Your purpose statement is the last section of your dissertation chapter one (unless your chair asks you to create a "key concepts" section, which sometimes is also included in the first part of your dissertation). This section pulls together everything you've said up to this point to articulate 1) what you actually plan to do in your study (the purpose), 2) state your research questions, and 3) describe the expected contributions of the project.

Crafting the Purpose Sentence(s)

The first sentence(s) of this section should articulate your purpose for the study—what you intend to do. The best way to think about the purpose: it is the dissertation equivalent to a thesis statement for an essay.

The purpose should logically follow your research rationale (which you wrote in the previous section). In fact, think of it as an extension of this statement. In your research rationale, you stated how your study will address the gap in research literature; now you are going to get even more specific.

Purpose statements are very formulaic. They include the following elements:

1. Signal word or phrase indicating you are explaining the purpose
2. A purpose verb
3. Your methodology
4. The central phenomenon under study
5. Your participants/context
6. Your theory/other details if they are central to your purpose/intent

A sample purpose statement might approximate the following structure:

> The purpose of this *(method/methodology)* study is to *(investigate/explore/discover/understand/describe)(the central phenomenon)* of/for *(participants)* at/in *(research site).*

Let's break down this structure.

Signaling the Purpose. As we discussed in chapter two, academic writing at the doctoral level supports your reader to follow the important parts of your argument. An appropriate scaffold to add here is a clear signaling phrase about the purpose. This phrase is the writing equivalent of tapping your reader on the shoulder and saying, *"Hello, please pay attention, I'm about to tell you what the purpose of this study is!"* As the first sentence in the example structure above shows, your signal phrase should simply and directly state that this is your purpose statement: "The purpose of this [methodology] study is..."

Methodology. Because the purpose sentence serves as an overall framing statement for your dissertation, it is a good idea to give a nod to the type of methodology you will be using. Naming the methodology lets the reader know what type of study you will be conducting.

However, including this also serves as an additional scaffold, because it will help the reader anticipate what will come later in the dissertation, when you describe the methodology in more depth as part of the methodology chapter. So, to keep the purpose statement succinct, I usually add the methodology as a modifier of "study"—e.g., a qualitative case study, a community-based participatory action research study, or a mixed-methods study.

Choosing a Purpose Verb. In terms of the purpose verb, you should choose it based on what you plan to do with your study. For example, is it an exploratory study? Then you may want to indicate that by choosing the verb "explore" or "discover." Is it descriptive? Then choose the word "describe." If it is an investigation, choose "investigate." And so on.

Stating the Phenomenon. The phenomenon is the "what"—as in, *what exactly you will be studying* (or investigating, or describing, or exploring, etc.) in your research. This should flow both from the problem entry point (which we discussed in the beginning of the chapter) and from your research rationale (see the previous section). For example, earlier I provided this narrowed problem:

> First-year teachers struggle to translate their learning about socioculturally based pedagogy into first-year practice and often revert to transmission-based methods.

I then provided the following research rationale:

> Researchers who have examined first-year teaching practices have identified many factors from multiple system levels that influence first-year teachers' instruction. These include teacher-level factors (e.g., the teacher's background, beliefs about teaching and students, and confidence levels); classroom-level factors (student diversity, student agency, class size, classroom dynamics, material space), school-level factors (e.g., colleagues, leadership, resources, school culture) and larger systems (testing, mandated curriculum, policy). However, these researchers have largely studied these factors in isolation or by taking a "slice" of the teaching system. Few studies consider the ways that factors at all educational system levels interact to collectively generate first-year teaching practices. Therefore, to provide a more complex and holistic portrait of the enactment of first-year teaching practices, this study will examine the ways elements at the teacher, classroom, school, and district/policy levels interact to jointly produce teaching.

The phenomenon here is *the construction of first-year teaching practices* (this could be stated multiple ways—that is the way I would say it).

Sometimes you have more than one phenomenon you are studying, although often when that occurs, the study is focused on the relationship between two or more phenomena. For example: *The purpose of this action research study is to examine the impact of a unit of socioscientific instruction on sixth grade students' use of argumentation.* In this case, the phenomenon is a specific *relationship* between the unit of instruction and a specific skill (argumentation). In other cases, there may be multiple phenomena and a relationship. For instance: *The purpose of this qualitative case study is to investigate what teachers learn from a professional development program regarding multilingual learner supports and how they enact that learning in their classroom instructional practices.* In this purpose statement, there are two phenomena being studied—teachers' learning from a professional development program, their subsequent classroom practices—as well as the relationship between the two.

Participants and Context. Typically, studies are bounded to a particular population and context; briefly detailing this information can scaffold for your reader by helping them to build schema about the important details of your project. However, it is also a trustworthiness measure—it situates your study and provides the reader with some initial information to help them determine the transferability of the research (that is, whether or not it might be useful for their own contexts). How much detail you provide is up to you.

Let's put this together. Figure 4.6 shows a sample purpose sentence for a qualitative study (the methodology) consisting of multiple case studies (the method). These case studies will *investigate* (the purpose verb) how three new science teachers (the participants) who teach high school (the context) translate their preservice learning into their first year teaching practices (the phenomenon).

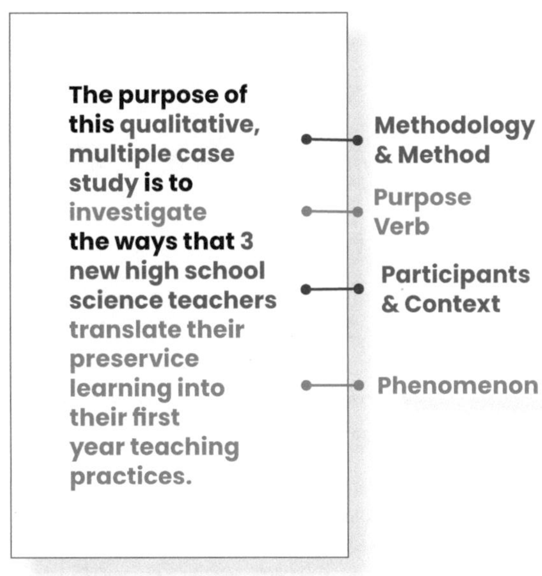

Figure 4.6: Annotated purpose statement

ACTIVITY 11. BUILD OUT YOUR PURPOSE STATEMENT	
First, list the elements of your problem statement. Then, use them to craft a sentence in the bottom row.	
	Elements
Signal Phrase	
Purpose Verb	
Method/Methodology	
Phenomenon/a	
Participants & Setting	
Purpose Sentence	

Research Questions

Your research questions should map directly onto your purpose statement. Although your language may vary slightly, to ensure that the reader of your dissertation can clearly see the connection between the purpose and research questions, I recommend keeping the language very similar, if not exactly the same. For example, consider the following purpose: *The purpose of this qualitative case study is to examine how three first-year high school science teachers negotiate their preservice learning and elements of their teaching systems.* My question mirrors this statement: "How do three first-year high school science teachers negotiate their preservice learning and elements of their teaching systems?"

In other cases, especially when more than one phenomenon is involved, you may want to break the purpose into two questions. For example, consider the purpose provided above: *The purpose of this qualitative case study is to investigate what teachers learn from a professional development program regarding multilingual learner supports and how they enact that learning in their classroom instructional practices.* Since the purpose is two-fold, consider breaking this into two parts: 1) *What do teachers learn from a professional development program regarding multilingual learner supports?* And 2) *How do they enact that learning in their classroom instructional practices?*

When you add your research questions to your purpose statement, make sure that you add a signaling phrase, such as "The research question that guides this study is..." If you have more than one question, consider adding a scaffold for your reader to signal that as well. For instance, "Two research questions guide this study: 1)..."

ACTIVITY 12. ALIGN YOUR PURPOSE STATEMENT & RESEARCH QUESTION(S)	
Add your research purpose and question(s) below. Then, edit the research question(s) to clearly show how they will meet the purpose.	
Research Purpose	
Research Question	

Contributions

The contributions of your study, which some might frame as your objectives or goals for the project, let your reader know how the research you are planning to conduct will advance practice, policy, and/or the field as a whole – things of that nature. What will it do, ultimately, to address the problem you have identified? What kind of knowledge and action do you think might result? How will this research *matter*?

Your contributions statement should meet three criteria:

1. It should reflect both concrete, short-term or local objectives.
2. It should speculate on potential long-term or global objectives.
3. It should point directly back to the problem (or parts of the problem) you identified at the beginning of your problem statement chapter.

Start by articulating your short-term or local goals. These goals should refer to what your study will concretely accomplish. Although you won't know exactly what the findings will be, you will generate knowledge of some kind. However, unless you are conducting an action research study, it is unlikely that your study will lead to direct change, so stay away from promising impact in the short-term portion of the contribution statement. Instead, I recommend that you begin by referencing the knowledge, understandings, or insights that this study will produce. For example: *This study will generate insights into the day-to-day instructional negotiations of teachers in urban science contexts.*

Next, articulate your longer-term goals, or global objectives. For these statements, speculate on how the knowledge you will generate (or other short-term outcome) might inform or impact the field. You can frame the long-term goals in terms of policy, practice, research, or whatever dimensions you feel are most relevant for addressing the specific problem driving your study. For this portion, because you are offering *possible* contributions, keep your language tentative: use words/phrases like *may, could, has potential,* and so on. Continuing with the example above, your "broader impact" statement might read as follows: *Such knowledge can inform preservice and in-service science teacher development that supports assets-based, linguistically responsive teaching.* Notice that I used "can inform" to avoid making too strong of a claim.

Finally, your contribution statement should point back to the problem you identified in the first part of your problem statement chapter. For instance, in the above examples, the problem is that multilingual learner instruction is often deficit-based and offers few opportunities for students to practice their langauge through dialogue. Therefore, the example above contains a direct reference to the problem with the phrase *that supports interactive, assets-based, linguistically responsive teaching.* This phrase directly addresses how the project will (hopefully) be relevant for addressing the problem identified—since research shows that asset-based classroom interactions can disrupt larger deficit-based patterns for multilingual learners.

ACTIVITY 13. BUILD OUT YOUR CONTRIBUTIONS STATEMENT
In the organizer below, free-write what your study's short-term outcomes and broader impact might be. Then, articulate how those point back to the problem; and identify the language you use to make those connections.

Short-Term Outcome (Concrete)	
Broader Impact (Speculative)	
Language Used	

ACTIVITY 14. PUTTING IT ALL TOGETHER
Use the exercises throughout this chapter to draft your problem summary, problem background, rationale, and purpose statement. Then, edit everything together using the scaffolds identified in chapter two.

ACTIVITY 15. REVERSE OUTLINE FOR LOGIC FLOW
You can check the logic flow and alignment with the following activity. ▪ Add 1-2 summary sentences for each section in the organizer below; check the logical flow from one section to the next. ▪ How does each section logically connect?

Problem	
Factors/Context that Explain the Problem	
Social Justice Rationale	
Research Rationale	
Purpose	
Questions	
Contributions	

Conclusion

This chapter focused on the problem statement, which frames your dissertation and usually comprises chapter one of your dissertation. The following summarizes the key ideas we discussed.

1. The ***problem statement*** identifies the impetus for your research. Your tasks are to explain the problem, convince the reader that the issue is indeed a problem, and then present your proposed study and describe how it will address (or begin to address) that problem.
2. The ***problem summary*** is the opening or introduction and usually is just a paragraph or two. It provides context, concisely names the problem, and provides additional details to understand the problem, who it affects, and why/how it's a problem.
3. The ***background of the problem*** section goes into further depth, describing where the problem came from, its contributing factors, and/or why it persists.
4. The ***rationale*** contains two parts: a *practical rationale* shows the problem's significance and urgency, and the *research rationale* communicates a specific gap in research literature around the problem.
5. The ***purpose statement*** lays out your goals for the study and briefly outlines what you plan to do, including your research questions.

5

The Literature Review

Contents

Introduction

This chapter introduces you to, and guides you through, what many students report to be one of the most challenging tasks of the dissertation proposal: the literature review. Again, I typically teach this topic over an entire semester—so use this chapter accordingly! Part of the reason this topic can take so much time is that reading and analyzing a body of literature is no small task. So along with the information and exercises in this chapter, I recommend that you carve out time to read and annotate texts for your literature review regularly (even daily, if possible). This will help with time management as well as offer processing time (it helps to think about the ideas over a longer time frame).

5.1 Purposes and Structures of the Literature Review

WARM UP

Jot down some ideas that come to your mind about the following questions:

- What do you know about empirical literature reviews?
- What questions or wonderings do you have about empirical literature reviews?

Purposes of Literature Reviews

There are multiple purposes of your dissertation literature review—and some of them will depend on the kind of study you plan to conduct and your specific needs. For that reason, I focus here on scaffolding a writing approach to craft an *empirical* literature review: that is, a review of research literature, or original studies that have been conducted on a particular topic (also referred to as "extant literature").

One of the most important purposes of an empirical literature review is *to provide an original analysis of the existing body of research* in relation to your proposed study. This purpose corresponds to the question, "What does the extant literature say about [topic or phenomenon you plan to study]?" or "What have researchers discovered about [that topic or phenomenon]?" The analysis typically offers a synthesis of the main ideas, evidence, and conclusions the studies have collectively yielded and organizes them into themes/patterns, trends, and/or major lines of thinking.

Such an overview of the research literature will ground your study by providing a baseline foundation of literature to which you will connect your own project. It also allows you to identify the key players in terms of research in a specific area and get to know (and honor) the work of those who came before you.

This analytic mapping of a defined portion of the field also sets you up for a second purpose: *to critically evaluate the state of the extant research* on your topic or phenomenon of interest.

Part of this evaluation includes *interpreting the synthesis* described above. Your interpretation will likely answer questions such as these: "what is the significance of the patterns and trends you identified in your overview of the main ideas, evidence, and conclusions offered by the extant literature? What do they mean or reveal in relation to the problem you laid out previously and/or the study you plan to conduct?"

A second part of this evaluation includes *identifying inadequacies or gaps* in terms of empirical research (and sometimes noting conceptual and methodological gaps as well). The empirical gap, also known as the research rationale (which was discussed in chapter four), should map onto the study that you plan to conduct—it should demonstrate that there is little or no research that addresses the specific aspect your study aims to examine.

Anatomy of a Literature Review

Prior to getting started with your own literature review, it may be helpful to become familiar with the anatomy of a typical empirical literature review. In other words, to write your own review, it is important to understand how literature reviews are typically structured to meet their purposes or goals.

While the structure may be slightly different based on topics, generally there are three parts to an empirical literature review: the introduction, the thematic analysis, and the statement of the gap. Below I discuss each of these briefly, and then expand on them in the sections that follow. Please keep in mind that these structures align with "typical" literature reviews—arts-based dissertations and other research genres that break with more traditional convensions may adopt other formats.

Introduction

The introduction provides a "road map" (see chapter two) that scaffolds readers' understanding of the overall dissertation topic by offering a summary of the major themes and previewing the gap in literature relative to that topic. In some cases, the introduction may also contain a summary of the literature review methods (that is, the procedures for conducting the review—what databases were used, key words used in searches, elimination processes, and so on). The inclusion of literature review methods varies by program or advisor—so check with yours to find out if you should include this information.

Thematic Analysis

The body of the literature review, or the thematic analysis, presents the "findings" or outcomes of your review process. Usually, this section is chunked into major themes. These tend to be broad categories which are further broken down into smaller sections or subthemes, which identify sets of specific findings within those larger themes.

Typically, each thematic section contains claims about the theme, providing explanations that draw both on subsets of studies and specific exemplars (i.e., discussions of individual studies providing details that support the claim/s).

Statement of the Gap

The final portion of the literature review is the statement of the gap. This section first offers a brief summary of the key contributions of the extant literature (i.e., what we currently know about the topic), then states the gap (what we don't know yet about your topic of interest, or what we don't know enough about). Finally, you will explain how your study will address this gap.

ACTIVITY 1. EXAMINING LITERATURE REVIEW STRUCTURE

Find a dissertation on your topic.

(If you have access to your library's databases, typically there will be one dedicated to dissertations; at my university it is called "Dissertations and Theses").

Once you have identified a dissertation, locate the literature review and answer the following prompts:

1. Find the literature review introduction.
    a. What information is offered there?
    b. Does the author provide a clear roadmap of their literature review structure and content? If not, what advice would you offer to make it clearer?
2. Find the thematic analysis and skim it.
    a. What are the key themes?
    b. How are the themes further chunked out or broken down into smaller ideas?
3. Find the statement of the gap.
    a. What is the gap?
    b. How does the proposed study address it?

5.2 Getting Started

Although this book is mainly focused on learning to write for the specific purposes of the dissertation, there are multiple steps involved in searching and analyzing literature that must be done prior to writing—and which are critical for creating the foundation to write a high-quality literature review. In the next two sections I briefly describe the steps involved in finding and analyzing your literature while also offering practical tips and activities aimed at helping you get started with your own review. To start, I will discuss setting parameters for your literature review, using library databases to identify and compile literature, and refining your literature review scope.

ACTIVITY 2. FREE-WRITE/MAPPING

Free-write or map out possible questions to guide your literature review.

Start with these question stems:

- What does the literature say about [problem driving your study]?
- What does the literature say about [phenomena you are interested in studying?

Determining Initial Scope and Parameters

First, you'll need to determine the scope of your literature review (what will be covered) and its parameters (delineators or boundaries, or what will not be covered). To determine the scope, draft guiding questions that spell out the topic/issue or phenomenon your proposed study aims to address. This will keep your search focused. For example, if I was crafting a study proposal that seeks to investigate how new teachers translate their pre-professional learning into first-year classroom practice, the questions below might guide my literature review.

1. What does the literature say about the role of preservice learning in new teachers' instructional practices?
2. What does the literature say about factors other than preservice learning that influence new teachers' instructional practices?

Once you have a general idea of the scope of the review, set some parameters—these will help bound your review and keep it manageable. Typically, you'll write parameters as inclusions and/or exclusions. For example, for a project looking at first year teachers' classroom instructional practices, you might create a set of the following inclusion parameters to narrow your search.

> **Inclusion parameters:** Include studies that focus on the practices of first-year teachers in public K-12 schools who graduated from university-based teacher preparation programs in the U.S.

From here, you would create a list of exclusions, such as the following:

a. Exclude studies that focus on teachers who are not in their first year of teaching
b. Exclude studies that focus on non-K-12 teachers (e.g., pre-K or college)
c. Exclude studies not taking place in public schools
d. Exclude studies that do not focus on some aspect of teaching practice (and you'd need to define teaching practice specifically)
e. Exclude studies with non-university-prepared teachers
f. Exclude non-peer reviewed works

As I previously mentioned, setting parameters will be a non-linear and somewhat experimental process. Treat your initial scope and parameters as flexible estimations—and once you delve into the literature, be prepared to adjust them based on what you uncover. For example, you may find that there are thousands of articles on the specific topic you've identified. In that case, you'll need to narrow your focus further. On the other hand, if your searches are yielding very few articles, you may need to broaden your scope and/or parameters.

ACTIVITY 3. SCOPE AND PARAMETERS

1. **Describe the scope of your study. What kind of articles or other sources will you include and why? What kind of questions will you ask to guide your search?**
2. **Set your parameters. Create inclusion parameters, then think through a list of related exclusions to narrow your search.**

Searching for Literature

After determining your initial scope and parameters, you will be ready to start searching, identifying, and compiling literature for your review. First you need to *create a list of search terms*. To do this, return to the scope of your study and note the main research focus. Then, write out that focus, phrasing it as many different ways as possible. I provide an example below. Given the focus of the literature review (teaching practices of first year teachers), can you think of other terms that might fit this search?

For a project looking at the teaching practices of first year teachers, you might use the following search terms:

- *New teacher + practice*
- *Beginning teacher + practice*
- *Novice teacher + practice*
- *First-year teacher + practice*
- *New teacher + instruction*
- *Beginning teacher + instruction*
- *Novice teacher + instruction*
- *First-year teacher + instruction*
- *New teacher + pedagogy*
- *Beginning teacher + pedagogy*
- *Novice teacher + pedagogy*
- *First-year teacher + pedagogy*

In addition to coming up with as many ways as you can to phrase the topic or issue, use *article keyword lists* to guide you. When you download articles, you can typically find the keyword list near the abstract. These will help you discover whether there are "standard" search terms for your topic and the related dimensions you are investigating. For example, when I began searching for articles on first-year teaching practice, my efforts did not yield many relevant articles. However, as I looked through what I did manage to find, I noticed that the keywords did not feature "first-year teacher." Instead, authors were using the keywords "novice teacher" and "beginning teacher." When I used these terms in my own search, I was able to locate many more articles.

ACTIVITY 4. DRAFTING SEARCH TERMS

What words will you use to search for literature? Create a "word bank".

- Try to find as many different versions of your search terms as you can.
- Examine a few articles on your topic to see if you might get ideas from the keywords they use.

To optimize your searches, make sure that you familiarize yourself with your library databases and use them strategically. You can conduct a general search, but you can also search by specific database or within a particular journal.

If you conduct a general search—for example, by using a cross-disciplinary database like EBSCO or JSTOR—make sure to refine your search using additional delimiters (categories that narrow your search). Most databases will provide options to choose a range of years of publications, limit your search to peer-reviewed publications, search only publications within a specific discipline, and so on. You can also experiment by asking the search engine to look for your search terms in the article keywords, abstract, or title (rather than searching the entire text for them) which may offer a more targeted approach.

For some disciplines, there are specific databases that may yield better or more tailored results. For instance, in education, two common databases are the Education Resources Information Center (ERIC) and Education Research Complete. Using these education-specific databases rather than general ones like EBSCO can help filter out publications outside your discipline.

You may also want to search within specific journals in your field. While each journal will have an option to use your search terms to search within the journal, you might also consider a "hand search." Prior to the digitization of libraries, a hand search entailed going to your physical library, identifying target journals, obtaining copies of those journals spanning a specified period of time (e.g., the last decade), and reading through the contents (usually the titles and abstracts) to identify any relevant articles you may have missed on your broader searches. Today, however, you can conduct a hand search merely by looking up the journals on your library website, going to each journal page, and looking at the lists of articles from each issue for a specified time period. For instance, if you are searching for topics on urban schools, you might go to *Urban Review* or *Equity and Excellence in Education* and read titles and abstracts for each article in each issue for the past several years.

Finally, when you locate articles that are closely related to your topic, mine their literature reviews and reference sections for publications you may have missed on previous searches. However, an important caveat here is that *you should always look up the original source and read it yourself.* Do it not only because it is ethical, but also because authors' interpretations are often very subjective. For example, one professor in my doctoral program had an activity called the "Lo Jack" assignment, named for a device that would help find stolen cars. In the activity, we chose a citation from a literature review, looked it up, and read the original source ourselves. We then compared our interpretation of the original article to the way it was summarized and/or cited in the secondary source. Often, these differed quite a bit.

5.3 Analysis of Literature

ACTIVITY 5. KEYWORDS AND HAND SEARCHES

1. **Go to your library's main web page. Find the periodical locator (a search engine to locate journals). Enter a keyword that you think a journal that published in your field might contain. Browse the results that come up and explore some of the journal websites.**
2. **From the journals you found, which three journals do you think would be productive for you to conduct a hand search? Why?**

Your next step is to begin to read and analyze the literature you've gathered. Much of this process parallels qualitative research analysis—but instead of analyzing original data like surveys or interviews, the body of literature you have compiled will serve as your data set. In the sections that follow, I will briefly discuss the literature analysis process and offer tools to use. In the initial phase of analysis, you will 1) take systematic notes on each article, book, report (and so on) using a charting tool; 2) conduct an initial analysis of text charts and generate first-level codes; and 3) write initial exploratory memos on those codes. In the second phase, you will 4) create axial codes, or emerging categories, and category memos; and 5) formalize your analysis into themes and write theme memos.

Charting

As you begin reading, you will need a process for notetaking in a systematic way that will support later phases of analysis. My suggestion: read the articles and take notes using a charting tool that will enable you to extract information along the same dimensions for each text. You may want to create separate charts using Word documents, or you may want to make a spreadsheet to enter your notes.

There are also online tools you can also explore, such as Zotero, to help you manage the articles and your notes. Because these tools evolve every year, I recommend conducting a search to find out what is available that might work best for you.

Typically, you will want to document the following information from an empirical text:

- ***Citation:*** The full APA citation (so you do not have to look it up later)
- ***Study Purpose and Research Questions***: What the study seeks to accomplish, any questions that guide the inquiry
- ***Theoretical or Conceptual Frame***: The theories, concepts, models, and/or perspectives that shape or inform the study
- ***Methodology/Methods***: Type of methodology/methods, participants, setting, data sources, analytic procedures, and any other relevant design details
- ***Findings:*** Summary of the authors' report of results or outcomes of analysis
- ***Conclusions and Implications***: Any relevant ideas from the authors' discussion of findings in terms of larger significance; any relevant implications for practice, research, policy, and so on
- ***Limitations or Critiques:*** Any limitations of the methodology or any critiques you have of the research.
- ***Powerful Quotes:*** Direct quotes that might be useful when you write your actual review later (tip: ALWAYS make sure to add the page number so you do not have to go hunting for it later!)
- ***Relevance for your Topic:*** Any notes regarding how the study relates to your specific study plans

An example of a literature review article chart is provided for you below.

Read through and notice the elements included and the level of detail. As you begin reading articles for your own review, you will likely start to notice repeated ideas and/or have emerging "a-ha" moments. Keep track of these a-has and then fold those notes into the initial analytic process that is described in the next section.

Citation	Strom, K. J. (2015). Teaching as assemblage: Negotiating learning and practice in the first year of teaching. Journal of teacher education, 66(4), 321-333.
Study Purpose & Research	▪ *Purpose*: To examine the construction of teaching practices of a first-year science teacher in an urban school setting; to illustrate the non-linear nature of teaching ▪ *Research Question*: "How does a science teacher negotiate his preservice learning within his first-year teaching environment as he constructs his practice?"
Theoretical Frame or Key Concepts	Rhizomatics- a non-linear theory of social activity; assemblage- a heterogeneous mixture of human and nonhuman elements that collectively produce something (e.g., a classroom)
Methodology *Type of methodology, participants/ setting, Data sources, other relevant design details*	▪ *Methodology*: Qualitative case study ▪ *Participant*: 1 teacher, Mauro, who taught 9th grade environmental science and 11th/12th grade earth science; he was Latinx, 25, and identified as gay. ▪ *Context*: NMUTR teacher residency program; a large urban district in northeastern US; very diverse student body ▪ *Data*: teaching observations over one semester of instruction; a 20-minute teaching debrief after each lesson observation; two semi-structured interviews with the participant. ▪ *Analysis*: situated analysis and rhizomatic mapping
Findings	Main takeaway: Mauro taught and interacted with students differently depending on what set of classes he was in. Each set of classes brought a number of student and contextual factors that were different, despite being within the same school; these shaped his pedagogy differently in each class. The Findings Summary: **11th/12th Grade Classes**

Findings	1. Context: $11^{th}/12^{th}$ grade classes were small, and the subject was one Mauro was familiar with. The subject was not tested. All of this gave Mauro a lot of flexibility. 2. Students were mature and focused on graduating. Mauro was able to build productive relationships with them. 3. Mauro was able to co-create a harmonious class environment and an interactive pedagogy characterized by group activity and plentiful opportunity for student discussion and investigations. **9th Grade Classes** 1. Context: Classes were large, subject was unfamiliar to Mauro, and the subject was tested, all of which were constraining factors 2. Students: were transitioning to high school and were quite rowdy. Mauro often had to navigate conflicts in the class which led to a lot of tension between him and students. 3. Mauro was not able to build the same kind of relationships; students were unpredictable in interactive lessons, and he often reverted to teacher-led, lecture-based activity which was the opposite of his teacher prep program's focus.
Implications and/or Conclusions	Teaching is complex phenomena with many moving parts; these parts, collectively, produce teaching and learning. Therefore, one must look at the relations of the assemblage, how all the parts work together.
Limitations and/or Critique	The methodological design is a single case study, which means that the findings are not generalizable.
Relevance for Your Topic; Other Notes	Provides an example of a study regarding a first-year teacher that examines the way teaching moves across time and space into first year pedagogical practice; also examines not just the teacher, but the way the teacher interacts with both human and nonhuman components of the classroom setting.
Relevant Quotes (with page number)	"In 'translating,' as highlighted by Mauro's case, teachers take their learning and make sense of it within a specific setting and set of circumstances, which may mean the product of that joint sense-making may look substantially different from one context to the next." (p. 330) "...the collaborative negotiations occurring between teachers, their students, and their contexts, and the teaching practices emerging from those collective negotiations, suggest that no straight line can be drawn between the experiences of learning to teach in a preservice program and the enacting of that learning in a classroom." (p. 330)

ACTIVITY 6. CREATING A LITERATURE REVIEW CHART	
Try out charting an article of your choice relevant to your dissertation topic.	
Citation	
Study Purpose & Research Questions	
Theoretical Frame or Key Concepts, Perspectives	
Methodology	
Findings	
Implications and/or Conclustions	
Limitations and/or Critique	
Relevance for Your Topic; Other Notes	
Relevant Quotes (with page number)	

Initial Analysis

Generally speaking, the initial analysis steps include data familiarization, initial coding, and initial memoing. Below I describe each of these briefly, and then I offer resources for the initial coding and memoing processes.

Data Familiarization

Once you have read and charted the articles in your pool, start with *data familiarization* (Braun & Clark, 2006). Familiarizing yourself with the data (in this case, your article charts are treated as your data) involves reading and re-reading the charts and taking informal notes on what you notice relative to your framing questions. Make sure to keep in mind the central problem or issue on which your literature review is focused. Once you've done this, write a summary memo in terms of ideas or a-has that surfaced during this first complete read-through. This memo should be informal—you can write it in paragraphs or in bullet form.

Initial or Open Coding

Once you've familiarized yourself with your charts, move on to initial coding (Charmaz, 2006). For this process, read through your charts a second time, labeling data with *codes*, or phrases/short sentences that summarize ideas. Essentially, these codes become units of meaning-making that you can use later to start identifying patterns and emerging categories.

Once you start to see repeating and/or similar codes, it's a signal that you need to start your *initial literature review codebook.* You can create your own in a spreadsheet, or you can use a coding template, such as the one provided below. You can also use qualitative coding tools or software, like Dedoose or In Vivo, but I prefer working with the codes myself because it stimulates additional thinking.

INITIAL/FIRST CYCLE CODES		
CODE	**EXPLANATION**	**ILLUSTRATIVE DATE/CITATIONS**

Figure 5.1: Suggested initial coding template

Read the example from a first-level codebook (below). I will use this example to illustrate the process of recording initial codes in your first-level lit review codebook, which I discuss in detail next.

CODE	EXPLANATION	ILLUSTRATIVE DATE/CITATIONS
STUDENT BEHAVIOR AFFECTS PRACTICE	If students do not behave in ways that are conducive to the lesson, it can influence teachers to adopt more traditional teaching practice because they feel a need to "control" the lesson or classroom.	Brashier & Norris (2008): Early elementary teachers reported that although they started off their year using developmentally appropriate pedagogy, like instructional centers, they cut down on their use of center activities because students tended to be noisy and rambunctious.

For each row, first add the code (i.e., the phrase/short sentence you've created). In the above example, I named the initial code "*Student behavior affects practice.*" Then, explain the code with as much detail and specificity as you can, making connections to the overall topic of the literature review if possible.

For instance, above I describe the code as follows: "*Students' behavior, particularly when it is perceived as disruptive or unruly, can influence teachers to adopt more traditional teaching practice because they feel a need to 'control' the lesson or classroom.*" For a literature review looking at the factors that shape first year pedagogy, this offers one possibility—how students respond to lessons in terms of their behavior can impact new teachers' instructional decisions. In this explanation, I tried to be concise, but also detailed enough so that the explanation itself stands on its own in the initial codebook. Without that detail, when you get ready to move on to the next stage of analysis, you may not remember what you meant, so you'll have to go back to the initial articles to find out more about the context in which you originally created the code (which will take you much more time).

Finally, summarize the evidence that supports the code, as well as a short corresponding citation (just the year and author/s). If you add quotes, they should be in addition to (not in place of) your own summary of the evidence. This will help you start to create usable text for later use when writing actual sections of your literature review. Above, I have noted the short citation (Brashier & Norris, 2008) and added a sentence to describe the evidence that illustrates the claim the code makes: Participants (first year early elementary teachers) were not using the developmentally appropriate pedagogies they learned about in their preservice programs consistently. The teachers explained that, during these times, they perceived students as being too loud and out of control, so they cut back on the use of center activities to cultivate a more orderly classroom.

Keep in mind that, depending on the focus of your analysis, you could have multiple codes for this piece of data. Here, my purpose is to examine collectively the factors and forces that shape first year teaching, and how that shaping happens. However, if my literature review focused on new teachers' understandings of pedagogy from their teacher preparation programs, this code might instead focus on the conflict between theoretical ideas learned in the teacher preparation program (e.g., learning is social and happens through talking) and teachers' need for a quiet, orderly classroom.

As you first start recording your codes, you will probably have many that apply to one study; however, as you read and code further, you'll start to see recurring codes and can add more than one study to the evidence column. In addition, your first iteration of a code might need to be adjusted as you read further. For instance, you might initially create a code, and afterard, read a few more articles with a similar focus but which give you a more nuanced perspective. In this case, you would refine your code to reflect your more complex understanding. Think of your codes as flexible labels in this initial stage of analysis.

Initial Coding Memos

As you go through your charts and make these refinements, start to write informal memos, which I call *initial coding memos*. These memos should explore the emerging patterns and connections you are seeing with the initial set of codes you are generating. They can be free-written and just a paragraph or two in length.

My process is as follows: writing off the top of my head—as if I'm having a conversation with myself—I articulate a pattern I am seeing. I explore how I think it relates to the overall problem and describe the initial evidence indicating that the idea might indeed be a pattern or significant in some way.

The purpose of these memos is to flesh out your thinking about particular ideas while also maintaining a holistic perspective. Codes are important tools because they break up the text into chunks of meaning that can be used to reconstruct a story. However, in isolation, they also can feel disconnected and decontextualized from the data. The initial memos help you reconnect and recontextualize those ideas in complex ways. Thus, coding and memoing are simultaneous micro-macro processes of decontextualization and contextualization, reduction and complexification.

Read the example memo below. Compare the codes by themselves to the memo. What kind of nuance does the memo, in combination with the codes, provide that the codes would not communicate on their own?

EXAMPLE INITIAL CODING MEMO

Codes:

- Struggle to enact preservice learning
- Non-developmentally appropriate instruction
- Authoritarian classroom management
- Need for control

In research discussions about the "theory-practice disconnect," the problem is presented in a fairly linear fashion: the teachers are taught how to teach effectively in their programs but can't seem to put it into practice—and so they tend go back to traditional teaching/classroom management. But through reading some of the in-depth qualitative studies (e.g., Brashier & Norris 2008; Hargreaves & Jacka) I'm seeing that it just isn't that simple or black-and-white of a process. For example, in Brashier & Norris (2008), elementary teachers talked about how they had to stop using centers and other student-led learning activities as much because students got so rowdy. They didn't give it up altogether, so it's pointing to a kind of modification or hybridizing of their practice—but not a total "washout" (like Zeichner & Tabachnik, 1981 call it). And, they were cognizant of their decision-making; they realized that teacher-led activities were not as developmentally appropriate, but the need to be able to control their classrooms was more important to them. Similarly, the teacher Hargreaves & Jacka (1995) focused on was cognizant of her decision to use more authoritarian methods of classroom management ("behavior modification") because she couldn't seem to wrangle her students otherwise—and she was torn up about it. Both of these studies point to a common need for teachers to "control" classrooms which interferes with their enactment of equity-based practices, but perhaps a more complex decision-making process is involved than previous literature might suggest.

In the above example, I am writing about data involving at least 4 codes I have already identified. However, these codes on their own do not tell the whole story—nor do they pick up fine distinctions in the same way the memo does by exploring the complexity presented by teachers' struggles in the two studies. By writing the memo based on the codes, I'm able to tease out the idea of *hybridization of practices* and further explore teachers' conscious decision-making based on a need to "control" the classroom.

ACTIVITY 7. INITIAL CODING AND MEMOING

Once you've read a few studies from your set, begin creating your initial codebook. Use the prompts below to create your initial memos.

- Articulate the pattern you are seeing or explore some of the connections in a "free write" manner, without worrying about organization of thinking, language, grammar, etc.
- How does this pattern, connection, etc. relate to the overall problem?
- What evidence do you have so far that this is, indeed, a pattern? Be as detailed as possible.

Second-Level Analysis

The next step involves building more complex codes, or *axial codes* (Charmaz, 2006), out of your initial codebook and memos. Think of a wheel with an axis: The individual spokes are the first level codes, and the axis is what connects them—i.e., the axial code. In axial coding, you refine and cluster like or connected codes into an "axis" (an emerging category). Axial coding will help you move your analysis in the direction of narrative "chunks" that can eventually form the major sections of your literature review.

There is a qualitative difference between first and second level codes in terms of their level of meaning-making. First-level codes tend to be mainly *descriptive*: that is, they answer questions about what is happening or what is there. However, axial codes begin to move toward *interpretation*. That is, they begin shifting toward "what does this mean?" or "how does this help us explain the phenomena we are interested in studying?"

Because by now, you've already been memoing on your initial codebook, you likely already have some ideas for axial codes. However, to be systematic, I recommend the following process: Read through your initial codebook and initial coding memos several times. Take notes on the ideas that relate or overarching ideas you notice. Then, go back to your first-level memos and fold additional meaning-making into these second-level notes, and use them to begin to move codes into related clusters.

As you form the clusters, give them flexible labels that express the relation or connection between the initial codes comprising them.

For example, if all the codes are clearly related to teacher identity, you might name that category "teacher identity" from the start. However, if you've got a cluster of codes that you know are related but aren't quite sure how to articulate the relationship, free-write a memo to try to figure out what the connection is, and then label it accordingly. You'll likely refine them as you go along, so don't worry if it isn't perfect.

Each cluster will become a category in your axial coding organizer (see below for a suggested format for creating yours).

AXIAL CODING ORGANIZER			
AXIAL CODE	**EXPLANATION/ CLAIM**	**SUBSUMED CODES**	**ILLUSTRATIVE STUDY(IES)/NOTES**

Figure 5.2: Axial coding organizer

When you add each axial code to your second-level codebook, make sure that you add a thorough explanation that describes the overall category (think of this as a brief memo). Write it in the form of a claim, if possible, and include enough detail/context that someone without a background in the topic could read and understand what you mean. This is very important because through the literature review process, you may come back to some of these codes and not remember details—so making sure not to skimp on this step will help you avoid having to go back to your notes, initial codebook, and/or articles. (The coding stages can be tedious and time-consuming, so you might be tempted to take shortcuts. Don't. You will thank your future self, I promise!) Then, add the subsumed codes and supporting studies, with a summary of the finding or other element of the study that supports the claim you are making with the description. Again, don't skimp with the study summaries—they will help you synthesize across studies later, and they are also often a scaffold for writing about exemplars that illustrate your themes and subthemes (discussed later in this section).

Examine the example axial coding entry below. Are there enough details provided to understand the meaning of the axial code as it is written? How are each of the initial codes folded in to the new codes? How do the examples identified support the claim? (Due to space limitations there are only 3 examples given in the example, but it should give you the idea.)

AXIAL CODE	EXPLANATION/CLAIM	SUBSUMED CODES	SUPPORTING STUDIES
School Environment shapes teaching practice	In the school environment, the teacher must interact with other teachers, administrators, parents, the collective school culture, and school policies and schedules, all of which have the potential for shaping teaching practice in unpredictable ways.	Administrators influence teaching Parents influence teaching Colleagues influence teaching School culture Influences teaching School structures influence teaching	Scherff, 2008: The administration supported parents over the 2 teachers, which created a power imbalance between teachers and students that contributed to classroom management problems. Saka, Southerland & Brooks, 2009: A teacher initially committed to inquiry-based teaching reverts to lecture style due in part to administrative pressure to teach more traditionally. Allen, 2009: 14 teachers who had been prepared to teach in socially constructivist ways mainly reverted to traditional teaching, partially from influence from their veteran colleagues.

Second Level Memoing

As you move further along in your literature review process, your memos should become more complex and start to synthesize across multiple points (often these correspond to your initial codes, albeit in refined form). At the same time, the memos also become more focused: for example, you'll need to create a memo for each axial code, or emerging category, and think through what that category means, why it is significant in the context of the focus of your project, and what evidence you have to support your reasoning.

On a conceptual level, second level memos help you flesh out your thinking with relation to axial codes and experiment with ways that the pieces might fit together to form a coherent whole. However, there is also a practical function as well: Second-level memos, along with your theme memos, begin to form a bridge to your actual writing. Often, you will repurpose text from these to use as you write the sections of your literature review. As such, taking your time with them is critical. Doing so will economize the time you spend later as you actually write your literature review.

Read the example literature review memo. What is the emerging pattern being articulated? How are the first-level codes being shaped and reshaped to form a coherent narrative? How do you see different pieces being woven together here to form a synthesis? In what ways does this memo push beyond mere description to more advanced analysis and interpretation?

EMERGING CATEGORY: *Struggling with instructional tasks contributes to transmission*

I'm seeing a pattern that shows that beginning teachers struggle with different facets of instruction as they enter the classroom, including curriculum, differentiation, and constructivist pedagogy. Studies show that struggling with these instructional components leads to frustration and feelings of inadequacy, which can contribute to new teachers' reverting to traditional, lecture based, and one-size-fits-all-practice. This pattern may connect to the theory-practice divide (Zeichner, 2010) which argues that university preparation is disconnected from practice and is another factor leading to "praxis-shock" (Smagorinsky et al., 2004). It also shines a light on specific areas that teacher preparation programs and induction programs may need to support more intensively.

- **Struggles with curriculum:** Several studies described teachers struggling with planning and organizing their curriculum (Beck, Kosnik, & Roswell, 2007; Fry; 2007; Griffin, Kilgore, & Winn, 2009).
    - Teachers in Beck, Kosnik, & Roswell's (2007) study felt totally unprepared to plan/create 9 months of instruction. One said, "...you really have to use your best judgment and decide when to teach certain things, trying to figure out what skills to teach in September, and in January, and in June" (p. 61).
- **Struggles with differentiation:** Several other studies showed that new teachers experienced difficulty differentiating instruction for specific student needs (Fantilli & McDougal, 2009; Grossman & Thompson, 2008; Tait, 2008).
    - Fantilli and McDougal (2009) found that teachers experienced difficulties modifying their curriculum/instruction to support academic achievement of special education students, which led to feelings of inadequacy or frustration on the part of the teachers and left their special education students worse off academically.
- **Struggles with constructivist pedagogy:** Other research demonstrated that novices experienced difficulties with the implementation of constructivist pedagogical strategies.
    - Livingston & Borko (1989) found that teachers struggled to engage in open ended questioning with students;
    - Teachers studied by Beck, Kosnik, & Roswell (2007) struggled to implement collaborative group learning.

ACTIVITY 8. CREATE AN AXIAL CODEBOOK			
Use the suggested format below to create your axial coding organizer.			
AXIAL CODING ORGANIZER			
AXIAL CODE	**EXPLANATION**	**SUBSUMED CODES**	**ILLUSTRATIVE STUDE(IES)/ NOTES**

ACTIVITY 9. AXIAL MEMOS

Use the prompts below to write your emerging category memos.

- What is the emerging category?
- What is the central claim or assertion for this category?
- What are the key ideas to highlight in this theme relating to the central claim or assertion?
- What studies provide evidence for/illustrate these ideas? Be specific and provide summaries with as much detail as possible.
- How does this category connect back to the central problem and/or emerging overall argument you are making? What other connections can you make to other categories or other research in the field?

Formalizing Analysis: Themes

The final step is to formalize your analysis into the ideas that will eventually structure your literature review. Typically, literature reviews are organized by major *themes* that articulate high-level patterns across the studies you reviewed. As I explain below, a theme can be either a formalized category, or it could be a cluster of categories. To determine whether to continue to cluster categories together, examine them and map out the relationships between them. Is it logical to join them together under a larger theme? What would your rationale be for doing so?

For instance, when I was writing my dissertation literature review, I had clusters of factors that influenced new teachers' practices: *teacher factors* (e.g., her background, beliefs and orientations, and preservice learning), *classroom factors* (e.g., students, materials, and physical space), *school factors* (e.g., leadership, colleagues, and school climate), and *district/state factors* (e.g., testing and policy). It made sense to cluster these together because they all described related systems of factors at different levels that helped shape teaching—and, together, they provided a more holistic picture of how teaching practice is "co-produced" by many factors, of which the teacher (and her preservice learning) is only one part.

Once you've identified a theme, outline it to create a scaffold for writing. Not only will this help you ensure your writing is logical and organized, but it will also help make sure that you have adequate evidence. Below is a graphic organizer I created to help students outline their themes. Keep in mind that you may have to modify it to fit your literature review findings.

THEME 1: CLAIM:			
Subtheme	**Main Assertion(s)**	**Studies that Support**	**Exemplar Studies & Major Details**

Figure 5.3: Theme outline organizer

In the graphic organizer above, start by naming the theme and creating an overarching claim that communicates the key idea of the theme. If you aren't sure what that is, then map out the subthemes first, and come back to it later.

Then, for each of the subthemes (which are typically created from your emerging categories), develop a claim that communicates the key idea of the subtheme. Record all the studies that correspond to the subtheme (use citations only) and then choose a few of those that you think make compelling exemplars (that is, you think they illustrate the claim(s) particularly clearly). Summarize each exemplar study, focusing in on relevant details for that subtheme only. Later, you will use these as part of your evidence in the body of your literature review.

Examine the example theme organizer on the next page, which builds out a theme and one of its subthemes. Take a few minutes to think through these questions: How does the theme claim relate to the subtheme and its main assertion? What kind of details are included in the summary? Also note that, due to space limitations, only two exemplar studies are provided.

THEME 1: Multiple influences and interactions of Teaching Practice CLAIM: Many factors, including the first-year teacher herself, her environment, and the work of teaching, work together to shape teaching practice.			
Subtheme	**Main Assertion(s)**	**Studies that Support**	**Exemplar Studies & Major Details**
The teacher system	The teacher herself brings multiple factors that shape her practice: her history and background experiences, personal qualities, preservice learning, and beliefs, all of which help shape her work.	History and background experiences (Birrell, 1995; Hargreaves & Jacka, 1995) Personal qualities (Hebert & Worthy, 2001; Tait, 2008) Preservice learning (Beck, Kosnik, & Rowsell, 2007; Grossman & Thompson, 2008; Towers, 2010) Beliefs (Bergeron, 2008; Grossman & Thompson, 2008)	*Preservice learning/ beliefs*: Grossman and Thompson (2008): analysis of the use of curriculum materials by 3 beginning teachers; one taught in a school that mandated a writing curriculum that was philosophically aligned with his preservice learning, which aided in his successful creation of curriculum in his first year. *Beliefs*: Bergeron (2008)- in depth study of one first year teacher; she had asset-based beliefs about students, which helped facilitate culturally and linguistically relevant practices.

ACTIVITY 10. THEME OUTLINE			
Use the organizer below to outline one theme. There is an optional activity at the end of this chapter if you would like to outline further themes.			
THEME 1: **CLAIM:**			
Subtheme	**Main Assertion(s)**	**Studies that Support**	**Exemplar Studies & Major Details**

Creating a Schema for Your Literature Review

Once you've decided on your themes and mapped them out, you'll need to create a schema for the body of your literature review—that is, you need to decide how to communicate the outcomes of your analysis to your readers through an organizational structure. To do so, you will need to think about how your themes relate to each other to tell a cohesive story or narrative. These linkages between the themes are the key to deciding how to organize your review in the most logical and coherent manner.

Sometimes, the relationships amount to a larger narrative that will be broken down into its constituent parts. For example, if I was conducting a literature review that examined the construction of new teachers' classroom practices, the whole narrative could be "Systems of First Year Teaching." The subsequent themes could be the teacher system, the classroom system, the school system, the district system, or state/federal policy. However, it might also be a linked narrative that builds logically: Theme one leads logically to theme 2, which builds to theme 3.

If the "story" is not apparent to you, create a concept map or flowchart and see if you can articulate relationships between the big ideas.

Let's look at an example of a literature review on teaching practices for multilingual learners in science.

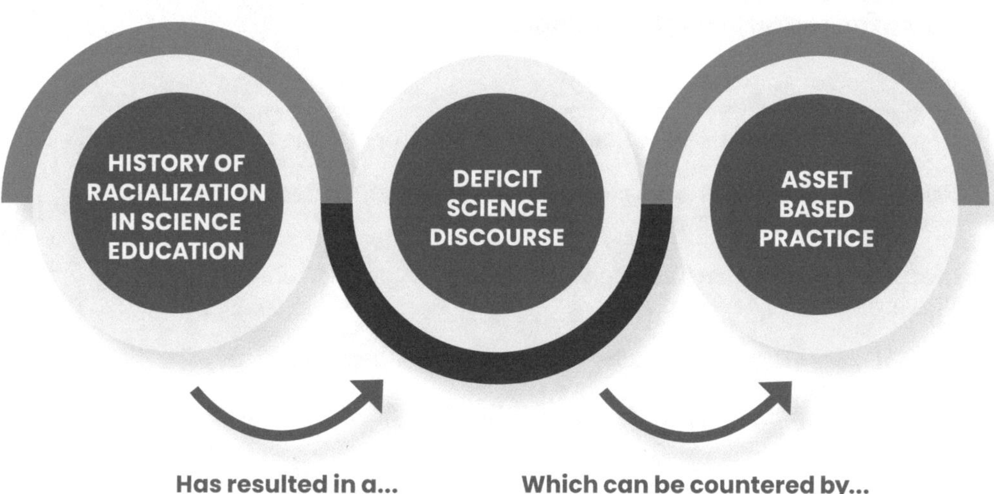

Figure 5.4: Example literature review schema

In the example above, I created an organizing schema using a process chart that makes visible the logic between the themes (these links are italicized, below). I start with a discussion of research showing how science has historically been taught in ways that emphasize white, western knowledge, discourse and practice (theme 1). This racialized history *resulted in* the creation of a deficit science discourse regarding multilingual learners, which negatively impacts their access to quality science education (theme 2). However, studies have shown that this inequity *can be countered by* asset-based practices that value multilingual learners' heterogeneous resources (theme 3). In this example, the logical links show that theme 1 created conditions for theme 2; and theme 2 can be corrected through theme 3.

ACTIVITY 11. CREATING A SCHEMA

Create a conceptual map or logic/process flow with your themes. How do the themes relate to each other? Is there a logical sequence, or do they form parts of a larger narrative? Depending on your answers, create a draft schema to organize the body of your literature review. If you have access to a partner, describe the schema to them, articulating the connections between the big ideas.

5.4 Building Out Themes: Levels of Claims

Now that you have your themes outlined and have determined the structure of the body of your literature review, it is time to start fleshing out the themes and bridging into writing. To do that, it is helpful to focus on three levels of claims organized from broad to specific, as outlined below.

Three Levels of Claims in a Literature Review

Level 1/Theme or Subtheme claims: Assertions that correspond to the main themes/subthemes

Level 2/Subset claims: Assertions that apply to specific subsets of studies in your review

Level 3/Exemplars: Single study claim + description that supports Level 2 claims

Level 1 Claims

Level 1 claims are high-level assertions that correspond to the claims you developed for your themes. They are framing declarative statements (often in section introductions or topic sentences) that represent a conclusion drawn from your literature review analysis. Basically, level 1 claims are literature review-specific topic sentences.

Take a look at the example below.

> **Level 1 Claim Example**
>
> **Theme:** The Teacher System
>
> **Main theme assertion:** According to the literature reviewed, teachers themselves bring a variety of individual factors or elements that help shape their practice, including their preservice preparation; beliefs about self, students, and teaching and learning; and personal qualities and background experiences. Studies showed that these elements functioned as constraining or enabling forces that, in combination with student and school environment factors, contributed to the teachers' adoption of fairly traditional teaching methods and authoritarian classroom practices.

This example develops an overarching claim for the theme "the teacher system." The assertion lists multiple factors that make up the teacher system, or the elements they bring to their teaching. Typically, including a list of elements, like this one, also serves as an organizing statement or mini-road map that tells the reader that each of these elements will receive its own subsection. There's also a second sentence—because the task of the literature review is not only to answer "what research has been done on this topic?" but also to address "what does that mean for my study?" In this case, the second sentence of this level 1 claim describes the significance of the teacher system; that is, it works in tandem with other systems to perpetuate dominant teaching methods (the problem I was hoping to disrupt with my research).

You will also develop level 1 claims for each subtheme. Any time you begin a new section, it should open with an assertion that serves as a framing analysis statement. Let's look at an example to illustrate.

> **Level 1 Claim Example**
>
> **Theme:** Teacher System
>
> **Subtheme 1:** Learning from Preservice Preparation
>
> - **Main subsection assertion:** Researchers have found that preservice preparation can serve as both an enabling and constraining factor in shaping first-year teaching practices.
>
> **Subtheme 2:** Beliefs about Self, Students, and Teaching and Learning
>
> - **Main subsection assertion:** The literature reviewed shows that teachers' beliefs regarding self, students, and views of teaching and learning exerted a strong influence on their practices.

Using the same theme as above, this example builds out two of its subthemes: teachers' learning from their preservice preparation programs and teachers' beliefs. The level 1 claims communicate findings from the literature review analysis: preservice learning is an influence that can be both positive and negative; and teacher beliefs are a very strong influence. In addition, both claims serve as organizing statements, which in turn scaffold for the reader so they can anticipate what is coming.

ACTIVITY 12. LEVEL 1 CLAIMS

Go back to your theme organizer (Activity 10). The overall assertion and subtheme main assertions are your level one claims. Use the following to evaluate and edit.

- Does the theme claim clearly state the overarching finding? Does it serve as an organizing statement for the subthemes? Edit as needed.
- Do the subtheme main assertions clearly unpack part of the theme claim? Does it serve as an organizing statement for the rest of the subsection? Edit as needed.

Level 2 Claims

Level 2 claims are assertions referring to specific subsets of studies. These assertions are smaller in scope and more focused. They should contextualize or unpack the level 1 claim. Level 2 claims also serve as one layer of evidence supporting the level 1 claim.

Read the example below. How do the four different level 2 claims unpack and illustrate the level 1 claim for the subtheme? What else do you notice about how the level 2 claims are structured? Think about or jot down your answer before continuing.

Subtheme 1: Learning from Preservice Preparation

- **Subsection Level 1 Claim:** Preservice preparation served as both an enabling and constraining factor in shaping first-year teaching practices.
- **Study-Specific Assertions (level 2 claims):**
    - 15 studies showed that teachers struggled to enact their preservice learning, often contributing to the adoption of more traditional practices.
    - 8 studies showed that when the school setting aligned to preservice learning, it could be a positive influence.

- Preservice education that included work around socio-cultural issues also influenced pedagogical practices and instructional interactions with diverse student populations, as two studies illustrate.
- Practicum experiences also informed professional practices adopted in the first year of teaching, as revealed in six studies, particularly when teachers are hired by the same school in which they completed their practica.

In the example above, each of the level 2 claims refer to a specific number of studies that illustrate that pattern, and clearly state the number of studies in that subset. Each of these claims also relate to the level 1 claim: The first two study-specific assertions describe constraining and enabling influences, while the second two describe particularly influential features of preservice programs.

However, we can't stop here. While these do provide some level of support for the higher-level claims that have been made, adding more specific detail is essential. Not to do so is the equivalent of "telling" readers what we learned from our literature review and expecting them to trust us that our conclusions are warranted. To provide detailed evidence that *shows* what we mean, we will need level 3 claims. But first...

ACTIVITY 13. DRAFTING OUT LEVEL 2 CLAIMS

Choose one of the subthemes from the theme you worked on above. What would be the level 2 claims? Draft at least one level 2 claim, then assess it: do you state the number of studies? Do you make a specific claim that clearly gestures back to the subtheme level 1 claim?

Level 3 Claims

Level 3 claims are study-specific assertions that, along with contextual information from the study, illustrate level 2 claims, while also serving as a "trustworthiness" measure. Trustworthiness is a concept from qualitative research referring to the degree to which readers find research to be ethical, credible, and rigorous (for more on trustworthiness, see Sarah J. Tracy's 2010 article, which provides an expanded definition). When you conduct your study, you will ensure trustworthiness through a variety of means, including a high level of transparency in the methods section, triangulating patterns across multiple sources of data, running emerging findings by your participants, and discussing findings with critical friends. However, for the literature review, a good portion of the trustworthiness comes from the examples you provide to support your higher-level claims. Therefore, exemplars used should be detailed enough that the reader can judge the veracity of the claim, *and* the description should provide brief methodological details. For instance, what was the focus of the study? Who were the participants, and how many were there? What was the methodology and/or methods? Where did it take place?

Let's look at an example. As you read, think about or jot down your answers to the following: How does this exemplar discussion support the Level 1 and 2 claims? What details are provided in the discussion of the exemplars?

> **Subtheme Level 1 Claim:** Preservice preparation served as an enabling and constraining factor in shaping first year teaching practices.
>
> **Subtheme Level 2 Claim:** Preservice education that included work around sociocultural issues also influenced pedagogical practices and instructional interactions with diverse student populations in two studies.
>
> **Level 3 Claims** *(Exemplars)***:** Bergeron's (2008) case study of a beginning white teacher who attended a culturally responsive teacher education program provides an illustrative example. The teacher's preservice preparation served as a foundation to help her build a sense of classroom community and provide linguistic support for the mostly English language learner students she taught. In a similar vein, He and Cooper (2011) found that preservice opportunities to examine their beliefs about diverse populations and to interact with students from diverse backgrounds in their preservice programs helped five new teachers in their study to establish productive relationships with diverse pupils and their families.

In the example above, I provide two brief exemplars. (As a side note, often you can use just one exemplar to demonstrate your 2 claims, but since there are only two studies in this subset, it makes sense to discuss them both.) The first exemplar describes a study by Bergeron (2008). I provide specific details about the study, including the method (case study), the participant (a white, beginning teacher) and some context (her program emphasized culturally responsive teaching). Next, I address the part of the study that supports the level 2 claim: the program helped her build community and support the language development of her emergent bilingual students.

I then transition (using the connector phrase "*in a similar vein*") to the second exemplar. My description offers details about the participants (five new teachers) and a summary of relevant findings (opportunities to examine their beliefs about and interact with diverse kids helped preservice teachers build relationships with diverse populations).

Both examples clearly show how preservice learning served as an enabling factor for new teachers' practices (level 1 claim) and specifically, how preservice learning experiences involving sociocultural development were helpful.

If you have a longer exemplar, make sure that you clearly signal to your reader, up front, the way that the exemplar links back to the level 2 claim. Otherwise, the purpose of the exemplar may get lost in the details. For example, compare the following two versions of an exemplar (example taken from Strom, 2014, p. 63). Can you spot the difference between them? What does the added text clarify?

VERSION 1

For example, Lambson (2010) conducted a qualitative, interpretive case study of three first-year teachers taking part in a school-based teacher professional learning community. The school at which the study took place had a long-standing and close relationship with the university as well as established school norms of participation in teacher inquiry groups. During the year-long study group led by a teacher educator from the partner university, the beginning teachers interacted with more experienced teachers at first as "peripheral participants" (Lambson, 2010, p. 1662, citing Lave & Wenger, 2001) and gradually took on more of a central role. As the year progressed, the teachers became more confident in their practices and an increasingly integral part of the teacher learning community.

VERSION 2

Lambson's (2010) qualitative, interpretive case study of three first-year teachers taking part in a school-based teacher professional learning community highlights the potential of the positive impact of productive interactions between colleagues. The school at which the study took place had a long-standing and close relationship with the university as well as established school norms of participation in teacher inquiry groups. During the year-long study group led by a teacher educator from the partner university, the beginning teachers interacted with more experienced teachers at first as "peripheral participants" (Lambson, 2010, p. 1662, citing Lave & Wenger, 2001) and gradually took on more of a central role. As the year progressed, the teachers became more confident in their practices and an increasingly integral part of the teacher learning community.

The difference between the two paragraphs can be found in the first sentence of version 2: "*Lambson's (2010) qualitative, interpretive case study of three first-year teachers taking part in a school-based teacher professional learning community highlights the potential of the positive impact of productive interactions between colleagues.*" Without this sentence, the reader may get confused over the purpose of the exemplar: it could just as easily be focusing on the positive role of university partnerships or teacher inquiry groups. Adding an additional phrase is important to frame this example as an illustration of the positive influence of collegial interaction.

ACTIVITY 14. LEVEL 3 CLAIMS

Read the paragraph below and answer the questions that follow.

Three studies found that the struggle which often occurs during the transition from preservice preparation to being a teacher of students in a particular school setting with real limitations can lead to feelings of frustration, despair, and failure (Allen, 2009; Chubbuck, 2008; Fantilli & McDougal, 2009). Such conflict is clearly illustrated by Chubbuck (2008) in a case study of a novice teacher committed to socially just teaching. The beginning teacher's previously held beliefs about a "right" way to

ACTIVITY 14. LEVEL 3 CLAIMS (CONT.)

teach, combined with high expectations for her own teaching abilities, conflicted with her actual ability to both manage the classroom and teach in a manner consistent with her ideas about social justice. Having not performed to her own standards and ideal conceptions of teaching, the teacher began to feel like a failure, internalizing "beliefs about her practice that interacted negatively, creating strong reality shock and leaving her mired in a slough of anxiety, guilt, and self-condemnation" (p. 322).

- What is the study-specific assertion? How do you know?
- What evidence is used to illustrate this assertion?
- What details are provided as part of the evidence?
- What language signals the focus and purpose of this example to readers?

Now, let's put the idea of exemplar to practice in the context of your own dissertation.

ACTIVITY 15. DRAFTING OUT EXEMPLARS

Working from the level 2 claim(s) you drafted, choose an exemplar or two from the set of studies illustrating that claim.

- First, outline the specific study claim (the part of the study that illustrates the level 2 claim).
- Then, make a note of some of the relevant methodological details (e.g., participants, method, context).
- Finally, edit these together; make sure that you've added language to frame the exemplar which explicitly states the purpose of the exemplar (often this is done in the transition).

Grounding Your Claims

As you craft your assertions, try to avoid making sweeping or broad statements. Chances are that you have not reviewed every article, book, or report that has ever been published on your topic. Instead, stay grounded in the specific literature you have reviewed. If you look back through the examples in this section, you can see how I have grounded myself.

Below are grounding sentence openers for each of the levels of claims. Can you think of any others to add?

As you are drafting your Level 1 claims, you might use sentence openers like the following:

- Generally, across the literature reviewed...
- My analysis of studies showed that...
- Researchers have found...

For second level claims, make sure you are clearly referring to a particular set of studies. Use language like:

- XX studies showed that...
- In X studies reviewed, researchers reported...
- [Claim], as xx studies reviewed illustrate...

For in-depth exemplars, make sure you are referring to one specific study. Use language like...

- In Researcher Name's (YEAR) study of...
- In this study...
- The researchers reported that...

ACTIVITY 16. GROUNDING CLAIMS IN SPECIFIC LITERATURE

Go back to the activities you've done in this section on claims. Assess the claims to ensure that they are grounded in the literature. Use some of the phrases above if you'd like or come up with your own.

5.5 Making an Argument with the Gap in Literature

ACTIVITY 17. FREE-WRITE

What are the gaps or shortcomings of the literature that you have analyzed? What is there not enough studies about? How does that relate to your proposed study?

Remember back in chapter three, when I mentioned that you would be making arguments in multiple places in your dissertation chapters? The final section of your literature review—the gap in research—is where you make an argument drawn from the synthesis you just provided. You may already have some thinking done around this from your problem statement (see chapter four) for your *research rationale*—that is, showing that there is a need to conduct more research on your chosen topic. In the concluding section of your literature review, you will build on that brief research rationale to make a more detailed case, supported by your review, that the study you are proposing will fill a gap (or gaps).

While the literature review conclusion typically articulates an empirical gap, you may have also identified conceptual and methodological gaps. Below, I define each of these types of gaps and offer examples of statements for each.

Empirical gap: There are few or no studies on the specific topic of your project.

- **Example:** Few studies exist that examine how asset-based teaching of MLLs in middle school science classrooms unfolds in micro-moments of every day instruction.

Conceptual gap: There is a lack of studies on your topic that take a particular theoretical lens.

- **Example:** Few studies exist that examine asset-based teaching of MLLs in middle school science classrooms from a positioning theory perspective.

Methodological gap: There is a lack of studies on your topic that take a specific methodological approach.

- **Example:** Few studies exist that examine asset-based teaching of MLLs in middle school science classrooms using qualitative micro-analysis.

Although your main literature review gap should be empirical, you may also want to point out methodological gaps as well if it will help you build the case that the study you are proposing is necessary. Also, keep in mind that some gaps may be both empirical *and* methodological. For example, many of my students are interested in qualitative research that centers the narratives of marginalized students. Quite often, the literature they review does not feature the voices of marginalized students at all, much less center their perspectives. In this case, the gap would be both empirical (understanding a phenomenon from marginalized students' perspectives) and methodological (featuring a method, like narrative or portraiture, that foregrounds students' voices and stories). However, I do recommend staying away from conceptual gaps in your literature review—if there is one, you'll use that as part of the rationale in your conceptual framework (see chapter six).

I like to build a statement of the gap with the following elements:

- A summary of the big ideas from the literature review (i.e., what we know);
- A critical evaluation of the literature in light of the study topic;
- A statement regarding what we do not know, or do not know enough about (the gap);
- A summary of how the project will address the identified gap; and
- A reminder why this research is important.

Let's look at an example of a literature review conclusion that includes these elements (excerpted from Strom, 2014, p. 4-5).

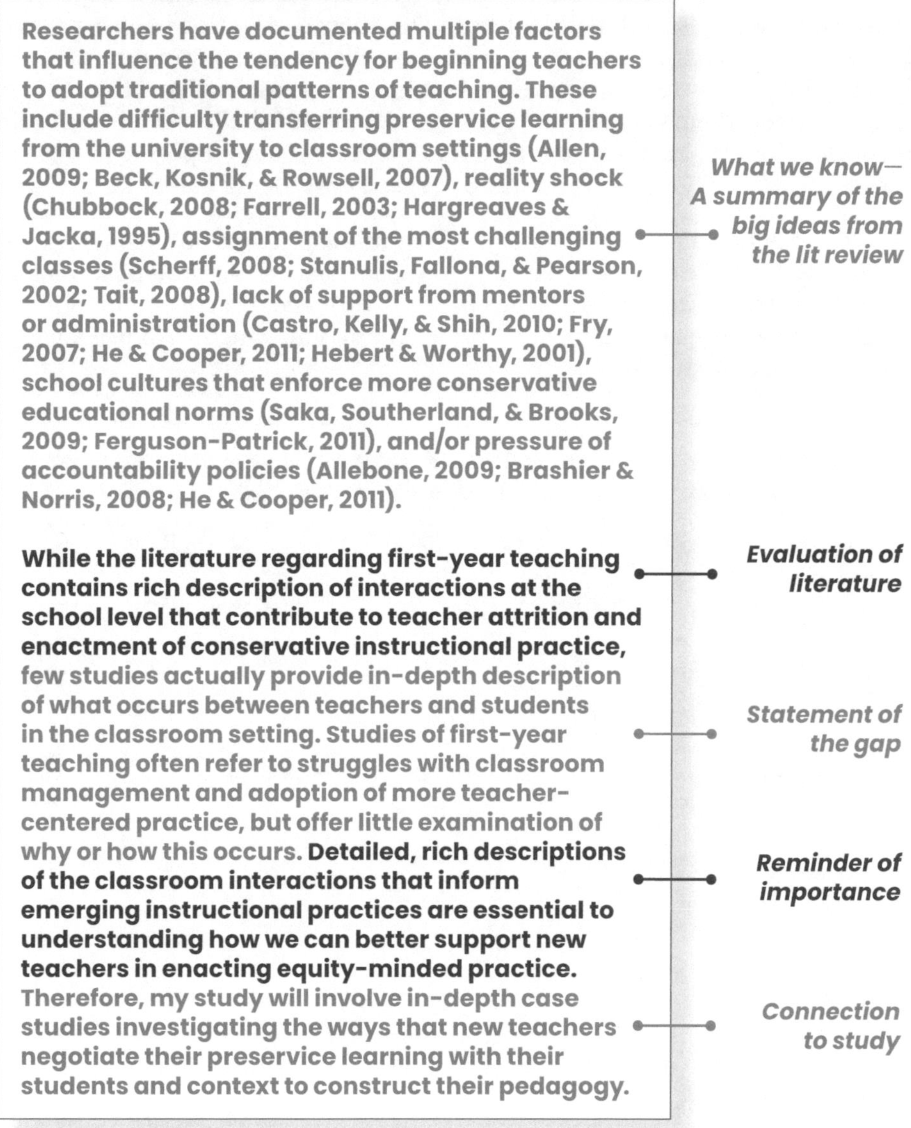

Figure 5.6: Annotated literature review conclusion

In the example above, I start off with what we know—a high-level summary of the findings of the literature review. I do not need to go into too much detail here, because I have already discussed these findings in depth in the body of the review. This is just a reminder to the reader before we launch into the gap.

Next, I provide a brief evaluation of the literature I've just summarized in relation to what I would like to study: these studies show plenty of interactions that contribute to the problem *at the school level.* Then the second part of this sentence states the gap: not very many studies closely examine student-teacher interactions *at the classroom level.* Notice the structure I used in that sentence—you can easily use the same structure when writing your own gap statement: *While the literature on [phenomenon] [state what it does look at], few studies [state the gap].*

I then offer another facet of the gap: we know first-year teachers struggle with classroom-level interactions regarding group dynamics and pedagogy, but there's not much research that looks deeply at how or why this happens. Next, I bridge to why this gap is important to address: We must deeply understand what is happening in classroom interactions that shape new teachers' practices to know how to support them to enact the type of practice that will disrupt long-standing inequities. Finally, I make a connection to the study I am proposing in terms of how it will address (or start to address) the gap I have identified.

You might also notice that the gap I've outlined here is both empirical and methodological: the empirical part is the student-teacher classroom interactions (and the way those work with other elements to influence practice), and the methodological part is the need for in-depth examination, which I am proposing to address with case studies.

ACTIVITY 18. GENERATING TEXT FOR THE STATEMENT OF THE GAP	
Use this graphic organizer to generate text that you can edit into a paragraph or two for your statement of the gap.	
Summary of What We Know from the Review	
Evaluative statement of Extant Research	
Statement of the Gap	
Reminder of importance	
How your Study Will Address the Gap	

5.6 Putting It All Together

Now, you are ready to start putting the pieces together. As a reminder, here is the general format of a (traditional) literature review:

I.	**Introduction: restates issue, summarizes major lit review themes, states gap**
II.	**Theme 1 (with as many subthemes as needed)**
III.	**Theme 2 (with as many subthemes as needed)**
IV.	**Theme 3 (with as many subthemes as needed)**
V.	**Statement of the gap summarizes what we know, what we don't know enough about (the gap in literature), and how your research will address this gap.**

I recommend building out your themes and statement of the gap first, then as a last step, write your introduction. The introduction should be a road map for the literature review: Remind the reader of the topic guiding the literature review, summarize the major "findings" you will be discussing (your themes), and preview the gap.

To build out your themes, always start by creating an outline. If you would like a little more scaffolding for your writing, there is also an optional additional writing activity at the end of this chapter that will provide targeted guidance for turning a subtheme into a paragraph.

Once you have edited all the pieces together, go back through your entire review with a scaffolding lens (see chapter two). Do you provide roadmaps in the beginning of the review and for each theme? Do you chunk your themes into clear subsections with headings? Do those headings communicate the gist of the section? Do you have transitions that connect all your sections as well as create flow from sentence to sentence? Specifically, do you have transitions for all your exemplars? Each example from the literature should have a transition that signals to the reader that you are moving into an example that supports a claim you've just made—such as:

- For example/for instance, Strom (2015) found that...
- As an illustration, Strom's (2015) case study shows...
- The work of Strom, Martin, & Villegas (2018) highlights...
- Strom and Viesca (2021) provide an instructive example...

For more ideas for transitions, look up the University of Manchester's Academic Phrasebank. (You can simply google "University of Manchester" + "Academic Phrasebank" and it will come up.)

OPTIONAL WRITING SCAFFOLDING ACTIVITY: MOVING FROM THEMES TO TEXT
1. Use your lit construction organizer/codebook to identify one theme, and one subsection from that theme, to build out. Theme: Subtheme:
2. Write the main theme and subtheme assertion. Main assertion of the theme: Subtheme assertion:
3. Write one specific study claim and identify an exemplar study that you will use to support that claim. Write WHY you will use that study (a rationale for how it supports the claim) Specific study claim: Exemplar & Rationale:
4. Put together one paragraph that starts with the subtheme assertion and then transitions to the specific study claim, followed by your exemplar. Make sure you have the following: 1) Transitions; 2) Scaffolding sentence that connects the specific study claim to the exemplar; 3) Language to show that this information is grounded in your lit review analysis. Paragraph:

OPTIONAL ACTIVITY: EXTENDED THEME OUTLINE

Use the organizer below to outline your themes, claims, subthemes, assertions, and evidence.

THEME 1:

CLAIM:

Subtheme	Main Assertion(s)	Studies that Support	Exemplar Studies & Major Details

THEME 2:

CLAIM:

Subtheme	Main Assertion(s)	Studies that Support	Exemplar Studies & Major Details

THEME 3:

CLAIM:

Subtheme	Main Assertion(s)	Studies that Support	Exemplar Studies & Major Details

Conclusion

In this chapter, we learned about the purposes of literature reviews, as well as how to search for and analyze literature, organize the review into themes, build out levels of claims, and finally, craft a gap statement. We discussed the following key ideas.

1. ***Purposes of literature reviews*** include providing an original analysis of the existing body of research in relation to your proposed study and critically evaluating the state of the extant research on your topic or phenomenon of interest. Part of this evaluation includes interpreting the synthesis and identifying inadequacies or gaps in terms of empirical research.
2. As ***first steps,*** you will need to determine the scope of your literature review (what will be covered), its parameters (delineators or boundaries, or what will not be covered), and your keywords or search terms. You will use these to search library databases, compile articles, and refine your set of literature using your parameters.
3. ***Analysis*** begins with charting articles to extract and record relevant information. Then, you analyze the charts using processes that mirror basic qualitative analysis (coding, categorizing, and memoing) to create your main literature review themes.
4. A ***schema*** refers to the organizational structure of the literature review. To create a schema, you will use the themes and determine their relationships to create a cohesive structure that communicates a narrative.
5. To make a strong argument, you will use three different ***levels of claims***. ***Level 1 claims*** are assertions that correspond to the main themes/subthemes; ***level 2 claims*** are assertions that apply to specific subsets of studies in your review; and ***level 3 claims*** are single study claims, accompanied by detailed description, that illustrate level 2 claims.
6. The ***gap in literature*** is the concluding portion of your literature review in which you use your previously discussed analysis to point out areas where more research is needed, and state how your project will help. The gap is an important part of your rationale for your study.

Kathryn Strom

6

The Theoretical Framework

Contents

Introduction

This chapter aims to help you structure and generate text for the section of your dissertation that explains the theoretical ideas that inform your study.

Theory, at its most basic, is an explanatory mechanism to help us understand the world around us—it is a system of ideas or principles that explains how something works.

However, as a foundation of your dissertation, theory is much more than that. It influences everything! Your theory (or theories) will shape how you frame the problem and make a case for its significance, the questions you ask, and the assumptions you bring to your literature review. It will influence the your research design, from your research questions to the methodology you choose and the way you analyze your data. It will also guide your decisions on how to structure and present your findings, as well as how you discuss those findings and create recommendations from them. It may even have influenced your interest in your topic in the first place!

(As you might have picked up by now from this introduction and my examples of my own work, I am really passionate about theory!)

There are two different terms for the theoretical section of your dissertation: *theoretical framework* and *conceptual framework.* Both articulate the ideas and assumptions that inform the study, how they will be used, and why. The only real difference is that a theoretical framework is a set of ideas or concepts that come from a particular theory (or theories); and a conceptual framework is a set of interconnected concepts that usually encompass both concepts from theory and previous research (I explain this further below). Regardless of which you go with, this section typically comes in chapter two of your dissertation, directly before or after the literature review, depending on your chair's preference and your disciplinary conventions.

In the sections that follow, I will discuss the purpose and elements of theoretical frameworks and provide guided exercises to generate text for each of the major elements. Please keep in mind that there is a vast amount of variety in terms of how to create a theoretical or conceptual framework—meaning that there are many equally valid and legitimate ways to organize it. This is especially true for conceptual frameworks, which may include both theoretical concepts and topic-specific concepts that may cut across perspectives (for example, "teacher identity" or "leadership for social justice"). For that reason, I focus mainly on *theoretical frameworks* and their common elements, all of which is transferable for a conceptual framework, in this chapter. The ultimate organization, whether you choose a theoretical framework or conceptual one, will be dependent on your specific needs, but the tools in this chapter will hopefully help you make that decision.

6.1 Understanding Theoretical and Conceptual Frameworks

WARM UP

What do you already know about theory and theoretical frameworks? What would you like to know?

Purposes of Theory

There are usually multiple purposes for a theoretical framework. Theory is typically used to *describe and explain phenomena*: you are using it to understand the world around us, and why and how it works in the ways it does. To meet these purposes, your writing needs to clearly articulate what theories or perspectives you are drawing from; provide definitions and important background information; outline the specific concepts that will inform your study; and provide a rationale for why you are using this particular theory or set of concepts—what will it do for you? How will it help you achieve your study goals?

Another purpose of your theoretical framework might be to *disrupt the status quo by providing a more critical, complex, or otherwise different perspective*. In that case, in addition to the above, you will need to also provide a critique of the status quo that shows its insufficiencies, as well as explain how the theory and/or set of concepts offers a different perspective, set of tools, etc. For example, my research is typically framed by some type of complexity theory, so part of my theoretical framework describes the shortcomings of dominant thinking (i.e., rational humanism) in relation to teaching; explains complexity perspectives as an alternative; and then lays out an argument showing how such perspectives can help us better account for the realities of classroom activity to support teachers.

Another purpose of the theoretical framework is an *ethical* one. As I mentioned in the beginning of this chapter, theory is not something separate from you and your study—it co-creates it, influencing every aspect of the project, including our very thinking (Barad, 2007). Being transparent about the ideas and assumptions informing your study is one way to practice accountability as a researcher.

For instance, you might notice that in many quantitative articles, there is no explicitly stated theoretical framework. However, none of us come to our research as empty vessels—we bring ideas about the world and how we create knowledge about it. These are theories (although they may not be articulated as such). If we do not name the theories and concepts that shape our research, and define them and discuss them in detail, *they still will influence our research*. However, they will do so in ways that we may not be aware of (and likely perpetuate the Eurocentric idea that research is neutral and objective).

Let me provide a little more illustration. Critical theoretical perspectives take, as a starting point, that inequities exist in the world—and they exist not because that's just the way it is, but because they are created and maintained by dominant groups through specific sociocultural processes, including the creation of knowledge (Freire, 1970; McLaren, 2009). This foundational assumption represents a particular belief about how the world works (i.e., ontology), and that will influence the focus and goals of your study—just to begin with. If you are using this perspective, you will likely be interested in addressing unequal power relations of some kind—which will then figure into the way the study takes shape. For this reason, your theoretical framework needs to be explicit about its ontological and epistemological perspectives (i.e., what the underlying assumptions are about the world and how we come to know that world).

What Goes into a Framework?

Although you may use just one theory, it is rare to find one that covers all the necessary aspects of your study. Therefore, most studies use combinations of theories (or specific combinations of concepts from multiple theories) that work together as a frame for the study (i.e., the *framework*).

Sometimes these mashups already exist, and sometimes they have to be created to meet your specific needs. For example, critical posthumanism is a theoretical framework that combines understandings from critical theory (such as an analysis of power relations) with the ontological and epistemological shifts of posthumanism (for example, a view of the world as relational, interdependent, and always changing). Remember, though, that the theories should be able to explain the phenomena we are studying, so we need to assess them to make sure they will be sufficient. If I am conducting a study on how teachers translate their pre-professional learning into their first-year classrooms, a critical posthuman framework will help me frame and analyze the activity of the classroom in complex ways. However, it does not provide explanatory power for teacher learning and pedagogy, which is implicit in my purpose—I am looking at what teachers do with what they learned in their initial teacher preparation programs, and that learning represents a particular type of pedagogical approach. So, my theoretical framework would likely combine critical posthumanism and some kind of appropriate teaching and learning perspective.

As noted above, a conceptual framework is similar to a theoretical framework. It is a set of concepts that, together, explain a particular phenomenon (or provide guidance for understanding it). However, not all the concepts may come from a unified theory. For example, if one of my students is planning a study in which "teacher identity" is a major part, I would expect identity—in some shape or form—to be included as part of the framework. But there's not *one* theory of identity—there's many, plus a lot of empirical work that has contributed to the theorization of identity specific to teachers. So likely there would be an articulation of the student researcher's particular definition of identity (which might be from a particular perspective, or a synthesis of multiple, kind of like the qualitative research definition activity from chapter three) and a discussion of the research that informs that definition.

THEORETICAL FRAMEWORK ELEMENTS	
RATIONALE	An argument for why you are choosing this theory; how it will help you meet the goals/purpose of your study; articulation of a conceptual gap.
DEFINITION	Detailed definition of the theory, its purposes and applications; situate in a particular tradition of necessary.
BACKGROUND	Roots, key theorists and developments, overview of traditions or lines of thinking, and major critiques.
KEY CONCEPTS	Detailed discussion of the concepts or principles from the theory that you will be drawing on, with clear connections to the study.
THEORETICAL CONNECTIONS	Articulation of connections between theories if there are more than one, or for conceptual frameworks, explanation of how the concepts all fit together.

Figure 6.1: Theoretical famework elements

Sometimes—although not always—the conceptual framework is synthesized into a cohesive structure. Take, for example, Lucas and Villegas' (2011) Framework for Linguistically Responsive Teaching (LRT). The framework proposes that LRT requires both a specific set of teacher beliefs and orientations as well as a distinct set of knowledge and practices. Therefore, the framework consists of two parts—a discussion of beliefs and orientations required as conditions for linguistic responsiveness, and a set of knowledge and practices for enacting that linguistic responsiveness. In each part, the authors introduce and define specific ideas (i.e., value for linguistic diversity) providing both theoretical and empirical support for them.

Given what we've discussed so far, we can identify five different elements to meet the purposes of the theoretical framework (see Figure 6.1, above).

These include a *rationale*, which encompasses an argument explaining why this particular theory is needed for the study you are proposing, how it will help you meet your study goals, and how it will fill a conceptual gap; a detailed *definition* of the theory, including its purposes and applications; a *background* discussion, providing an overview of the roots of the theory, important theorists and developments, any divergent lines of thinking, and any important critiques; and an in-depth discussion of each *concept* or principle you will be using from that particular theory, along with connections between the concept and the study. Finally, because you will likely be using concepts from multiple theories, you will need to make explicit linkages between them; if it is a conceptual framework, you will show how the concepts are interrelated to form a coherent whole.

Two more important points: first, you need include these elements for every theory you use. Second, these elements may be organized in a different order. For example, it is common to offer a rationale in multiple places throughout the framework. Moreover, you can structure your framework in the way that makes the most sense to you: maybe you will choose to integrate the theories completely (such as in the case of DisCrit) or discuss first one, then the other. You could also discuss the relevant theories' definitions and backgrounds, and then chunk all the concepts and rationales together.

ACTIVITY 1. THEORY FREE-WRITE

What are the theories or big ideas you would like to use in your project and why?

If you are not sure about the theories, start with the major concepts involved in your study. Can you identify any major perspectives or theories they come from or connect to?

6.2 Pre-Writing Supports for Theoretical Frameworks

Before we jump into learning about and generating text for the theoretical framework, I want to suggest some supports for reading and note-taking about the theories/concepts you will be working with.

First, you need to create a way to record systematic notes, just like you did for your literature review. In a way, writing your theoretical frame is another kind of literature review, just with a focus on conceptual ideas rather than evidence from empirical studies. So, you will also need to locate appropriate literature, create spreadsheets to keep track of your theory-focused readings, and carefully annotate them. You'll be drawing on two types of texts: 1) theoretical texts that help you build understanding of the "what" of the theory/concept, and 2) empirical texts that demonstrate the "how" (that is, how that particular theory has been used or taken up by other researchers).

Reading and Notetaking: Theoretical Texts

The first thing you will want to do is determine who the foundational thinkers are for your chosen theory or concept(s). If you are not sure who they are, explore a few articles that use that theory and examine who they cite. Usually, you will be able to determine a theoretical "lineage"—for example, Lev Vygotsky is generally regarded as the originator of sociocultural theory, followed by theorists like Jerome Bruner, Mikhail Bakhtin, and Jean Lave/Etienne Wenger.

Other times, a theory may have a very long evolution, so you will have to decide where to "bound" your reading: for example, if I am using rhizomatics, I would trace it to Gilles Deleuze and Felix Guattari's 1987 book, *A Thousand Plateaus*, where they introduce it as a philosophy. However, they draw heavily on the concepts of philosophers like Spinoza and Bergson to do so. This means I would have to decide: do I need to read the original Spinoza and Bergson? Or is it enough to give them a mention, perhaps in the background section of my framework (which we talk about later)?

Still other times, you may need to locate yourself in a particular "school" or line of thinking of a theory. As mentioned previously, for example, Paulo Freire is largely credited as the "father" of critical pedagogy, but there are also arguments that critical pedagogy originated with Black thinkers like W.E.B. Du Bois. Again, you would have to do a little exploratory reading to make a decision here, likely informed by your study focus and purpose. Does your study focus on a range of oppressions, or perhaps simply disrupting the status quo through critical inquiry? Then you probably would locate yourself in the Freirean tradition. If you are focused on race and/or antiblackness and pedagogy, you might want to situate yourself in the Black educational studies tradition.

Other theories have very relevant antecedents that you may need to start with. For example, critical race theory has many offshoots, like Latcrit, Asiancrit, Discrit, Deafcrit, Tribalcrit, and so on. To understand each of these fully, however, requires a solid grounding in critical race theory. This is because each of these offshoots uses the main principles of critical race theory as its foundation, with some adjustments. For example, in Discrit, an important idea is "ability and whiteness as property," or the idea that things associated with ability and whiteness (e.g., language, ways of behaving, physical spaces) are more valued. This idea builds on the critical race theory principle of "whiteness as property," which you'd need to understand to grasp the more intersectional version.

Once you've determined where you want to bound your reading and/or locate yourself, create a spreadsheet to take detailed notes. I suggest that you set up the spreadsheet by creating columns to record information that will help you build out the major areas of your theoretical framework (that is, information that will help you draft the theory definition, background, and key concepts). By doing this, the spreadsheet will become a scaffold for writing the sections of your framework.

Below is an example of a chart for a theory I use frequently, critical posthumanism, and a text by Rosi Braidotti (2013). Although Braidotti has earlier books, I am choosing to start with this one because it is where she first outlines the critical posthuman perspective in detail. As I read, I record notes on information that will help me create the definition of the theory and its purpose; information for the background section; and definitions of important concepts or ideas. Although I've summarized the chart for the purposes of this book, the actual chart would likely be lengthier.

Citation	Definition/Purpose	Background	Key Concepts or Important Ideas
Braidotti, R. (2013). *The Post-human.* Polity Press	Critical Posthumanism disrupts rational humanist, Eurocentric ways of knowing and being, which have been used to justify colonialism/enslavement and perpetuate white supremacy. Instead, posthumanism offers a process/decentered onto-epistemology that is characterized by relationality, multiplicity, non-linearity, affirmative difference, vitalism, affect, politics, and mobility. For education, posthumanism offers a way to think differently about teaching as decentered, jointly-produced activity shaped by a multitude of factors, including history, politics, local contexts, material realities, physical spaces, dominant discourses, and so on.	Posthumanism is the meeting of two major bodies of thought: 1) anti-humanism, the resistance to the idea of human as conflated with rational white European man and his ways of knowing-being, and the expansion of the subject to one that is relational, part of multiplicities, always becoming-different, difference-affirmative; and 2) post-anthropocentrism, the resistance to human supremacy/extractive capitalism and the expansion to understanding life and agency as pertaining to collectives that include humans and nonhumans or materialities. Important thinkers include Spinoza, Deleuze & Guattari, Foucault, Haraway, Said.	1. **BECOMING:** The shift away from "to be," static reality, to a state of always changing in relation to (whatever one is in assemblage with). 2. **DIS-IDENTIFICATION:** The purposeful distancing from rational humanist ways of knowing and being. 3. **POLITICS OF LOCATION:** The idea that we speak from where we are, embodied and embedded, in particular locations that are geo-political; as an ethical imperative we have to account for how our political locations shape our knowledge/practices. 4) **RADICAL IMMANENCE:** The idea that all matter is connected and alive and self-organizing; there is nothing above or below, nothing that can be extracted, so there is no such thing as universals or transcendent knowledge free of context; everything has to be defined and understood in terms of what it is in relation with.

ACTIVITY 2. THEORY READING AND NOTE-TAKING			
Read several texts and take notes using a graphic organizer with the elements below.			
Citation	Definition/Purpose	Background	Key Concepts or Important Ideas

Reading and Notetaking: Empirical Texts

While you do not need to provide a lengthy review of studies that have drawn on the theories and/or concepts you plan to use for your study, it is important to read them for a few reasons. One, in your theoretical framework you will need to state whether you are offering a unique theoretical contribution, or if you are drawing on the work of others who have used it empirically. If it is the latter, you will need to offer a brief summary of applications (this will become part of your "definition" section, as discussed later). Second, these serve as *mentor texts* for you in terms of research application of theory. It is one thing to be able to explain a theory and its key components; it is another thing entirely to be able to *put it to work* in your project. Examining empirical articles that employ the same theoretical frame/ concepts you are considering can help provide detailed examples of the ways that you can use theory as well.

To analyze empirical studies in terms of their use of theory, focus in on specific elements and examine whether, and/or how, the ideas are shaping that element. My suggestion: after recording the study and the theory or concept, look at the front or framing sections of the article (problem statement, purpose, lit review); the research design/methods; and findings/discussion. The following chart is an example of an organizer that can help you analyze empirical works for their use of theory. In this example, I've outlined the three article sections mentioned previously. How has the author(s) put theory to work in each of these sections?

Study/ Theory	Framing	Methods	Findings and Discussion
Strom, 2015 Rhizomatics, assemblage	The problem – we need more complex ways to understand how teacher learning affects practice Assemblage informs the question- practice as negotiation between multiple factors, a joint construction The lit review structured via "systems" of teaching	Methods are post-qualitative, which is aligned with the theoretical perspective on epistemology and ontology rhizomatic mapping based on the figuration of the assemblage	Findings: focus on negotiations and influence of multiple factors on teaching- the way the learning "morphed" or adapted based on interactions Discussion: uses assemblage and its insights to draw implications (learning will morph, but it is visible; but cannot draw a straight line) and recommendations (teacher prep needs to help teachers learn to negotiate)

This chart annotates Strom (2015), an article in which I use a framework of rhizomatics. I focus on the concept of "assemblage"—a temporary grouping that has human, nonhuman, material, and discursive components—which I suggest helps conceptualize teaching in a more complex way (e.g., rather than an act done solely by the teacher *to* students, teaching is an assemblage of teacher-students-context-history that collectively produces teaching). As you can see from the chart, the rhizomatic frame and concept of assemblage profoundly influence each major section of the article.

First, the theoretical framework affects the way I frame the problem: we tend to look at the relationship between teacher learning and classroom practice as "transfer," which indicates a one-to-one correspondence; we need more complex ways to understand how teacher learning moves into practice. The theory then informs the question I ask: how does a science teacher negotiate his preservice learning with his students and context to construct practices in his first year of teaching? This contains assumptions informed by the theory that teaching is an active process (a negotiation, a construction) involving multiple actors and conditions (here, students and context).

The theory also shapes the literature review, which looks at different assemblages or systems involved in teaching: the teacher herself (her beliefs, background, preservice learning); the classroom (students, pedagogy, interactions, physical surroundings, etc.) and school (climate, leadership, colleagues, etc). In addition, the methods are informed by the theory in multiple ways: the approach is post-qualitative, meaning that the methodology is grounded in post-foundational philosophy; and the analysis method is "rhizomatic mapping," which maps out the assemblage and its connections.

The findings describe the ways that teaching was negotiated, with attention to how elements like students and context influenced those adaptations. The discussion then used the notion of assemblage to draw implications (e.g., we can expect learning to morph in relation to other elements in the teaching assemblage; we cannot draw a straight line from teacher preparation to first-year practice).

Finally, the recommendations suggest focusing on teaching as negotiation, as well as providing ongoing support, since teacher learning-practice adaptation is ongoing.

ACTIVITY 3.1. THE ROLE OF THEORY IN EMPIRICAL RESEARCH

- **Search for empirical articles on your topic that use the theory or concepts you are considering. If there are not any on your topic exactly, find a few in a related area.**
- **Use the elements below to create a graphic organizer and take notes. Then, write a reflective memo (see instructions below).**

Study/Theory	Framing	Methods	Finding & Discussion

ACTIVITY 3.2. REFLECTIVE MEMO

What are some of your takeaways from analyzing the way theory was "put to work" that can be useful for your own project? How?

6.3 The Theoretical Rationale

Back in chapter three, in our discussion of arguments, I mentioned that you would be making multiple kinds of arguments throughout your dissertation. The theoretical rationale is one of those arguments. Specifically, in the rationale, you will need to make a convincing argument that the theory/theories or concepts you are using are appropriate and necessary for the study you will be undertaking. You will do this in multiple ways, but the first is to illustrate that there is a *conceptual gap* when it comes to your topic.

The Conceptual Gap

I like to make the conceptual gap part of my introduction to the theoretical framework. I first remind the reader of the problem and topic, and then offer a brief assessment of the ways that the topic has been conceptualized in the extant literature. Next, I use that assessment to make a case for what's missing (the gap)—and how the theory/theories I am using will address that conceptual gap.

To support assessment of the ways a topic has been theorized by previous research, I created the following chart which records the study citation, the theoretical frame, and provides room for a summative memo (your free-written sensemaking that documents "a-has" and patterns across multiple articles).

Citation	Theoretical Framework/Concepts	Memo
Bianchini, J. & Cazavos, L. (2007). Learning from students, inquiry into practice, and participation in professional communities: Beginning teachers' uneven progress toward equitable science teaching. Journal of Research in Science Teaching, 44(4), 586-612.	No detailed theoretical framework, but two concepts listed with mention of social theories of learning. 1. Inquiry based teacher learning: researching one's own practice 2. Professional communities and teacher learning, with a mention of social theories of learning	

Now, how can you complete this assessment of your topic in relation to theory without having to go back and completely re-read all the articles in your literature review? Well, if you take high-quality notes in your literature review annotation charts, you shouldn't have to. You can go to those detailed charts and copy each citation along with the notes you've already taken on the connected theoretical framework or major concepts. Create a new spreadsheet, copy them over, and you have a ready-made annotated list of theoretical perspectives and major concepts from the body of literature on your topic ready for you to analyze. (See Activity 4).

To conduct your assessment, read through the charts and take notes on what you see. Ask yourself: what are the major theories and concepts that have been used to study your topic? What is still missing?

As you assess the ways theory has been used in relation to your topic, keep in mind that not all articles have conceptual/theoretical frameworks. This is particularly true for articles using quantitative methodologies. So, if many of your articles do not have frameworks, don't panic. This is an important point in and of itself to record because it likely is an indication that this area is under-theorized. You can include that as part of your conceptual gap.

ACTIVITY 4. IDENTIFYING AND ARTICULATING THE CONCEPTUAL GAP

1. **Create a new spreadsheet in Excel or Google Sheets (or your preferred program).**
2. **Copy over the citations from your literature review spreadsheet in one column.**
3. **In a second column, paste just the theoretical frame or major concepts cell for each study. If there is no theoretical frame or major concepts discussed in the study, note that by either color-coding the cell red or black.**
4. **Read through the annotations.**
5. **Write a memo, either in a third column (see below) or in a different document, that notes the patterns, the theoretical contributions of the studies, and possible gaps you see from these annotations. Use some or all of the following prompts to help guide your writing:**
6. **What theories or conceptual frameworks have other researchers used to study your topic? What have those added to our understanding? What theoretical patterns do you notice? What is lacking theoretically in relation to your topic? Given the gap(s), what theory/theories do you plan to use contribute to this body of research?**

Citation	Framework or Concepts	Memo(s)

The next step will be to formalize some conclusions and formulate your gap statements. First, craft pattern statements. For example, a literature review regarding the factors that affect first-year teachers' enactment of pedagogy might reveal these broad patterns:

- Multiple studies draw on pedagogical perspectives with critical and cultural emphases, such as critical pedagogy and culturally responsive teaching.
- Many studies also feature sociocultural theories attending to teacher learning.
- A few studies adopt more complex frameworks, like complexity theory, to examine the enactment of teacher learning.

Once you have crafted these pattern sentences, critically evaluate them in relation to your topic. What have these theories contributed to our understanding (what do they do)? What areas do they *not* address (what *don't* they do)?

Then, create a statement from this evaluation that points toward what they do not do (i.e., the gap), or maybe pointing out that they don't go far enough. Keep in mind that the purpose of formulating the conceptual gap is to *build a case* for the necessity of using the particular theory or concepts you are proposing—so you want to craft these in a way that they logically build toward the theory and concepts you will be using.

Consider the gap statements that I've added onto the example pattern sentences below. As context, I am aiming to build a case for the use of a complex theoretical framework that can better account for the multidimensional influences that "co-create" first-year teaching.

> Multiple studies draw on pedagogical perspectives with critical and cultural emphases, such as critical pedagogy and culturally responsive teaching. However, these attend to the pedagogical characteristics and an evaluation of their success in enacting those, rather than the ways they enact it and the factors that contribute to it.

In the above example, my evaluation points to the theoretical perspectives' focus (the kind of teaching methods) and how those theories are applied (an evaluation of that teaching). The last part gets to the conceptual gap: it doesn't help us study the process of enacting teaching practice and all the things that influence that enactment. This builds a case for a complexity perspective like rhizomatics that *does* allow a look at the collective process of constructing practice.

> Many studies also feature sociocultural theories, which allow the analysis of interactions between teachers and cultural-historical context. However, typically the interaction focus is not holistic, but rather focuses on one set of interactions (such as the role of teacher professional communities in enactment of practice).

Above, I offer an evaluation that concedes that this set of perspectives does look at interactions, which is essential for being able to understand how teaching is constructed. However, as I point out, the way sociocultural perspectives have been used in the body of research I analyzed has been narrow—often looking at the influence of one element on teaching, rather than understanding how a whole system co-constructs the practice. This again bolsters my argument for a complexity perspective.

A few studies adopt more complex frameworks, like complexity theory, that allow for the study of multiple interacting factors.

Finally, I acknowledge here that a handful of studies *have* taken an explicitly complex perspective. My point here is that there have not been very many—and my next step would be to transition into an argument that, to gain in-depth understanding of the relationship between teacher learning and its enactment in practice, we need more studies that attend to the collective construction of teaching practice using perspectives that can account for a whole multi-tiered system of contributing factors.

ACTIVITY 5. BUILDING OUT AND EVALUATING THE CONCEPTUAL GAP STATEMENT

Using your chart and memos from the previous activity in this section:

- **Formalize your thinking into 1-3 sentences that summarize major perspectives used in the literature on your topic; then evaluate the use of those perspectives in a way that points out what they do and what they don't do (i.e., the conceptual gap).**
- **Now, assess your writing: does this statement explicitly show the need the theory/concepts you plan to use? Write a brief explanation of how.**

Creating a Cohesive Introductory Paragraph

Now that we have identified the parts of our theoretical framework introduction, we want to pull everything together into a coherent paragraph that succinctly restates the problem, summarizes what we know about how others have conceptualized the issue, identifies a conceptual gap, and then introduces your theory/theories/concepts as a way to fill that gap.

There are many ways you could go about structuring this paragraph, but if you like a formulaic approach, I suggest something along the lines of the following:

1. Start with an introductory sentence foreshadowing the conceptual gap.
2. Summarize the ways other researchers have conceptualized this topic.
3. State the conceptual gap or lack, based on your assessment.
4. Last, provide a statement of the theory you will use and describe how it will address this gap.

It might look something like this:

> Researchers agree that [*something about your topic that can segue into the discussion of related theories*]. However, most of the research conducted on [*your topic*] has been studied from perspectives like [*theory*], [*theory*], and [*theory*]. While these studies [*positive aspect*], they do not [*conceptual gap*]. Therefore, I will use [*your theory/concepts*], which can [*how it will address the theoretical gap*].

For example:

> Teacher education researchers agree that teaching is highly complex and situated. However, the majority of studies on teachers' translation of their preservice learning into practice are conducted using lenses like culturally responsive pedagogy and sociocultural theory. While these perspectives illuminate characteristics of powerful pedagogy and situated learning, they do not account for the many human and nonhuman elements that collectively shape teaching. Only a few studies have adopted more complex frameworks, like complexity theory, that allow for the study of multiple interacting factors. Therefore, in this study I draw on rhizomatics, which offers conceptual tools to explain how human, nonhuman, material, discursive, and sociocultural-historical factors shape teaching collectively.

If the theories cannot be neatly clustered together, you will need to briefly discuss them. The example below is the same conceptual gap statement, with a theoretical perspectives discussion that has been elaborated.

> Teacher education researchers agree that teaching is highly complex and situated. However, the major frameworks used to study the ways that first year teachers translate their teaching into practice fall short in terms of their ability to help us understand this complexity. In the literature, multiple studies draw on pedagogical perspectives with critical and cultural emphases, such as critical pedagogy and culturally responsive teaching. These lenses attend to the pedagogical characteristics and an evaluation of teacher success in enacting those, rather than the ways teachers enact pedagogy and the factors that contribute to it. Many studies also feature sociocultural theories, which allow the analysis of interactions between teachers and cultural-historical context. However, typically the interaction focus is not holistic, but rather focuses on one set of interactions (such as the role of teacher professional communities in enactment of practice). Only a few studies have adopted more complex frameworks, like complexity theory, that allow for the study of multiple interacting factors. Therefore, conducting a study with a rhizomatics lens, which offers conceptual tools to explain how human, nonhuman, material, discursive, and sociocultural-historical factors shape teaching collectively, would help to understand the process of translating new teachers' learning into practice in ways that can better account for its immense complexity.

ACTIVITY 6. DRAFTING THE CONCEPTUAL GAP STATEMENT

Use the work you have completed in this section to draft a conceptual gap paragraph. Use the supports below.

Elements of the conceptual gap paragraph/introduction to the theoretical framework:

1. **Introductory sentence foreshadowing the conceptual gap**
2. **Summary of the ways other researchers have conceptualized this topic.**
3. **Statement of the conceptual gap or lack**
4. **Statement of the theory you will use and how it will address this gap and/or meet the goals of your study.**

Sample sentence stems:

Researchers agree that [something about your topic that can segue into the discussion of related theories]. However, most of the research conducted on [your topic] has been studied from perspectives like [theory], [theory], and [theory]. While these studies [positive aspect], they do not [conceptual gap]. Therefore, I will use [your theory/ concepts], which can [how it will address the theoretical gap and/or how it can meet the aims of your study].

In addition to the conceptual gap, throughout the entire theoretical framework section you will need to emphasize what this theoretical framework and its parts can do to meet the goals of your study. Each time you reinforce this message, you will build a stronger argument for why you are using the theory/concepts you have chosen. I will discuss ways that you can emphasize and reinforce your conceptual rationale in the sections below.

6.4 Theory Definition and Purpose

ACTIVITY 7. FREE-WRITE

Take one theory or major concept from your framework and free write:

- **What is your theory about?**
- **What is the purpose (what does it help us understand, or what problems does it help us address)?**

The next element of your framework will be a general theoretical overview, which includes a definition of the theory and a discussion of its purpose(s) in relation to your specific research project. Keep in mind that if your theoretical framework involves multiple theories, you will need to do this for each theory.

Theory Definition

The definition of the theory can range from a few sentences to a couple of paragraphs, depending how complex it is and whether there are multiple interpretations. The definition should answer the question, "What is [theory]?" Typically, you will offer a sentence or two of concise definition, and then add information as necessary so the reader is able to get the gist of the theory as a whole. The purpose of the definition is to provide the reader with a *macro-level* understanding, so be careful not to get lost with too many details here. In addition, you may need to foreshadow some of the key concepts, depending on how central they are to the definition of the theory—but remember that you will be discussing each of the concepts you will be drawing on in your study later in the framework. So, to avoid repetition, don't get into them here beyond a quick mention, and only if necessary.

Now that you've got the basics, let's look at an example of a definition. For context, this theoretical framework corresponds to a research project examining the ways that teachers enact culturally- and linguistically-affirmative science instruction with multilingual learners.

> Critical sociocultural theory is a way of understanding teaching and learning that combines insights from both sociocultural theory and critical perspectives on education (Vossoughi & Gutierrez, 2016).

The sentence above provides a very high-level definition of critical sociocultural theory with two components: One, it's an explanatory mechanism for teaching and learning; and two, it is actually a combination of two separate theories: sociocultural theory and critical pedagogy. However, unless the reader is very familiar with both of these perspectives—and we cannot assume they are—they will need more information to understand what critical sociocultural theory is and how it is relevant for this project.

Now, look at the additional sentence below. What information does this add, and how does it help the reader understand the theory better?

> Critical sociocultural theory is a way of understanding teaching and learning that combines insights from both sociocultural theory and critical perspectives on education (Vossoughi & Gutierrez, 2016). According to sociocultural theory, teaching and learning are social, historical, and culturally-situated acts that are mediated by language and other tools (Vygotsky, 1978). Critical perspectives view teaching as a political act that can either perpetuate social inequities or disrupt them (Freire, 1970; McLaren, 2009).

The first added sentence provides more detail about what sociocultural theory is (a perspective that sees "*teaching and learning as social, historical, and culturally-situated acts that are mediated by language and other tools*"). The second makes clear why critical pedagogy adds something important that sociocultural theory does not: it brings an explicitly political perspective on teaching and learning.

As a note, I've made explicit here how these theories are relevant to teaching and learning, generally, but I have not yet contextualized them to teaching and learning for multilingual learners in science. I will get to this in the purpose section. But first, let's pause and generate some text for your definition.

Theory Purpose

ACTIVITY 8. BUILDING OUT A THEORY DEFINITION	
Take 10 minutes and work with the free-write from Activity 7, plus notes from your theoretical annotations, to generate ideas regarding the definition.	
General Definition (1-2 Sentence Overview)	
Additional Details about the Theory	

While the definition tells us what the theory *is*, the purpose states what the theory *does*: what it helps us understand, how it helps us think differently or in more complex ways, and/or what problems it helps us address. Importantly, you will need to contextualize this purpose to your particular project—which will help you continue to build out your rationale, as mentioned in the previous section. One way to do this is to first state the general purpose, and then add a second project making it clear what this theory can do for *your* project specifically.

Read the example below. What is the general purpose, and how does that relate to the specific project at hand (investigating how teachers enact culturally and linguistically affirmative pedagogy for multilingual learners in science)?

> Critical sociocultural theory helps us to understand the process of teaching and learning, and especially the ways that cultural-historical factors, language, and power influence knowledge-construction processes (Vossoughi & Gutierrez, 2016). All three of these elements are important considerations in terms of education for multilingual

learners: these students often bring sets of cultural, linguistic, and experiential resources which differ from those valued by dominant western science, and as such, are often constructed from a deficit perspective and denied culturally- and linguistically-affirmative meaning-making opportunities (Kayumova & Strom, 2023). Critical sociocultural theory can help examine and make visible teacher moves that reinforce these inequities, or alternately, moves that disrupt them by supporting learning opportunities in science that encourage use of multilingual learners' full repertoire of meaning-making resources.

In the example passage, I first describe how critical sociocultural theory can help understand teaching and learning more generally: it facilitates the examination of how multiple dimensions (culture, history, language, power) shape and mediate these processes. Next, I make a connection to how these dimensions are important for teaching and learning *in relation to multilingual learners in science* and the inequities they tend to face (the focus of my specific study). I then offer an argument which further strengthens the rationale for using this theory, explaining what sociocultural theory can do for my specific project: it will help me "*examine and make visible teacher moves*" and how they help or hinder multilingual learners' science learning opportunities.

If you are not sure about the purpose(s) of your theory, or perhaps how to articulate it, free-writing using the general purposes of theory discussed earlier may help. Below, I've formatted them into sentence stems that you can use both to think with as you free-write, and as a writing support for building out your definition and purpose paragraph (which I discuss next).

- [Theory] explains...
- [Theory] helps us understand...
- [Theory] disrupts...
- [Theory] helps us to think differently about...
- [Theory] helps us to address [xxx issue] by...

ACTIVITY 9. THEORY PURPOSE FREE-WRITE

Jot down your thoughts on some of the purposes of your theory and how it relates to your project. Use the sentence stems above and these prompts:

- **Generally, what does the theory help us understand or do?**
- **What problems does it help us address?**

Crafting Definition and Purpose Paragraph(s)

The final step is to take the text you have generated for your definition and purpose and edit it into a cohesive paragraph or two. Keep in mind that there is more than one way to sequence the ideas in a logical way that both helps the reader get a general gist of the theory/concepts you plan to work with as well as make a clear case for why and how you will use it/them. As the writer, you have agency to organize your writing in ways that you think makes the strongest argument and presents information in the clearest way—this is part of developing your writing voice (see chapter three).

That said, there is an important caveat: Every linguistic choice you make needs to serve the purpose of the element you are working with (in this case, the definition and purpose paragraphs of your theoretical framework). You should be able to explain how every sentence in your paragraph(s) for this section does one or more of the following: 1) provides a definition; 2) unpacks the definition or provides additional important information for the reader to get the gist; 3) describes the purpose; and/or 4) contextualizes the purpose to your project so your reader understands how/why you plan to use the theory and/or concepts.

Let's take a look at the example below. For each sentence, I describe how it meets one or more of the purposes noted above.

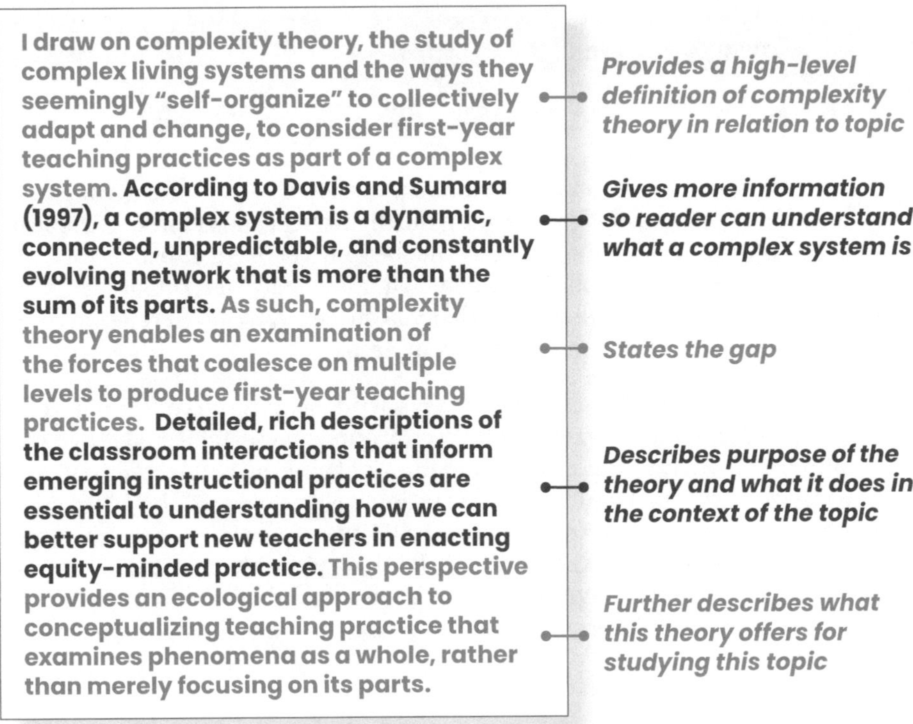

Figure 6.2: Annotated theory and purpose paragraph

ACTIVITY 10. DRAFTING THE THEORY DEFINITION AND PURPOSE PARAGRAPH(S)

Using notes from your readings and the text you have generated so far, write 1-2 paragraphs that contain:

1. **A definition of the theory (with enough details to get the gist of what it is); and...**
2. **A discussion of the purpose of the theory (what it is meant to explain, help understand, or do).**

Make sure that you use citations to show what readings are informing the definition/purpose. If you use a quote, make sure to explain what the quote means, using "in other words..." or something like that to interpret the original meaning for your reader.

6.5 The Theory Background

ACTIVITY 11. THEORY BACKGROUND FREE-WRITE

Free-write for 5 minutes on the following prompt: What do you know about your theory's background (e.g., where it comes from, important theorists, developments over time)?

One of the purposes of your dissertation is to show that you've read widely and developed in-depth knowledge regarding the theoretical and empirical literature on the topic of your dissertation. In terms of your theoretical framework, the *background of the theory* is one way that you demonstrate that you demonstrate that you have done so. It's also a way that you situate yourself in relation to the theoretical work that has been done in your area.

The components of the background may vary depending on your framework—including how long the perspective has been around, how established it is in your discipline, and whether it has diverging lines of thinking connected to it. This means that, as with much of your dissertation writing, you will have to make a decision based on your own circumstances. However, there are some common elements, which include a discussion of the theory's roots or antecedents, key theorists and their major contributions, theoretical developments over time, different traditions or interpretations, and major critiques. I discuss examples of these below.

Roots or Antecedents

Often the first information you discuss in the theoretical background section is the theory's history—where did it come from, what was the context in which it came about, and for what reason? What are its theoretical forebears?

This discussion can range from a couple of sentences to a couple of paragraphs, depending on how involved the history is and how important those roots are for developing your rationale for using the theory and the key concepts you will build out later on.

Let's zoom in on an example to demonstrate what I mean. Discussions of the history of critical race theory often begin with a nod to critical legal studies scholars, who birthed the perspective as a framework in the 1970s for understanding why the legal victories of the Civil Rights movement were not successful in permanently dismantling systemic racism. These scholars were influenced by both critical theory (which comes from a Marxist lineage and focuses on power relations) and legal realism (which held that the law could not be interpreted in an objective and neutral way—it was always influenced by a range of factors, including local contexts, social norms, and the judges' personal experiences and beliefs).

You'll have to make some decisions around how to bound this lineage discussion. If I was conducting a project with a critical race theory lens, I would decide what to include in my discussion of the background of critical race theory (and how in-depth to go with those inclusions) based on the particulars of my topic. If my project emphasized racialized power relations, for instance, I would likely nod to the legal realist scholars but spend more time discussing how the critical perspective influenced critical race theory today.

In other circumstances, you may decide where you want to start, which could be part of your positioning yourself within or in relation to the theoretical literature in your area. For instance, intersectionality is a concept that was popularized by Kimberle Crenshaw (1989), and she is commonly cited as its originator. However, the idea that the intersection of gender and race creates oppression specific to Black women was referenced by many of the Black feminists of the 1960s and 1970s, such as Angela Davis (1972) and the Combahee River Collective (1977)—and can be traced back as far as Sojourner Truth's "Ain't I a Woman?" speech. If you are using intersectionality in conjunction with critical race theory, simply citing Crenshaw is probably fine. However, if you are using intersectionality in the context of Black feminisms, it would be remiss not to start with some history on the use of the concept before its formal coining.

Let's look at two more examples.

> Complexity theory, also known as complexity thinking or complexity science, arose from a number of disciplines in the earlier part of the twentieth century. It has roots in both catastrophe and chaos theories (Mason, 2008; Alhadeff-Jones, 2008), which emphasize seemingly chaotic systems' non-linear, interconnected dynamics. These perspectives responded to the mechanistic view of Newtonian

> physics, a resistance to the notion that absolute prediction of complex phenomena was possible.

In the example above, I introduce several ideas. First, I acknowledge that complexity theory doesn't have one singular trajectory in terms of its history by referring to its multiple names and that it arose from multiple disciplines. Second, I note that its antecedents include catastrophe and chaos theories, and then offer a brief summary of the main ideas, focusing on their contributions to complexity theory. In these first two sentences, the language that I use strategically corresponds to the task: by using language like "*arose from*" and "*has roots in*," I am signaling to the reader that I am discussing theoretical origins. Finally, I offer some information about the context in which it was created—that is, in response to the inadequacy of traditional (Newtonian) perspectives and making predictions about complex systems.

Read the next example below. How do I signal my purpose to the reader? How do I organize the information to support understanding?

> New materialisms emerges from what Rosi Braidotti (2019) terms the "posthuman convergence," referring to the meeting of two trans-disciplinary perspectives. These include 1) post-anthropocentric theories from science and technology studies (SST) that desettle the notion of human supremacy (e.g., Haraway, 2004); and 2) poststructural and feminist perspectives that disrupted the Cartesian subject and its connected, binary "mind/body" and "self/other" logic (Foucault, 1976; Braidotti, 1994).

In the example above, I lean on theorist Rosi Braidotti's organizing schema of a "*convergence*" of two lines of thinking that explains how New Materialisms developed. I use "*emerges from*" to signal that I am explaining the history of the theory, and I offer a clarification to make sure that the reader knows what I mean by "*posthuman convergence*." Because it is a meeting of two perspectives, I need to discuss them at the same time. So, to make sure that the information is digestible to the reader, I offer a scaffolding phrase—"*These include*"—so the reader knows I am about to provide additional information on the two perspectives. I then provide an organizing structure, numbering the two perspectives and separating them with a semi-colon. Both supports help the reader by making the information easily distinguishable and helping them navigate the long sentence.

Major Theorists

Another component of the theoretical background includes individual or groups of scholars who are major contributors to the development of the theory. This becomes especially important when theories have different traditions or if you are using a specific interpretation. Also remember that the theorists you highlight will situate you in relation to the theory.

I'll illustrate by going back to the example of critical pedagogy's contested roots: If you focus on Paulo Freire and Henry Giroux and their contributions, this situates you in a theoretical genealogy that descends from Karl Marx and the Frankfurt School of critical theory, and as such tends to foreground social class struggle. If you focus on W.E.B. Du Bois and Carter G. Woodson, this situates you in a Black studies genealogy, focusing on schools and teaching as sites for Black resistance and liberation.

Alongside determining the "who," make sure that you clearly describe their contribution to the development of the theory—this communicates to the reader your purpose for including discussion of the specific theorists you highlight in this section. In the example below, I discuss one of the key theorists of new materialisms, Karen Barad. Notice the ways that I highlight two of her contributions to the development of this perspective: one drawn from quantum physics (the notion of entanglement) and one from feminist philosophers of science (politics of research accountability).

> New materialisms is generally credited to feminist physicist Karen Barad, who fleshed out this perspective in her 2007 book, *Meeting the Universe Halfway.* Barad situates new materialisms as emerging, in part, from principles of quantum physics. Drawing on the thinking of atomic physicist Neils Bohr, she advances the idea of entanglement: in other words, nature-culture or material-discursive aspects of life are not separate and distinct, but entangled and co-constituted (in other words, they make each other). Additionally, Barad employs the work of feminist philosophers of science to establish the situated, co-produced nature of knowledge. Building on the work of Haraway (1988) and Harding (1980) in particular, Barad argues that researchers have an ethical and political responsibility to account for how, and with what knowledges and tools, they conduct research, and the ways these shape the analysis and interpretations produced.

Developments, Traditions, and Critiques

What else might you want to add to your theoretical background? Again, this will depend on the specific theory, how established it is, and so on. Many theories that have been in use for some time will probably have changed or expanded in some way over time, so you may want to dedicate a few sentences or a paragraph to discussing that. For example:

> Over the past four decades, critical race theory has evolved from a set of ideas used mainly for legal analyses into a framework used across multiple disciplines to understand how racism works in different systems (like education). In addition, after Crenshaw (1989) introduced the concept of intersectionality, critical race theorists began to pay more explicit attention to the ways that race intersects with other oppressions.

You may also want to address important critiques or controversies regarding the theory you have chosen, or different perspectives and interpretations. For instance, new materialisms has come under fire in recent years from indigenous scholars and researchers from the Global South. To address these critiques, I might add the following to my background section:

> New materialisms has also been critiqued by indigenous and postcolonial scholars, who point out that ecological perspectives that do not separate out humans, nature, ideas, and other elements have been around for millennia (Tuck, 2009; King, 2017). As a result, some scholars have adopted the term neomaterialisms—since the perspective is not exactly new—and give nods to indigenous scholarship in their writing (Strom, Mills, & Abrams, 2021).

There may also be different traditions or interpretations of a theory. Make sure you've done enough exploration to know whether there are multiple "kinds" of theories or interpretations in your perspective. Not only should you describe these differing perspectives, but you need to situate yourself in relation to them. Do so by explicitly stating which line of thinking your framework follows and citing the appropriate researchers.

For example, if I was using a feminist framework, I would need to be clear about which type of feminism I was using. There are many traditions, and they vary widely. Liberal feminism, for example, is critiqued by many for working mainly for white women and failing to account for the intersections of gender and other oppressions like race and ethnicity. Given my social justice commitments, this kind of feminism would be problematic for me. I would be more likely to draw on intersectional and ecofeminisms, which are more relational and attuned to the complexities of multiple marginalizations. So, I would likely give a nod to the different feminist perspectives and then clearly affiliate my study with a critical tradition (and explain why) to ensure theoretical coherence.

Or, as a second example, complexity theory concepts from mathematics and science have been taken up by social science researchers and applied in somewhat different ways—so I would make sure that I note that and cite the social science school of complexity theory, to appropriately situate myself (and avoid getting criticized). I've provided an example below.

> There is not one agreed upon conception of complexity theory, but rather, more of a range or continuum that spans scientific disciplines and quantitative and qualitative research. For the purposes of this study, I adopt a notion of complexity theory used in social science research (e.g., Butz, 1997; Byrne, 1998; Clarke & Collins, 2007; Cillers, 1998; Davis & Sumara, 1997, 2006; Mason, 2008; Richardson, Cillers, & Lissack, 2001). Complexity theorists from the social sciences use constructs from complexity science as metaphors to explain human behavior in systems (Cilliers & Richardson, 2001; Davis & Sumara, 2006).

ACTIVITY 12. GENERATING IDEAS AND TEXT FOR THE THEORY BACKGROUND

Bullet out information in response to the prompts below.

1. **Theory Roots: Where does the theory come from? Does it have antecedents? Explain them.**
2. **Key Theorists: Who are the main people credited with the theory's development?**
3. **Theory Evolution: Has the theory evolved since its conception? If so, what has that evolution entailed?**
4. **Differing Viewpoints or Perspectives: Are there different traditions of the theory, or different perspectives? If so, what are they? Do you need to situate yourself in a specific one?**
5. **Critiques, Controversies, or Other Important Background Info: Are there any controversies or differences of opinion, or different traditions in this theory? Explain.**

Putting Everything Together

Finally, edit together the pieces you've generated for the background section. For each sentence, you should be able to articulate the component it addresses (history, development, traditions, etc). Make sure to use transitions and connector words to build logical flow and include appropriate citations.

The two paragraphs below put together the deconstructed pieces shared throughout this section from two theoretical background examples (one on complexity theory and one on new materialisms). As you read, see if you can identify each component of the background, as well as scaffolding strategies to support the reader (for a review, see chapter two).

Example 1: Complexity theory, also known as complexity thinking or complexity science, arose from a number of disciplines in the earlier part of the twentieth century. It has roots in both catastrophe and chaos theories (Mason, 2008; Alhadeff-Jones, 2008), which emphasize seemingly chaotic systems' non-linear, interconnected dynamics. These perspectives responded to the mechanistic view of Newtonian physics, a resistance to the notion that absolute prediction of complex phenomena was possible. There is not one agreed upon conception of complexity theory, but rather, more of a range or continuum that spans scientific disciplines and quantitative and qualitative research. For the purposes of this study, I adopt a notion of complexity theory used in social science research (e.g., Butz, 1997; Byrne, 1998; Clarke & Collins, 2007; Cillers, 1998; Davis & Sumara, 1997, 2006; Mason, 2008; Richardson, Cillers, & Lissack, 2001). Complexity theorists from the social sciences use constructs from complexity science as metaphors to explain human behavior in systems

(Cilliers & Richardson, 2001; Davis & Sumara, 2006).

Example 2: New materialisms emerges from what Rosi Braidotti (2019) terms the "posthuman convergence," referring to the meeting of two trans-disciplinary perspectives. These include 1) post-anthropocentric theories from science and technology studies (SST) that desettle the notion of human supremacy (e.g., Haraway, 2004); and 2) poststructural and feminist perspectives that disrupt the Cartesian subject and its connected, binary "mind/body" and "self/other" logic (Foucault, 1976; Braidotti, 1994). New materialisms is generally credited to feminist physicist Karen Barad, who fleshed out this perspective in her 2007 book, *Meeting the Universe Halfway*. Barad situates new materialisms as emerging, in part, from principles of quantum physics. Drawing on the thinking of atomic physicist Neils Bohr, she advances the idea of entanglement: in other words, nature-culture or material-discursive aspects of life are not separate and distinct, but entangled and co-constituted (in other words, they make each other). Additionally, Barad employs the work of feminist philosophers of science to establish the situated, co-produced nature of knowledge. Building on the work of Haraway (1988) and Harding (1980) in particular, Barad argues that researchers have an ethical and political responsibility to account for how, and with what knowledges and tools, they conduct research, and the ways these shape the analysis and interpretations produced. However, new materialisms has also been critiqued by indigenous and postcolonial scholars, who point out that ecological perspectives that do not separate out humans, nature, ideas, and other elements have been around for millennia (Tuck, 2009; King, 2017). As a result, some scholars have adopted the term neomaterialisms—since the perspective is not exactly new—and give nods to indigenous scholarship in their writing (Strom, Mills, & Abrams, 2021).

ACTIVITY 13. WRITING A DRAFT OF THE THEORY BACKGROUND

Using your notes from the graphic organizer above (Activity 12), craft a paragraph or two for your background. Make sure that you can identify the purpose of each sentence (i.e., the component of the background it addresses).

6.6 Key Theoretical Concepts

The final element in the theoretical framework is key concepts—a discussion of the big ideas or theoretical principles that you will be drawing on in your study. The purpose of this section is to narrow your theoretical focus specifically in relation to the project you are conducting. Most theories or perspectives have many ideas connected to them, and you only need to provide an in-depth discussion of those that will play an active role in your project.

For example, critical race theory is one of the most common theories students use in my doctoral program. It has at least eight connected principles: racism is culturally sanctioned and makes up the fabric of daily life in the U.S.; racism is bound up with other oppressions; racism is the foundation of capitalism; whiteness is a property that provides value to its owner; changes toward racial justice are dependent upon interest convergence with those in power; the experiential knowledges of people of color are important and valuable; and research should be carried out in pursuit of racial justice. However, most students do not actively draw on all 8 principles in their projects. Therefore, they would introduce each of them in brief form, but the key concepts section would only provide an in-depth discussion on the ones that are central to the study at hand.

Each key concept discussion should feature the following components:

- Introduction to the concept (topic sentence)
- Definition of the concept with elaboration/details as necessary to build understanding
- Examples or connections to illustrate the concept and its importance
- Connection to your topic that illustrates how the concept will be used or be useful for your study

Let's look at an example together:

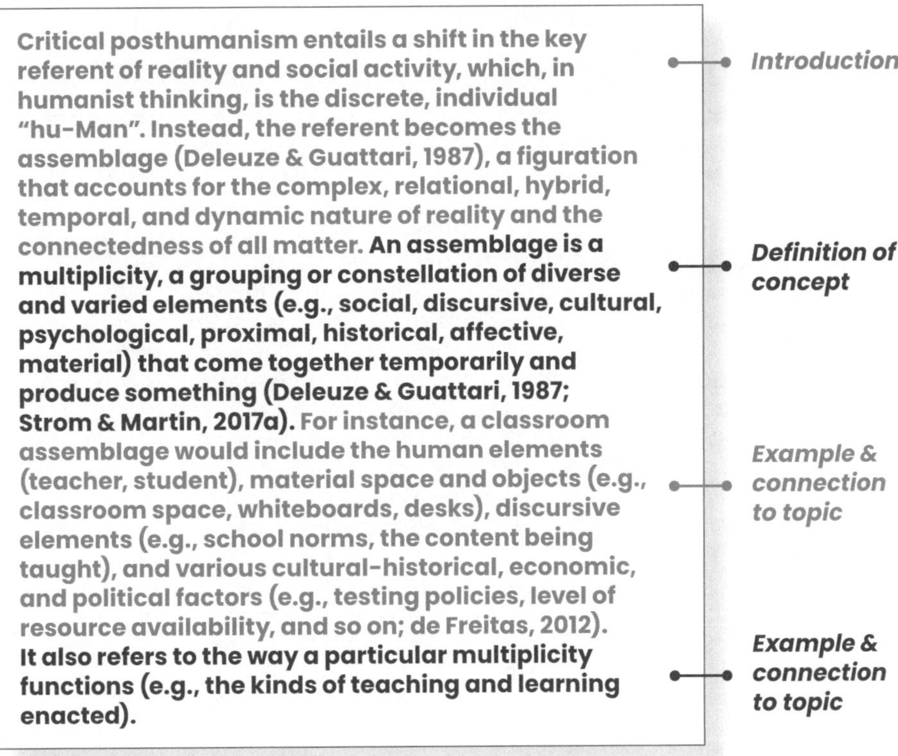

Figure 6.3: Annotated theoretical concept discussion

In this excerpt (Strom & Martin, 2022, p. 2), I offer a discussion of a key concept, *assemblage.*

The first two sentences serve as my framing for the paragraph. They introduce the idea of assemblage as well as describe a major shift that this concept entails (moving from thinking about the world as consisting of individuals, to seeing it as made up of connected systems or groupings).

Next, I provide a definition of the concept, describing an assemblage as a heterogeneous mixture that works together to produce reality. I then contextualize the idea, showing its relevance to my study by providing an example of a classroom as an assemblage. Notice that even within this example, I scaffold further by detailing some brief possibilities for each type of factor or element I introduce. This helps support the reader by translating abstract ideas, like "*discursive elements,*" into concrete, recognizable ones (like classroom routines).

I then build on the definition offered earlier, pointing out that an assemblage refers to both substance and process. I end with a parenthetical explanation that contextualizes to my topic (teaching and learning) as well as offers a brief example. Throughout, I also support my reader's understanding by using synonyms for the main concept, which provides multiple entry points for understanding: assemblage=system=multiplicity=mixture=constellation=grouping.

In this next excerpt, identify the introduction, definition, and example, as well as the explicit connection that spells out why the concept is important to the study.

> Networks of systems allow for feedback loops, an important characteristic of complex systems (Clarke & Collins, 2007). Feedback loops are cycles in which information is communicated to an actor about their actions, thereby influencing future behavior and moderating the system overall (Battram, 1998; Clarke & Collins, 2007). Negative feedback serves a regulatory function (Morrison, 2008), whereas positive feedback amplifies the actor's behavior (Johnson, 2001). In first-year teaching, for example, novices receive feedback about their teaching from multiple actors, including students, leaders, and colleagues. These messages influence the teachers' pedagogy, which then spurs more feedback from the local environment, creating feedback loops that either reinforce or regulate their pedagogy (typically the latter). As an illustration, first-year teachers who attempt to implement progressive pedagogies often receive negative messages from school administrators or colleagues, either explicitly or implicitly, about these practices, which tend to influence them to adopt traditional teaching behaviors (Newman, 2010; Saka, Southerland, & Brooks, 2009; Stanulis, Fallona, & Pearson, 2002). I argue that studying pedagogical feedback loops in classrooms and schools can offer insight into the processes by which new teachers construct their practices.

ACTIVITY 14.1 BUILDING OUT A THEORETICAL CONCEPT	
Pick one concept and generate text, using the prompts below.	
CONCEPT:	
Sentence that introduces the concept	
Definition and other important details	
Examples that contextualize the concept	
How the concept will be used in your study	

ACTIVITY 14.2. EDITING INTO COHESIVE PARAGRAPHS
Edit the notes above into 1-3 paragraphs that builds out the key concept, with appropriate references. Be sure to use transitions, signaling language, and other scaffolds to support your reader. Then, repeat this activity with each major concept you plan to use in your study.

ACTIVITY 15. PUTTING EVERYTHING TOGETHER
Use the work you completed in this chapter to draft out your theoretical framework. Remember to use scaffolding strategies to support your reader's understanding.

Conclusion

In this chapter we learned about the theoretical foundation of your dissertation, known as the theoretical framework (and sometimes the conceptual framework). Both of these articulate the ideas and assumptions that inform the study, how they will be used, and why. In relation to the theoretical framework, the following key ideas were discussed.

- The ***purpose of your theoretical framework*** is to describe and explain phenomena (the "what" of what you are studying). It can also be used to disrupt the status quo by providing a more critical, complex, or otherwise different perspective. There's also an ethical purpose: being clear about the ideas and assumptions, and how they shape our understanding, is a way to practice accountability as a researcher.
- ***Elements of theoretical frameworks*** typically include the following: a rationale for using the framework, a definition and background of theory or theories, and a discussion of the key concepts of the framework.
- The ***rationale or conceptual gap*** offers a brief assessment of the ways that the topic has been conceptualized in the extant literature. Then, use that assessment to make a case for what's missing—and how the theory/theories you are using will address that conceptual gap.
- The ***definition and purpose paragraphs*** provide a high-level summary of the theory or theories, along with what the theory is intended to do, so the reader can build a general understanding.
- The ***background of the theory*** (or theories) shows you have developed in-depth knowledge regarding the theoretical literature of your topic and situates you in relation to that work. While elements of the background vary, it is common to see description of a theory's roots, antecedents, development, major theorists, different perspectives, and critiques.
- The ***key concepts*** section provides a discussion of the specific concepts or ideas that you will be drawing on in your study. For each concept, make sure to introduce and define the concept, provide details and examples, and show how the concept is relevant in relation to your study.

7

The Methodology Chapter

Contents

Introduction

The methodology chapter of your dissertation is where you spell out how you plan to carry out your research project. This chapter will guide you to build out that explanation. As with the previous chapters, I recommend that you take your time working through the sections and exercises—it will likely be overwhelming to complete them in one or two sittings. Your patience moving through this chapter will ensure your successful completion of this critical aspect of your dissertation.

As you read, keep in mind that this chapter covers the basic elements of a **qualitative-oriented dissertation**, because that is my area of expertise. However, many of the ideas and activities you will find here are also applicable to mixed methods or quantitative projects. And, as always, make sure you check with your program director and/or dissertation chair to ensure that you are meeting your particular program's requirements in this area (since they can vary).

Finally, your methodology chapter will be written in two steps. First, you will write the methodology chapter that will be included in your dissertation proposal. At the proposal stage, the methodology chapter is an *initial research plan* that you will present to your committee. After you conduct the study, you will go back to the methodology chapter and edit it to show what you actually did, which usually entails fleshing out initial procedures, modifying anything that was adjusted during the study, and adding specifics that could not have been known in advance. As such, the major difference between the methodology of the proposal and the full dissertation is detail (and, of course, verb tense). In this chapter, I will mainly focus on writing the methodology chapter for your dissertation proposal, although I will offer some examples of both versions.

7.1 Elements and Purposes of the Methodology Chapter

WARM UP

What do you already know about the or methodology chapter? What do you need to learn more about? What questions or concerns do you have regarding this chapter?

Your methodology chapter is probably the most formulaic part of your dissertation, with many of the sections predetermined. Below, I provide an overview of the elements of the chapter (see Figure 7.1), in the order they typically appear in a dissertation.

On the left are the major sections of the paper, with a brief description on the right. I will expand on each of these elements in more depth later in the chapter.

ELEMENTS OF THE METHODOLOGY CHAPTER	
METHODOLOGY	Describes the overall research approach, including philosophical assumptions; provides a rationale for the methodology.
PARTICIPANTS & SETTING	Describes who will participate in the study; how they were chosen (sampling); describes the setting, if relevant, and any important background information.
DATA SOURCES & PROCEDURES	Provides detailed explanations of each data source, how it will be collected, and how it will answer the research questions.
ANALYSIS	Describes the procedures that will be used to organize, analyze, and interpret the data to create the findings.
TRUSTWORTHINESS	Describes 1) the measures that will be taken to ensure the study findings are credible, rigorous, and transferrable; and 2) limitations.
POSITIONALITY	Grounds the study in relation to the researchers' identities, background, and experiences and the ways these may shape the study.

Figure 7.1: Typical elements of the methodology chapter

The methodology (usually chapter three of your dissertation) is the "how" chapter of your dissertation. For your dissertation proposal, the central purpose win this chapter is to describe, in clear and detailed terms, the plan you will follow for conducting your study. Your goal in doing so is to show your committee that you have designed a feasible study (i.e., you have the access, time, and other resources to carry it out) with a design appropriate for helping you meet your study aims. Because the focus is on what you *will* do, the methodology chapter for your proposal will be written in the future tense. In your full dissertation, the chapter is edited into past tense (to reflect that the study has been carried out) and sections are fleshed out as needed to be as transparent as possible about the specific steps you actually took to complete the study.

Figure 7.2 provides a detailed list of the purposes of the methodology section, with accompanying strategies to achieve them. I briefly introduce each and then elaborate on them further in the sections that follow.

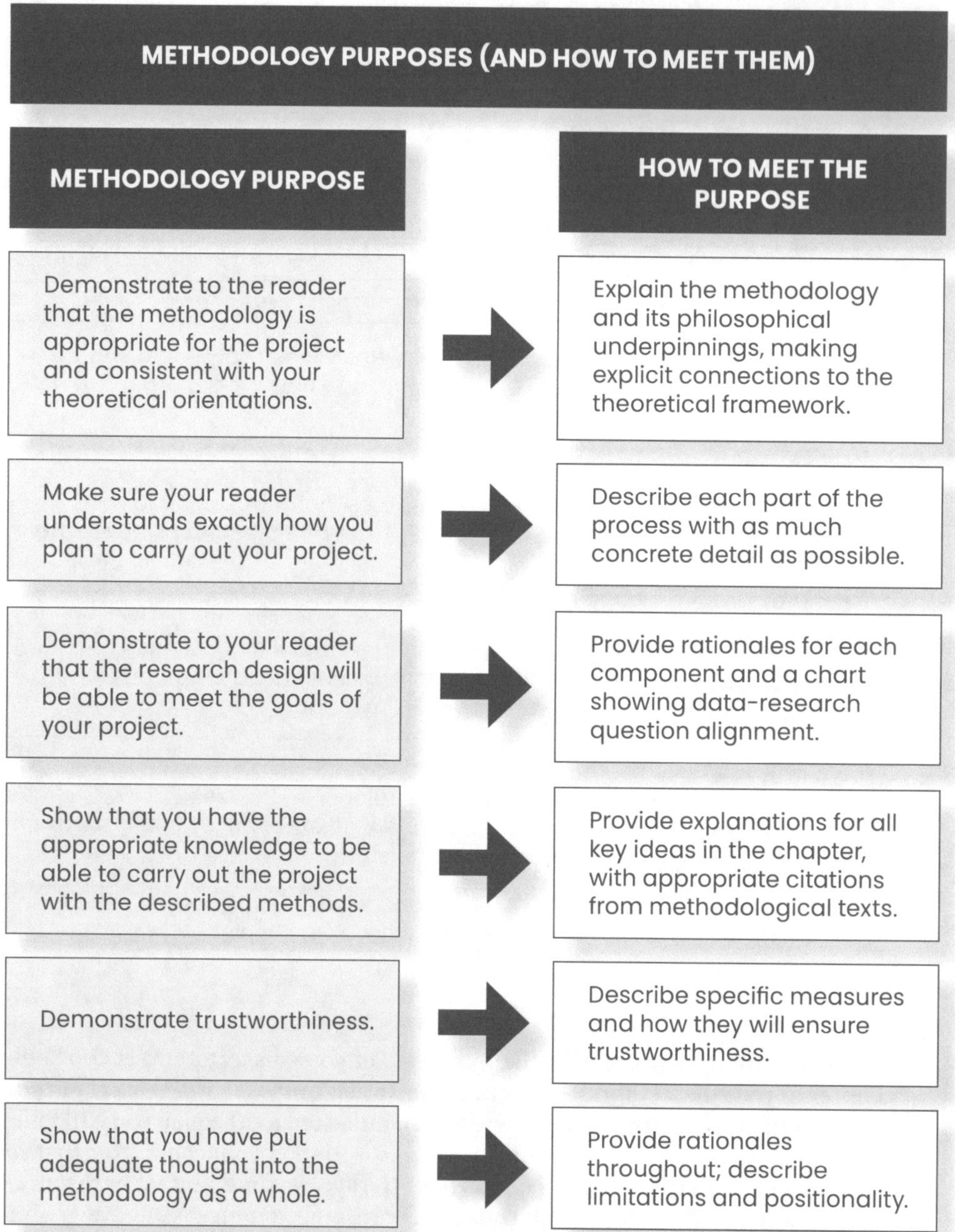

Figure 7.2: Purposes of the methodology chapter and how to meet them

First, you need to demonstrate that the proposed methodology is appropriate for your project and consistent with its framing ideas. Your overall methodology needs to help you answer the research questions that guide your study and must be aligned with its theoretical framework. In the first section (methodology description), you will need to show this by providing a substantive description of the methodology you are using, making direct connections to the theoretical framework to show coherence, and providing a rationale that shows why the overall methodology will support your project.

One of the most important aims of the methodology chapter is to ensure the reader understands how exactly you plan to carry out the research project. The key here is striving for clarity and detail as you write about each component of your study: who your participants will be, where the study will take place, background information (for example, interventions, programs, or other context necessary to understand the study design), types of data you will collect, how you will collect them, analytic procedures, and trustworthiness measures.

You also will need to show how each methodological decision made—from sampling to methods of data collection to analysis—will help you answer your research questions and meet the aims of your study. You can do this by providing clear rationales in each section that explain how your choices support the study goals and creating strategic charts that provide an "at a glance" look at the data to be collected aligns to the study questions.

Throughout the methodology chapter, you will need to demonstrate that you have an appropriate level of knowledge about the methods you are describing to successfully engage in them. This purpose can be addressed by providing clear definitions and explanations of major ideas (e.g., the type of methodology, the sampling strategy, method of data collection, and so on). These explanations should be accompanied by corresponding methodological references that align with your approach and theoretical orientation.

Another central purpose of the methodology chapter is to show your reader that you have planned a trustworthy project (that is, they can trust that you will conduct a high-quality research study). To do this, you must ensure you are practicing transparency in your writing, which can be achieved through detailed, clear explanations of each step in the process and your related decision-making. Additionally, you need to describe a specific set of measures that you will take to help you meet the trustworthiness criteria (e.g., triangulating your data across multiple sources, engaging with critical friends, sharing emerging analysis with participants for feedback, and so on).

Finally, throughout the chapter, you need to demonstrate that each decision you make and each step you propose has been carefully thought out, and that you have critically reflected on your positionality and the constraints of the project. This can be demonstrated by offering rationales that make your thinking visible; crafting a discussion of the limitations of the project; and writing a positionality statement that explores how your identity markers, background experiences, professional positioning, and research agenda may shape your research design, analysis, and interpretation.

ACTIVITY 1. ANATOMY OF A METHODOLOGY CHAPTER

For this activity, find a dissertation in your area with a methodological approach similar to the one you are thinking about taking (e.g., qualitative case study, ethnography, arts-based, mixed methods, etc). Locate the methodology chapter (typically chapter 3). Using the chart below, identify the major sections of the chapter (as denoted by headings) and record them in the left-hand column. In the righthand column, describe what methodology elements you find in that section (e.g., description of research setting) and their content (e.g., student demographics and an overview of programs).

When you have finished, reflect:

- How do the major elements included in the chapter you read compare to those laid out in Figure 7.1?
- What differences or additions did you notice?
- If different/additional sections or elements exist, do you think they are relevant for your project? Why or why not?
- What are your overall takeaways from this activity regarding what types of information to include in a methods section (or anything else)?

Major Heading	Description of Section Purpose/Content

7.2 Methodology Description

ACTIVITY 2. METHODOLOGY FREE-WRITE

What is your current thinking in terms of your overall research approach (quantitative, qualitative, mixed methods, arts-based, etc.)?

After the introduction to your methodology chapter (which I will discuss at the end of this book chapter), the first major element is the methodology description. Typically, this section will consist of two parts: 1) a discussion of the general research approach (i.e., quantitative, qualitative, mixed methods) and its theoretical underpinnings; and 2) the specific methodological approach (i.e., case study, action research, autoethnography, etc.). For each part, you will need to define and discuss the approach and provide a rationale to explain your decision in relation to the study goals and/or theoretical perspectives.

General Methodological Approach

Begin by locating your overall approach in one of the major research traditions—such as quantitative, qualitative, mixed methods, action research, or arts-based research (note that there may be substantive overlaps between qualitative, action research, and arts-based research). Then, bridge into a definition of your methodology, with attention to details that show why you chose this specific approach. Keep in mind the difference between *methodology* and *method.* Methodology is macro-level: it is a description of the overall approach, including its underlying philosophical orientations (i.e., ontology and epistemology). The purpose of the methodology is to explain the reasoning and theoretical underpinnings of the research design. *Method* is micro-level—its purpose is to provide a detailed plan of the actual data collection strategies you plan to use (e.g., interviews, surveys, observations, etc).

Take a look at the example below, which describes the overall research approach for a project investigating classroom instruction. How is qualitative methodology defined? How are the parts of this definition structured to show relevance for investigating pedagogy?

> In this study, I employ a qualitative methodology, which supports the investigation of lived phenomena in natural settings (such as classroom teaching) (Denzin & Lincoln, 1995). This approach is well suited for exploring "why," "how" and "what" questions that seek to understand and explain, rather than to measure (Merriam, 2009). In this type of research, the focus of the inquiry is teasing out meaning, rather than emphasizing control and prediction (Lather, 1992). Qualitative methods lend themselves well to the study of complex, non-linear, contextually situated phenomena such as teaching.

In the example above, I begin with signaling language that communicates to the reader exactly what the methodology is: "*In this study, I employ a qualitative methodology.*" I then offer a general definition of qualitative research—the study of real-life happenings—and provide an example in parentheses that supports its use for my study. I then describe the type of questions and inquiry focus it supports (which shows alignment to my questions and focus). Finally, I make an explicit connection to both my theoretical framework (complex, non-linear perspectives) and the central focus of my study (teaching).

Beyond defining the overall approach, you also need to situate yourself within a particular onto-epistemological stance (that is, perspectives on knowledge and existence). Quantitative approaches are typically positivist or post-positivist (e.g., generally believing in objectivity, universalism, neutrality, reduction), although a critical quantitative movement (QuantCrit) is growing. Qualitative research spans a range of onto-epistemological orientations, including post-positivist (see above), critical (foregrounding critique of systems and structures to combat unequal power relations), and post-foundational (emphasizing relationality, multiplicity, politics, constant change, and heterogeneity). Situating yourself in this way also provides another opportunity to explain how the onto-epistemological orientation you are describing aligns with your theoretical frame and/or your study as a whole.

In the example below (adapted from Strom, 2014, pp. 71-72), I get more specific about the onto-epistemological stance of my methodology. I also make explicit connections to my theoretical framework (rhizomatics) and study focus (how teachers translate their preservice learning into practice). As you read, jot down thoughts that come to you or think about these questions: How do I situate myself in a more specific onto-epistemological orientation regarding knowledge and existence/reality? What characteristics do I highlight about this stance? In what ways do I describe the alignment between this methodological approach, my theoretical framework, and my study focus?

> Specifically, I position my study in a post-foundational orientation, what St. Pierre (2011) refers to as "post-qualitative research." This perspective insists that all knowing is partial (Ellsworth, 1989; Richardson, 1994; St. Pierre, 2000) and research is inherently value-and perspective-based (Altheide & Johnson, 2011). Because post-qualitative orientations disrupt traditional research methods, which are based on the arborescent, tree-type thinking and the knowing subject that Deleuze and Guattari critique (St. Pierre, 2004/2011), this methodology is consistent with the rhizomatic frame that undergirds this study... Questions supported by a post-qualitative frame take up a performative, process-oriented approach—that is, they focus on "practices...as well as the productive effects of those practices and the conditions for their efficacy" (Barad, 2007, p. 49). Because of this processual orientation, a post-qualitative approach is also well-suited for exploring questions regarding the processes of teacher learning and its translation into practice.

In the excerpt above, I use signaling language to let the reader know that I'm further locating myself in terms of the methodological approach *("Specifically, I position my study in..."*). I then go on to describe post-qualitative research and some of its major characteristics before pivoting to offering rationales in relation to my theoretical frame. More specifically, I describe two areas of alignment. First, post-methodological approaches seek the same disruptions to Eurocentric onto-epistemology—in other words, this methodology and my theoretical framework both aim to disrupt dominant ways that we come to know (i.e., through arborescent thinking) and think of our existence (i.e., as knowing subjects). Second, they both focus on materially-embedded processes, not static or stable subjects or objects (an ontological characteristic). Finally, in the last sentence, I make a connection to show that post-qualitative methodology's process ontology can support my research focus, which is process-oriented in nature.

ACTIVITY 3.1. GENERAL METHODOLOGICAL APPROACH PRE-WRITE

Bullet out your thoughts for each element. First, think through the general approach and its major characteristics, as well as how it aligns with and supports your theoretical frame and study goals. Then, do the same with the specific onto-epistemological stance you will take.

	Definition & Details	Theoretical Alignment	Support for Study Goals
General Approach (Qualitatitive/ quantitative, mixed methods, action research, arts-based)			
Situation in Particular Onto-epistemological Stance (Positivist, post-positivist, critical, post-foundational)			

ACTIVITY 3.2. GENERAL METHODOLOGICAL APPROACH PRE-WRITE

Use the notes you generated above to draft one or two paragraphs that describe your general methodological approach and situate your study in a specific onto-epistemological stance. Remember to use topic sentences, signaling language, transitions, and other scaffolds for coherence and to support the reader's understanding.

Specific Methodological Approach

The second part of your methodology description narrows down to a more specific approach that corresponds to your study goals. While a description of all the specific methodological approaches is beyond the scope of this book, whatever you choose should ultimately allow you to "answer" your research question(s) as well as align with your theoretical framework and your previously stated onto-epistemological stance.

In this subsection, start by naming and defining the approach and its characteristics. Then discuss the methodology in relation to your study in particular, making make sure to justify your choice in that discussion. These elements correspond to three purposes we discussed earlier in the chapter: striving for clarity in terms of what approach you will be using, demonstrating that you have knowledge about the approach, and convincing your reader that the approach will meet the goals of your study.

First, let's talk about citations, which are an important part of showing that you have the appropriate methodological knowledge. Make sure that you know who the foundational methodologists are for the approach you have chosen—that is, those scholars who have contributed to the development and/or evolution of the methodology you are discussing. Additionally, be aware of how the methodologists you cite align with your theoretical framework and onto-epistemological orientations. Ensure they are coherent with your positions (or acknowledge the tension and provide a convincing justification explaining why you have chosen to use it regardless).

As an illustration, when I discuss grounded theory, I begin with a nod to the folks credited with its initial development, Glaser and Strauss (1967). Then, as I move into a more substantive discussion of the methodology, I intentionally draw on Kathy Charmaz's (2006) more recent interpretation of the approach, because her work is more closely aligned with a post-qualitative, rhizomatic stance.

Let's look at an example together using a case study approach. Due to space limitations in this book, I present a condensed version of this description, so keep in mind that your own discussion needs to be longer than a paragraph. As you read, identify how I:

- Signal to the reader about the specific methodology I will be using.
- Define case study and describe its central characteristics.
- Contextualize to my own topic/study.
- Justify why I have chosen this approach for my study.

With a grounding in the philosophical tenets of post-qualitative methodology, I turn to case study to begin structuring the actual design of the research study itself. Case study refers to "an in-depth description and analysis of a bounded system" (Merriam, 2009, p. 40). This approach allows researchers to gain deeper and more holistic understanding of complex phenomena, like teaching, that involve multiple interacting factors (Merriam, 1998)—such as the interrelated set of institutional, political, developmental, and personal factors that shape teaching (Stake, 1995). Designing a case study requires the identification of a phenomenon to be studied within the case and determination of a case boundary. Miles and Huberman (1994) visualize these two features as a heart inside a circle: the heart represents the phenomenon under investigation, and the circle bounds the area of study. Accordingly, for each case study, the unit of analysis will be the interactions that occur between the teachers and the various elements that shape their teaching practices. The classroom will serve as the boundary of each case.

In the example above, after transitioning from the previous section, I signal to the reader what my specific methodology will be ("*I turn to case study...*"). I then provide a definition of case study. Here, I deliberately quote Merriam (2009), a qualitative case study methodologist with an interpretivist perspective who is the closest theoretical match for my study. I then provide a justification for choosing this methodology, using a signaling phrase: "*This approach allows...*" My justification hits both a theoretical note (i.e., with a reference to complexity) as well as supports the focus of my study (the complex phenomenon of teaching) by being able to account for multiple, simultaneously interacting variables. Following this rationale, I provide more information about the characteristics of case study—the necessity of determining the phenomenon/unit of analysis and the boundary of the case. I then describe these two elements in relation to my own study, which helps the reader begin to see concretely how I plan to apply this approach.

ACTIVITY 4.1. SPECIFIC METHODOLOGY PRE-WRITE

Bullet out your thoughts for each element. Include references if you can.

	Specific Approach (e.g., case study, ethnography, narrative)
Definition	
Important characteristics	
Methodologists who contributed to its development	
Contextualization to your own study	
Rationale: how it aligns and supports study goals	

ACTIVITY 4.2. SPECIFIC METHODOLOGICAL APPROACH DRAFT

Use the notes you generated above to draft two to three paragraphs that describe your specific methodological approach. Use appropriate references, contextualize the approach to your own study, and provide a rationale showing how this approach matches up with your theoretical framework and supports achieving your study goals. Remember to use topic sentences, signaling language, transitions, and other scaffolds for coherence and support.

7.3 Participants and Context

The next section is a description of your participants and context. In this part, you will first describe who exactly will take part in your study and how you selected them. That should be followed by a discussion of any necessary context, which may include the setting of a study and important background information, such as descriptions of interventions or programs connected to the research project.

Participants

In the participant section, you discuss your sampling strategy (the way you will choose your participants) and offer details about who will be taking part in your study.

In terms of writing about your sampling, there are three main linguistic moves involved: 1) name and define the sampling strategy, 2) explain your reasoning for using it, and 3) describe the actual process (including any specific inclusion and exclusion criteria). Below, I have provided an excerpt from a previous student's dissertation (this comes from his completed methodology chapter, as the past tense indicates). Can you identify the three linguistic moves in this paragraph?

> Purposeful sampling, a strategy used by researchers to seek out specific participants or cases, is used often in PAR [participatory action research] to collect optimal data (Leavy, 2017, p. 235). As such, I sent an email with a call to collaborate to secondary English Language Arts teachers in Cutting Edge School District (district and school names are pseudonyms) to ensure that this study was situated within a literacy classroom. *(Dolid, 2021, p. 53)*

The first sentence names and defines *purposeful sampling*, or intentionally selecting participants who meet certain criteria important to the focus of the study. He explains that this method is often used in participatory action research (PAR) to collect "*optimal data*." In this case, he was specifically looking for a collaborator who taught in a secondary literacy classroom (his inclusion criterion), as his project sought to examine culturally sustaining digital literacy practices. He then describes his process, which involved sending an email to all the teachers in his school district who fit that description.

Next, offer details about your proposed participants. The level of detail and depth of that description may vary based on your approach and the number of participants. Generally, however, you want to give the reader a sense of the demographics and backgrounds of your participants, as well as any important information about them which is relevant for your study.

Below is an excerpt from another former student providing an example of a participant description (again, this comes from her full dissertation, which is why it is written in past tense). Her study examined how elementary teachers who had participated in science professional development enacted the practices they learned, especially with multilingual learner students. As you read the paragraph below, notice what kind of information is provided beyond demographics. Why might the researcher have included these details?

> The first focal teacher in this study, Heidi, was a white, monolingual veteran teacher with 22 years of classroom teaching experience, 21 of which had been at her current site, Buena Vista Elementary School. Heidi taught fifth grade during her participation in the study, though she had also taught fourth and sixth grades during her career. She commuted nearly an hour to work each day and greatly valued the relationships she had with her colleagues. She felt largely unsupported by the school district and found support in aligning herself with teacher-leaders at her site. Heidi's pedagogical approach was grounded in direct instruction, consistent over many years of teaching. *(Ansari, 2021, p. 52)*

In the paragraph above, Ansari (2021) first uses signaling language to let her reader know her purpose: *"The first focal teacher in this study..."* She then adds relevant demographic information regarding race and language. Note here that Ansari included a descriptor of Heidi as monolingual because it was relevant due to the study's language-learning elements.

She then moves on to the teacher's background, sharing that, of the participant's 22 years of teaching experience, 21 had been spent at the same school. Ansari's method, case study, integrates context into the analysis, so the fact that Heidi had taught at her current school site for over two decades was important to know (and later, the researcher theorized that this continuity of experience was an enabling factor for Heidi being willing to take risks with new teaching moves).

Ansari provides further contextual information about Heidi's teaching experience, pointing out Heidi's commitment to her school site and colleagues: *"She commuted nearly an hour to work each day and greatly valued the relationships she had with her colleagues."* However, Ansari goes on to explain that while Heidi felt supported by her local leaders, her participant did not think those at the district level were supportive (another factor that would later become relevant in Ansari's contextual analysis). Finally, the researcher offers a brief characterization of Heidi's pedagogy—*"grounded in direct instruction, consistent over many years of teaching."* Again, this is contextual information that is relevant in relation to focus of the study (how Heidi integrated the new teaching practices from the PD into her classroom instruction). Later, in her discussion of findings, Ansari referred back to this background information to emphasize just how far Heidi came in her pedagogical journey.

ACTIVITY 5. PARTICIPANT INFORMATION PRE-WRITE		
Bullet out information to include in your participant section in terms of demographics, background, and any other information relevant for your study.		
Participant	**Demographics**	
	Background	
	Other Relevant Information	

Setting

The setting refers to the context in which you are conducting your research, which is particularly salient for qualitative approaches.

Because a fundamental assumption of qualitative research is that research is situated and shaped by context, readers need to understand the specific context in which the study takes place to 1) grasp how the findings correspond to that context, and 2) to decide whether, given the context, the findings may be transferrable to their own setting.

Like many other sections of the methodology chapter, what you include in the setting may vary based on the methodological approach and the specific focus of your study. It could include descriptions of a city or area of town, a demographic description of the general population (beyond your participants) living in the geographic area where the study was conducted, political or historic patterns that shape(d) the setting and/or its population, and anything else that is important for the reader to know. For instance, in my dissertation study, I even described the physical layout of the school buildings to give the reader a more vivid sense of where my research took place.

Let's look at an example of a paragraph from the setting description of one of my former students (Bravewomon, 2018), drawn from her full dissertation (as indicated by the past tense). As you read, identify the different elements the author describes to help the reader understand where her study took place and other important information about the setting.

> The study took place at Cherryland Elementary School, which is located in a densely populated, unincorporated area of Alameda County in the Hayward Unified School District (HUSD). Although designed to serve 500 students, today the school serves approximately 750-800 students per year. In the 2016-2017 school year the school served 775 students. Approximately 650 students are Latino/x. The school offers a Bilingual Alternative program for students in Transitional Kindergarten and two academic programs in grades Kindergarten to Sixth: Structured English Immersion (SEI) and Bilingual Alternative (BA).
> *(Bravewomon, 2018, p. 60)*

The setting paragraph above offers an overview of Cherryland Elementary School, the setting of Bravewomon's (2018) participatory action research (PAR) study. To communicate the context of the school, she describes its *geographic location* and offers a couple of details about the area—"*a densely populated, unincorporated area*." Bravewomon goes on to describe the size of the school in terms of the total students served, while also showing that the density of the student population mirrors its geographic location. Bravewomon adds demographic detail regarding the students which shows that the vast majority of the students are Latinx, followed by a description of its academic programs, which are tailored to meet the needs of its population.

ACTIVITY 6. SETTING INFORMATION PRE-WRITE		
Jot down information to include in your setting (if appropriate). Consider: what would your reader need to know about where the study took place (will take place if the reader is in the proposal writing phase) to make sense of the findings?		
Setting	**Relevant Demographics and Other Descriptions**	

Additional Contextual Information

Beyond the setting and participants, readers may need other background information to understand your study's findings. For example, if your study involves an intervention, initiative, or program of some kind, that will likely need to be described in this section.

As an illustration, let's return to Ansari's (2021) study. The researcher examined how teachers who took part in a multi-year science professional development initiative enacted their learning with multilingual students; she did not investigate the PD itself, but rather, its impact. However, without a description of the PD initiative and its main ideas/practices, readers would probably find it difficult to understand the researchers' descriptions of the ways teachers took up those ideas in their classrooms. Below is one paragraph from Ansari's description of the initiative. As you read, see if you can identify the kinds of information she highlights from the professional development.

> The focus of The Science Project was to provide three-dimensional, inquiry-based science professional learning to 3rd through 5th-grade teachers, and to support administrators in facilitating the enactment of standards-aligned science instruction. The overarching goal was to provide more high-quality science education to historically underserved student populations. Student discourse and science and engineering practices—particularly scientific modeling—were key components of the pedagogy and content PD sessions. University science faculty, county office of education staff, and elementary science specialist teachers from local school districts partnered in this multi-year project to provide a variety of professional learning opportunities for practitioners, ranging from classroom teachers to district administrators, involved in different capacities. During each year of the multi-year project, two weeks of summer PD and three Saturday workshops during the school year were provided to all participating educators. Additionally, Lesson Study was offered yearly to select districts in the full-treatment group. Teachers participated in Lesson Study in grade-alike groups, led by county office staff to collaboratively create lessons, observe each other teaching the lessons, analyze and discuss student learning based upon artifacts created by students during the lesson, and plan for next steps. Full-treatment teachers also had the opportunity to participate in a book club, afternoon [technology] sessions offered monthly, and interactive technology platforms to share ideas.
> *(Ansari, 2021, p. 46)*

In the example above, Ansari includes a concise description of several elements of the professional development (PD) initiative: its focus, its goals, its participants, its key ideas/practices, its partners/facilitators, its format, and its activities. In the first sentence, Ansari introduces the initiative and its two aims: to provide "*three-dimensional, inquiry-based*" science professional development to elementary teachers; and second, to help administrators support teachers' enactment of these practices. She also integrates information about the PD participants into this first sentence (elementary teachers in 3-5th grade and their administrators). Next, she references the ultimate goal of the PD: to increase the quality of science instruction for minoritized students.

Following this, she moves into a brief description of the pedagogical and content foci of the PD—student discourse and science/engineering practices with an emphasis on modeling. Ansari then describes the collaborative nature of the Science Project's leadership and facilitation team, along with a description of the team's composition (university faculty, local county office of education staff, and elementary science specialist teachers). In the same sentence, the researcher explains that these groups partnered "*to provide a variety of professional learning opportunities.*" This phrase serves as a scaffold, signaling to the reader that she is going to describe these opportunities in the next sentence(s). She goes on to do so, explaining that the activities encompassed two weeks of summer PD, followed by three Saturday workshops during the school year, and yearly lesson study cycles (i.e., collaborative, in-depth investigations of teaching). She concludes with a description of resources "*full treatment*" teachers also had access to—a book club, technology-focused training sessions, and opportunities to discuss with other teachers via an online platform.

This paragraph also provides an example of writing with precision and specificity, which, as I discussed earlier, is essential to meet the purposes of the methodology chapter of your dissertation. Notice, for instance, that she does not just refer to participants as elementary teachers; she specifies that they were 3rd- through 5th-grade teachers. She is also careful to provide details regarding timing and breadth of the professional development, which the reader needs to get a sense of how the PD initiative operated. The researcher notes that the PD was a *multi-year* initiative with a structure that encompassed a *two-week* summer intensive with *three* follow-up sessions during the year which were held on *Saturdays*. With the phrase "during each year ..." she also ensures that the reader knows that this institute and follow-up workshops were held every year, for all three years of the project.

ACTIVITY 7. ADDITIONAL CONTEXT	
Add any additional contextual information below. Do you need to add information regarding interventions, programs, or descriptions of other elements important to the study? Bullet out this additional context (if appropriate).	
Contextual Information:	

ACTIVITY 8. 1. ROUGH DRAFT OF PARTICIPANTS/CONTEXT SECTION

Draft out your participants and context subsection. Use the text you generated in the previous pre-writing exercises to develop paragraphs.

ACTIVITY 8. 2. QUALITY WRITING ASSESSMENT

Use the following criteria to assess the above paragraphs:

- Does the first sentence of each paragraph use signaling language to gesture to its purpose?
- Does your participant description clearly describe demographics, background, and other relevant contextual information for your participants (or as much as you know at this point, if you are at the proposal stage)?
- Does your setting provide enough information for the reader to get a sense of the context in which the study will take place?
- Is there an intervention, program, etc. connected to the study's focus? Have you provided adequate description of that contextual element?

7.4 Data Sources and Collection Procedures

ACTIVITY 9. DATA COLLECTION FREE-WRITE

What kinds of data are you going to collect to answer your research question(s)? Why?

Now that you have drafted out your participants, setting, and any other necessary background, it is time to delve into the nitty-gritty details regarding *the methods.* This section describes, with as much specificity as possible, how you plan to actually carry out the methodological approach described at the beginning of the methodology chapter. The elements of this section typically include *data sources* (sometimes called *instruments*), and *data collection procedures.*

Alongside these components, you will also need to show how those data sources will help you answer your research question(s). For each type of data you plan to collect, you will need to explain how those data will support "answering" your research question(s)—which I refer to as "data source alignment." In fact, I like to start with this activity as a way to generate text to use as I write this section.

Data source alignment means thinking through exactly how your data sources will enable you to answer your question(s). I've created a graphic organizer to help you do this, but first, let's examine an example data alignment exercise (see Figure 7.3).

Figure 7.3 articulates the connections between three data sources—teaching observations, debriefs of those observations, and semi-structured interviews—and one research question. (Keep in mind that if you have more than one research question, this exercise needs to be done for each of them.)

For the first data source, I explain that directly observing my participants in their classrooms teaching over several months will allow me to see, first-hand, their practices and document them. Once I have data documenting what they do pedagogically across multiple lessons, I can analyze that observation data to tease out the ways major ideas from their pre-professional preparation may be showing up in their daily practices.

However, the observations by themselves won't provide a complete picture—my observations are limited by my own perspectives, *and* I need access to teachers' thinking about their lessons. As such, the second data source—20-minute debriefs with the teacher after each observation—will enable me to talk to the teachers about what I saw, to hear their reasoning and reflections, and to generate a more holistic understanding of the observation and how it might be informed by their preservice learning and other factors. In other words, this data can help confirm, problematize, or expand on my emerging observation analysis, and serve as a method of triangulation (which I discuss further in the trustworthiness section).

Data Source	How it will answer the research question: *"How do 3 high school science teachers enact their pre-service learning in their first year of teaching?"*
Observations of Teaching Practice	Observing multiple lessons over five months will help me document the enacted instructional patterns of the teachers and analyze them for the ways the key ideas and practices from their preservice learning materialize.
Observation Debriefings	By being able to talk to the teacher about each lesson, I will be able to clarify any questions I might have about practices I viewed during the lesson. I can probe the teachers' thinking about planning the lesson, carrying it out, and any modifications that may have occurred during the lesson. This will triangulate my own observations and flesh out my understandings of the ways the teacher is translating her preservice learning into practice, challenges she is facing doing so, and so on.
Semi-Structured Interviews	I can use these interviews to ask teachers to reflect on the ways that their practices have evolved (or not) over their first semesters in the classroom, the successes and challenges of enacting their preservice learning, and their perceptions of the mediating factors in enacting that learning. I can also use this time to "member check" my emerging analysis and triangulate data.

Figure 7.3: Data source and research question alignment

Finally, the semi-structured interviews are a more focused approach to surfacing teachers' thoughts on their practices, and how their preservice learning and other factors have played into them, over a longer length of time. In this study, semi-structured interview data serves as another way to triangulate findings. It also gives me an opportunity to have "member checks" with my participants (i.e., to share emerging analysis with participants and get their feedback).

In addition to helping generate text to strengthen your data sources and procedures section, this exercise provides the opportunity for you to assess whether the data sources are appropriate for your study and related questions. However, keep in mind that many students have difficulty completing this exercise in isolation. If you find that you are struggling to articulate how the data source will help you meet the goals of your study, don't panic. Work with a partner to talk through your reasoning for choosing the data sources. If you are still stuck, ask for a check-in with your advisor. They can help you determine whether the data source in question is a good fit for your study, or just needs to be adjusted to meet your needs (and provide subsequent guidance on how to do so).

ACTIVITY 10. DATA SOURCE ALIGNMENT

Use the graphic organizer below to explore the alignment between your planned data sources and your research question(s). In the lefthand column, add your data sources; in the middle and righthand columns, add your research questions at the top. Then, in the rows underneath, articulate how each data source will help you "answer" that question. (If you have multiple research questions, you may have data that corresponds to specific questions, so don't worry if you have some blank spaces.)

DATA SOURCE	Research Question 1:	Research Question 2:

Now that you've done some thinking around your data sources and decided which to use, it's time to begin sketching out the data source descriptions.

Before getting started with this task, a quick note on language. Sometimes the term "data sources" are identified as "instruments"—a term that typically refers to specific tools of data collection (e.g., surveys or observation protocols). I deliberately use "data source" because, in my experience, "instrument" tends to have a positivist connotation. In other words, I am purposefully making a linguistic choice based on my own research orientations. However, it is best to check with your advisor before deciding for your own writing since some doctoral programs or individual dissertation chairs may require "instruments" as a specific section.

Going back to data source descriptions: for each type of data you plan to collect, you will need to 1) provide a detailed definition and discussion of the data source; 2) describe exactly what participants will do; and 3) describe how the data will be shaped into an analyzable format, if appropriate.

To generate these descriptions, first outline all the needed information. In terms of the *data source definition and description,* bullet out what you know about the data source—what is it? Is there a "textbook" definition? How does that definition match up with what you plan to do? What methodological tradition or approach is this data source affiliated with? Are there any connected concepts that need to be defined/discussed? Are there different views or kinds of this type of data source, and if so, which might you be using? Which methodologists should you cite? Are there accompanying materials or tools you need to describe? What are some concrete examples you can give the reader to enable them to visualize the data source?

For example, in studies investigating teaching practice, researchers often use *observations.* If I was using this data source, I would need to define what I mean by "observation" to show that I have read some of the important methodologists in this area and understand what an observation is—it is a data collection method often used in ethnographic studies in which a researcher directly views a phenomenon in its naturally-occurring setting, records it, and interprets it (Merriam, 2009).

I'll also need to contextualize the data source to my study (i.e., describe how and why this method will work for me and my goals). If my aim is to investigate the ways that teachers translate their preservice learning into practice, logically, at least part of my data should be able to show how they do that. Observations, a common tool for studying pedagogy, will allow me to go into my participants' classrooms and document their practice as well as identify factors that might be influencing its construction (like interactions between teachers and students). If I conduct these observations over time and systematically record what I see, then I can analyze this data set and construct an argument regarding how the teacher is co-constructing pedagogical practice with students as well as the contextual elements of the setting. I also might mention that observations are important because they enable me to triangulate (that is, to confirm or disconfirm) analysis from teacher interviews, which are second-hand accounts of practice.

However, I'm not done yet. If I am using an established method of data collection, there are probably different *kinds* of that data source, which in turn may entail different approaches to collection.

For example, if I'm using interviews, at the most basic level I need to describe how structured the interview will be (structured, semi-structured, unstructured) and explain why I have chosen that approach. And beyond structure, there are many other types of interviewing influenced by different theoretical or onto-epistemological approaches—such as feminist, phenomenological, hermeneutic, and emancipatory (Roulston, 2010). If I'm using any of these, I need to state that, explain what it means, and provide a rationale that is theoretically coherent with my project.

Going back to the example of teaching observations, I would need to describe the specific method I am adopting for my note-taking process (in this case, I use two: scripting and field notes).

First, I would describe how I will approach scripting, which is to alternate between the overview and scripting methods (Acheson & Gall, 1992)—meaning that I plan to switch off between capturing what is being said and what is happening with as much detail as possible.

Second, I would introduce the idea of interpretive field notes, which include my own thoughts about what is happening in the observation that I keep separate from the script. (Although objectivity, in my view, is never truly possible, keeping your own initial interpretations separate helps with organization and keeps the initial notes as strictly descriptive as possible.)

Below is an example of a chart thinking through the elements I need to include in the first part of my data source description. Read through it, and then complete your own.

	Data Source: Classroom Observations
Definition	Observation is a research tool for qualitative data collection in which the researcher systematically records and interprets phenomena during direct encounters in their naturalistic setting. (Merriam, 2009, chapter 6)
Important Methodologists	Merriam (2009), Adler & Adler (1998), Acheson & Gall (1992)
Contextualization to My Study	◗ Observations are a method to directly document and analyze teacher practices in the classrooms (the naturalistic setting) as they occur over time; as well as the interactions between teacher and students (and other elements) that influence the development of those practices. ◗ Observations are a common tool used in research focusing on pedagogy because it is a first-hand account of instruction. ◗ This will be an important supplement to teacher interviews about their practice, which are second-hand accounts and "self-reports".
Tradition	Ethnography: observations are generally considered an ethnographic method because they help the researcher collect and analyze data over time to describe how communities function.
Connected Concepts or Approaches	"Participant observer": a "peripheral membership role" (Adler & Adler, 1987, p. 85) because the very presence of a researcher may affect what is happening during the observation. ◗ As a participant observer, the teacher and students will know I'm there as a researcher.

	Data Source: Classroom Observations (Cont.)
Connected Concepts or Approaches	◗ I will not intentionally take an active role in classroom happenings, but I still might influence teacher and student behavior simply by being in the room.
Tools, Materials, or Processes	◗ Field notes: For each observation, I will keep separate field notes to record my own thoughts. Field notes will include new insights, connections to theory or other data, methodological decisions, or personal reactions to what I am seeing. ◗ During each observation, I will combine the overview and scripting methods of note-taking (Acheson & Gall, 1992), alternately capturing what is done and said during the lesson with as much detail as possible.

ACTIVITY 11. DATA SOURCE PRE-WRITE	
Use the chart below to think through each of the elements below and generate text for writing your own data source descriptions. Complete one chart per data source.	
Data Source	
Definition	
Important Methodologists	
Contextualization to My Study	
Tradition	
Concepts or Approaches	
Tools, Materials, or Processes	

Now, let's put this all together. Read the paragraph below (adapted from my own dissertation proposal) and compare it to the data source chart I completed above for classroom observations. Locate the definition of the data source, the contextualization to my own project and rationale, and additional concepts/approaches.

> Observation is an ethnographic method for qualitative data collection in which the researcher systematically records and interprets phenomena during direct encounters in their naturalistic setting (Merriam, 2009). Observations will serve as a central data source because they facilitate the direct documentation of teacher practices in the classrooms (the naturalistic setting), as well as the interactions between teacher and students (and other elements) that influence the development of those practices, over time. In addition, observations are first-hand accounts of instruction, which can help triangulate the second-hand accounts provided in the teacher interviews.
>
> In the observations, I will serve as a "participant observer." Adler and Adler (1987, p. 85) describe the participant observer as a "peripheral membership role" because the very presence of a researcher may affect what is happening during the observation. Although I will not intentionally take an active role in classroom happenings, I still may influence teacher and student behavior simply by being in the room.
>
> To ensure systematic observation, I plan to combine the overview and scripting methods of note-taking (Acheson & Gall, 1992), alternately capturing what is done and said during the lesson with as much detail as possible. I will also record separate field notes, another ethnographic method (Emerson, Fretz, & Shaw, 1995), to capture my thoughts and emerging interpretations. Field notes will include new insights, connections to theory or other data, methodological decisions, or personal reactions to what I am seeing.

Once you have thoroughly described the data source, it is time to add fine-grained detail in terms of the logistics of how you will collect that data. As you write the methodology for your dissertation proposal, complete this section with as much detail as you have at that time; and, once you have completed your data collection, come back and flesh these descriptions out in terms of what you actually did.

The elements of this logistics section include *who, when, where, how many,* and *for how long.* First, from *whom* will you be collecting this data source? This is especially important if you have multiple types of participants (for example, in a study in which you are collecting data from both teachers and students, you likely will be collecting different kinds of data from them).

Next describe *when* the data will be collected: for instance, in a study conducting interviews, specify the intervals—if there are two interviews per participant, these might be done at the beginning and end of the study, five months apart. In addition, specify *how many* of that data source you plan to collect, both per participant and total, as well as *how long* it will take to collect the data. For an interview, for example, you would note an approximate length of time you will be speaking to the participant; if you were observing a class, you would likely cite the length of the class period. Finally, include any other details specific to the kind of data source, and add concrete examples to help the reader visualize those details. For instance, when describing the interviews you will conduct, you might share how many items will be on the protocol or interview guide and offer some examples of what those questions might look like.

The graphic organizer below shows an example of thinking through the logistics of collecting a set of interviews. Read through it, and then go on to complete your own.

	Data Source: Teacher Interviews
Who	◗ All three teacher participants.
When	◗ At the beginning and the end of the study, approximately 5 months apart.
Where	◗ At a location of the participants' choosing.
How Many	◗ 2 interviews per participant, for a total of six.
How Long	◗ Each interview will last between 60-90 minutes.
Other Details	◗ The interviews will include ten questions each. ◗ Examples include: "What have been your successes so far?" "What have you found to be challenging, and why?"

ACTIVITY 12. DATA COLLECTION LOGISTICS PRE-WRITE

Use this organizer to think through each of the elements below and generate text for writing data source descriptions. Complete one chart per data source.

	Data Source
Who	
When	

ACTIVITY 12. DATA COLLECTION LOGISTICS PRE-WRITE (CONT.)	
	Data Source
Where	
How Many	
How Long	
Other Details, Examples	

Now, let's look at an example of a paragraph describing the logistics of a data source—in this case, observations. What kinds of concrete details are provided?

> My total number of observations varied for each teacher. Because I was interested in the construction of practice, I made the decision to observe each study participant for the length of one instructional unit, so that I might see several consecutive lessons that supported a larger learning objective. For June and Mauro, whose classes were eighty-minute periods, this meant I observed seven and five classes, respectively. However, for Bruce, whose classes were only forty minutes, one unit spanned ten classes. In addition to the complete unit, I observed each teacher two to three times in September, as their schedules allowed, to get an understanding of classroom dynamics. Finally, I observed a "mini-unit," which consisted of three to four classes for each teacher, toward the end of the first semester, to note any additional changes or developments that might have taken place since the observed unit. Because each class is a unique composition of the teacher, students, content, forces, and objects that can shape what the teacher can do, I planned my data collection schedule to observe as many different periods as time allowed. *(Strom, 2014, pp. 80-81).*

ACTIVITY 13. DATA SOURCE DRAFT

Using all the activities you completed in the data source section, edit the text into cohesive paragraphs. If you have more than one type of data source, chunk them into subsections with subheadings clearly labeling each.

As a final note, if you are planning a project with several different kinds of data sources, you may want to create an "at-a-glance" chart. For example, the chart below (Strom, 2014, p. 80) summarizes my set of data sources, including classroom observations, observation debriefings, semi-structured interviews, field notes, and a researcher journal.

Data Source	Description
Classroom Observations	I conducted 2-3 observations per participant during the first month of school. I observed one full instructional unit with each teacher between October and December. I concluded with a mini-unit for each teacher of 3-4 observations. I scripted each observation.
Observation Debriefings	Each lesson observation during the full instructional unit was followed by a short post-observation interview. During this time the participant reflected on the lesson, discussed instructional choices, and answered other questions that arose from the observation.
Semi-Structured Interviews	For each participant, I conducted 2 semi-structured interviews of approximately 60-90 minutes in length, one at the start and another at the conclusion of the study to provide an understanding of the work of teaching taking place beyond observations, probe teacher thinking about practice, and present preliminary study themes.
Field Notes	I recorded my own interpretations before, during, and after observations in the form of field notes, which I later typed and use to supplement observational scripts.
Researcher Journal	I maintained a researcher journal to record methodological decisions and the thinking that accompanies them. The journal also served as a method to record ongoing sensemaking as well as my own emotional responses to the unfolding research.

Figure 7.4: At-a-glance data source chart

ACTIVITY 14. AT-A-GLANCE DATA SOURCE CHART

Create an at-a-glance data source chart to add to your data source section. You may want to edit it neatly into a table to add the front of the data source section as a scaffold for your reader.

Data Source	Description	Number

7.5 Analysis

This section describes your analysis—that is, the way you plan to systematically make meaning of your data. For your dissertation proposal, the analysis may be more of a sketch of your initial thinking; once you have completed your study, however, you will return to this section and flesh it out with concrete details of how you conducted your analysis.

The analysis section is comprised of five tasks. In it, you need to 1) identify the analytic approach(es) selected; 2) define it/them and any connected ideas; 3) justify or provide a rationale showing alignment to the theoretical framework and/or how the analytic approach(es) support(s) the study goals; 4) describe the analysis step-by-step, in as much detail as possible; and 5) offer examples to illustrate the analytic process. (Please note that you can only complete this last step after actually conducting the analysis, since you won't yet know these details when you write this chapter for your proposal.)

Let's look at an example from my work that illustrates the first three elements (identifying, defining, and justifying the approach). In the excerpt below I describe the analytic method of "situational analysis," a type of grounded theory.

> "Situational analysis" (Clarke, 2003, p. 558) is more explicitly relational and postmodern, distancing itself from traditional grounded theory's objective researcher/data outlook and moving from a focus on social process to a more "ecological root metaphor" (p. 558) of social situations and the negotiations that occur within them. This method also adds an analytic layer of maps that show situational elements in their collectivity, how these elements interact and negotiate, and the issues, discourses, and/or positions that contribute to social processes within the situations under study. From these maps, researchers proceed to produce memos and engage in substantive theorizing (consistent with a focus on process rather than a product of substantive theory). The philosophical stance underlying this variation of grounded theory, the potential to explain processes of change, the ecological focus on the collective situation (which I paralleled to the concept of *assemblage*), and the situational map-making all aligned with my conceptual frames and study aims. *(Strom, 2014, pp. 86-87)*

Here, I begin by defining situational analysis in terms of its onto-epistemological foundations—it is "*relational*" (foregrounding connection and networks/systems) and "*postmodern*" (it promotes a view of reality as situated, fluid, always-changing, collective, and heterogeneous). I reference its movement away from more traditional forms of grounded theory (which tend to see researchers and data as objective) and describe the shift to focus on "*social situations*" (i.e., temporal collectives or systems).

I go on to describe how it works (but only very briefly, since I will come back to this in more detail later, when I describe my own step-by-step situational analysis process). I explain that the situational analysis process includes mapping out the collective, examining how the elements in that collective work together and what influences that behavior, and memoing and theorizing. Finally, I point out the dimensions of the approach—the underlying philosophy, process focus, ecological perspective, and mapping—that align to my study.

As you identify, define, and justify the analytic approach(es) for your own study, don't forget to cite the methodologists credited with them (or those who have influenced your decision-making regarding which analytic process you plan to use).

ACTIVITY 15. GENERATING TEXT FOR THE ANALYSIS SECTION

Think through your general analytic approach in terms of the three elements described in the example above. If you have a combination of approaches, complete a row for each method of analysis you plan to use.

Approach	Definition	Justification

Next, create a step-by-step description of the analytic process you plan to follow, being as specific as possible (again, you will come back to this text and flesh it out after completing your data collection and analysis). For this section, if you introduce any new terms, be sure to briefly define them and cite methodologists, as appropriate. As an example: *"I will first engage in initial coding, also known as "open" or "free" coding (Saldaña, 2013). In this first-cycle coding method, researchers take an exploratory lens and create tentative codes, or units of meaning, which tend to be descriptive in nature."*

Let's look at an example of a paragraph from my own dissertation proposal describing an analytic mapping process via the software Inspiration. As you can see, I use future-oriented language ("*I plan to*") as well as tentative language ("*may help me*"). Although I describe what I plan to do—use the software to cluster key ideas and link them, creating "webs of ideas" that can be converted into a linear outline format—at this point, I am limited in terms of the detail I can add.

> Taking a cue from Bowles (2001) and Waterhouse (2011), I plan to use the data software Inspiration to record connections from the data sources, group similar ideas together, and make further linkages across data, thus simulating a version of a discovery and coding approach (Bogdan & Biklen, 1998), but focusing on connections and interactions rather than categories. Quotes from data sources, connections from the literature, thoughts from my researcher journal, or any other supporting text can be added to boxes that contain the main ideas or linkages that are being

> made, which can then be expanded into fuller vignettes. The software allows the construction of webs of ideas to visually represent thinking, but also has a function that converts visual representations to outlines. Going back and forth between the two expressions of my emerging findings may help make further connections.

Now, let's look at the same paragraph, fleshed out in the full dissertation.

> Taking a cue from Bowles (2001) and Waterhouse (2011), I used the data software Inspiration to record connections from the data sources, group similar ideas together, and make further linkages. This simulated a version of a discovery and coding approach (Bogdan & Biklen, 1998), but focused on connections, interactions, and processes rather than categories. I moved ideas from the data into an Inspiration document, with my research question at the top. Using circles with dotted lines to connote the open and fluid nature of these data, I entered main ideas and clustered them together in ways that related to the facets of constructing practice, such as "Negotiating NUTR practices," "Constraining conditions," and "Negotiating with students." From these I linked more "open" circles, adding data from observation scripts, debrief and interview transcripts, field notes, or my journal, which supported the linkages that were being made. As I plotted these, I began to make connections between and among the concepts, indicating these with non-directional, irregularly curved lines.
> *(Strom, 2014, pp. 88-89)*

In this example, the first two sentences are pretty much the same as those from the proposal paragraph above, adjusted in terms of verb tense. However, from there, I was able to articulate my process in a more specific way, describing a relational process of clustering connected ideas. I also provided explicit examples of the topics of the clusters, which I explained as relating to dimensions of construction of practice (the main focus of my research question).

Let's look at one more example that describes the analysis in a study already completed. In the excerpt below (Dolid, 2021, p. 64), which of the analysis tasks we've discussed in this section can you identify? What kind of *linguistic moves* does the author make to scaffold understanding for the reader?

> In the second cycle of coding, I used axial coding to relate and connect the initial codes. I attempted to remain open to various forms of axial coding that were appropriate based on the initial codes, such as focused codes or process codes. Saldaña (2013) defines focused coding as a "streamlined adaptation" (p.213) of axial coding, which allowed me refine and reorganize codes into categories, understanding

> that some categories might have shared features or that codes might have different degrees of belonging within those categories (Saldaña, 2013, p. 213). For example, I eventually grouped "Building Understanding of Community Practices" and "Building Asset Based Knowledge of Identity" under the broader code "Building Understanding of Identity" because of the shared features of those two former codes. Process codes allowed me to capture the "conceptual action" and "observable activity" (Saldaña, 2013, p. 96) occurring through the planning, teaching and reflecting phases in an action-research cycle (Anderson et al., 2007).

In the above excerpt, Dolid (2021) begins with a signaling transition that lets the reader know he is going to describe the process he used for his second cycle of coding. He identifies the overall approach—axial coding—and describes it as an emergent process (he "*attempted to remain open to various forms of axial coding*" based on initial analysis). Dolid scaffolds for the reader by introducing two specific approaches—focused coding and process coding—each of which he goes on to discuss in turn. First, he defines "focused coding," referring to Saldaña (2013), and describes how this analytic method worked for him. Using a transition ("*for example...*") to signal his intent to provide an illustration, Dolid provides concrete details of codes he grouped under a larger umbrella ("*Building Understanding of Identity.*") The researcher then moves on to the second term, process coding, offering a sentence that combines a definition (codes that "*capture 'conceptual action' and 'observable activity'*") with an explanation of his own use of the method (to illuminate processes of the action research cycle).

ACTIVITY 16. ANALYSIS STEPS PRE-WRITE

Outline the process you plan to take to conduct your analysis, step by step. "Name" each step according to the analytic approach you and your advisor have settled on, which should also align with your overall methodological approach. For example, if it is a general interpretive qualitative study, you will likely engage in data familiarization, coding cycles, memoing, and themeing—each of these should be discussed with concepts defined as needed and methodologists cited as appropriate.

Step	Detailed Description (with Citations)	Concept Definitions (with Citations)

ACTIVITY 17. ANALYSIS SECTION DRAFT

Using your notes from the two activities above, draft out the two parts of your analysis section: the discussion of the analytic approach and the detailed description of specific steps you plan to take. Remember to use topic sentences, signaling language, transitions, and other scaffolds for coherence and support. Signaling transitions like "first," "next", "finally," etc. are important for helping your reader understand a sequence description of activities (like the analytic process you are discussing).

7.6 Trustworthiness

Toward the end of your methodology chapter, you will need to add a section that addresses the trustworthiness of your study. Broadly speaking, *trustworthy* means exactly that: worthy of trust. That is, the reader can trust that your study is of high quality. Therefore, your purpose in this section is to show your reader that 1) you have thought through measures to ensure that your study will be conducted in an ethical, rigorous manner (for your proposal) and 2) that you enacted those measures (for your full dissertation). Generally, in your trustworthiness section, you will offer a definition of your chosen trustworthiness approach or framework with a rationale; then describe in practical terms how you will carry this out. While trustworthiness is generally associated with qualitative research, quantitative or mixed methods studies still require an ethics/quality assurance section of some kind (likely addressing reliability, validity, and other dimensions more associated with positivist research). Despite the differences, you can still apply the general ideas I offer regarding the structure and elements of an ethics/quality section to measures that are more appropriate for quantitative research.

To get started, first decide whose definition of trustworthiness to use (or perhaps which combination of definitions). Multiple methodologists have offered criteria for trustworthiness, including Lincoln and Guba (1985), Lather (1986/1993), and Ellingson (2009). Personally, I like to use Tracy's (2010, p. 840) "big tent" criteria for excellence in qualitative research. These include: 1) a worthy topic that is timely/important; 2) rigor in terms of both theory and methodology; 3) sincerity or transparency regarding positionality and methodological processes; 4) credibility; 5) resonance with readers; 6) significant methodological, theoretical, and practical contribution; 7) ethics; and 8) coherence or alignment across the study goals, theory, research design, and outcomes.

Whichever you descide, it will serve two purposes: it will indicate a particular orientation (which needs to align with your theoretical and methodological approaches) as well as provide an organizing structure for the rest of the section.

For example, in the excerpt on the next page, I define trustworthiness using Lincoln and Guba's (1985) and Merriam's (2009) definitions.

> The concept of trustworthiness is an argument that a study's findings are "worth paying attention to" (Lincoln & Guba, 1985, p. 290). Rather than asking if a study's findings match reality or can be reproduced exactly, trustworthiness seeks to establish credibility and transferability (Merriam, 2009). As such, trustworthiness is more suited to my purposes than validity for demonstrating that the research is rigorous, authentic, and contributes to understanding.

The definition above describes an understanding of what constitutes quality research that aligns with a particular onto-epistemological orientation (e.g., the nature of knowledge and existence is not fixed and unified, but is contextual and mobile). It also describes the corresponding quality criteria I am aiming to meet: to establish credibility, to be transferrable to conduct a rigorous and authentic project, and to contribute to the field's understanding of the phenomenon I am studying.

I can then use these criteria (credibility, plausibility, rigor, authenticity, and contribution to understanding) as elements to organize what I write next—a description of the actionable measures I will take to ensure that my work meets high quality standards.

ACTIVITY 18.1. TRUSTWORTHINESS PRE-WRITE	
Below, write out your definition of trustworthiness, along with a citation to an appropriate methodologist. If you are drawing from multiple definitions, bullet them out. **Then, think through and generate a list of trustworthiness quality criteria from this definition.**	
Definition of Trustworthiness (with citations)	
Corresponding Quality Criteria	

ACTIVITY 18.2. TRUSTWORTHINESS DEFINITION DRAFT
Using the ideas you generated above, edit the definition and the list of criteria into a few sentences or a paragraph.

Once you have settled on your quality criteria, create a table to articulate exactly how you will meet each criterion, one by one. This will serve as a scaffold for you to build out a section explaining to your reader how you are ensuring that you are conducting a trustworthy study.

The table below shows an example of a pre-writing scaffold to think through your measures of trustworthiness. In it, I use the five quality criteria described earlier, drawing from Lincoln and Guba (1985) and Merriam (2009).

Read through the table, then fill out your own to build out text for writing the trustworthiness criteria description.

Criterion	Measure(s) to Address Criterion
Credibility	◗ Triangulation or crystallization between multiple data sources ◗ Substantiating evidence that supports my claims ◗ Member checking: Presenting emerging findings to participants ◗ Critical friends: Discussing emerging findings with peers, advisors
Transferability	◗ Providing detailed descriptions of context and participants ◗ Reporting findings through thick description/explanation, including direct quotes from participants
Rigor	◗ Explaining data collection and analysis processes in detail to show they are robust and aligned with research goals ◗ Providing in-depth examples and evidence to substantiate claims
Authenticity	◗ Being transparent about my goals, my positionality ◗ Critically reflecting on how my positionality may influence/influenced the study design, analysis, and interpretation ◗ Disclosing challenges encountered during the study
Contribution to Understanding	◗ Supporting readers to follow and clearly understand major arguments and contributions through multiple linguistic scaffolding strategies ◗ Offering direct statements that illuminate theoretical, methodological, and practical contributions

ACTIVITY 19.1. TRUSTWORTHINESS CRITERIA PRE-WRITE	
Taking the criteria you generated from the previous activity, use this organizer to develop trustworthiness strategies that correspond to each criterion and build out text for writing the description.	
Criterion	Measure(s) to Address Criterion

ACTIVITY 19.2. TRUSTWORTHINESS CRITERIA DRAFT
Using the ideas you generated above, edit into 1-2 paragraphs.

7.7 Positionality and Reflexivity

An important part of trustworthiness includes practicing reflexivity, or critical reflection regarding the ways your positionality (the constellation of identities you bring to your research) shapes the study and the knowledge produced from it. Although reflexivity might be considered a strategy for trustworthiness, many social justice-oriented researchers create a separate section for positionality. Making this choice is a way to enact a particular onto-epistemological stance (i.e., a belief about the nature of knowledge and existence). For example, if I believe that...

- Knowledge is co-constructed, rather than found "out there" (an epistemological belief); *And...*
- Researchers do not transcend time/space/place, but occupy particular material locations and "speak from where they are" through their positionalities (an ontological belief); *Then...*
- This means that my positionalities will influence or shape everything—from the way I perceive the initial problem driving my research, to the goals of the study, to the theories I work with, to my research design decisions, to my readings of the data, to the ways I represent the outcomes of my analysis, to the ways I discuss those outcomes and draw recommendations from them for various audiences.

If researchers' positionalities co-produce their research, then scholars claiming the above onto-epistemological orientation must be accountable for how that co-production happens. The positionality section, then, becomes a vehicle through which we—researchers—can engage in reflexivity or self-analysis of the afore-mentioned co-construction. Creating a separate section emphasizes the importance of interrogating our positionalities in relation to our research as a reflexive exercise and provides a space to do so in a substantive way.

ACTIVITY 20. IDENTITY MAPPING EXERCISE	
Think through your positionality using the prompts of identity factors below. If there are other salient factors that influence your positionality, be sure to add them to this list.	
Identity Markers (social, cultural, gender-based, etc)	
Current Role/Context	
Beliefs Related to Your Topic	
Interests and Professional Goals	
Personal Experiences and Background	
Professional Experiences and Background	
Theoretical/Onto-Epistemological Orientations	

Like other parts of your methodology chapter, your positionality/reflexivity section will evolve between your dissertation proposal and your final dissertation. *For the dissertation proposal,* you will be discussing your positionality and how it shaped/is shaping the elements you can speak to at that early stage (i.e., the information contained within the proposal). Some questions to ask yourself as you get ready to write this section of your proposal: how have your identities, experiences, and various personal-professional connections shaped the issues you care about—including the selected topic? How might this constellation of factors have shaped the way you framed the problem? How might this mix of ideas and beliefs have turned you toward particular theories? How might it have influenced the methodological decisions you are making?

As part of your proposal, you will also need to speculate about how your positionality and socio-material locations may affect the later activities of your project (e.g., interacting with participants, data collection, analysis/interpretation, reporting findings) and describe how you might address ethical or political issues implicated therein. For instance, are issues of power likely to arise from your positionality in relation to participants, and if so, how will you mediate them? As an illustration, if I wanted to investigate the ways my scaffolded writing instruction is impacting my doctoral students' scholarship development, I would need to think through my positionality (I am their instructor, a position of authority) and related issues of power (I determine their grade). Given my positionality and power relations, it is reasonable to conclude that my students could feel coerced to participate in the study and/or not feel comfortable expressing their true thoughts about my instruction. To address this concern, I could ask our department administrator facilitate consent form signing and keep the forms locked away until after the semester is over and grades are assigned. That way, students would know that there would be no threat of retaliation if they did not consent to participate in my study, since I would have no idea who agreed or not. As another measure, I could ensure that all communication is through anonymous questionnaires or focus groups facilitated by other faculty.

Let's look at an excerpt from a positionality section from a dissertation proposal. Read the example below and answer the following: what personal and professional identities does the researcher identify, and how does she think they might shape her research? How does she plan to address this potential issue?

> As a White, English-speaking, female scholar-practitioner from outside of the school community that I am researching, I run the risk of making comparisons "between the culture of the 'studied' and that of the 'studier'" (Wilson, 2013, pp. 16-17) that could position English monolingualism as the norm or ideal, and multilingualism as a condition in need of remedy. Mindful of the potential I have of reinforcing a negative positioning of ML students, I strive to understand and portray the "complexity, contradiction, and self-determination of lived lives" (Tuck, 2009, p. 416), and in doing so, elevate the voices and experiences of the research participants, from which we can all benefit and learn. Fundamental to this work is highlighting the existence and effects of white privilege and questioning the "majoritarian stories" based on white privilege (Solórzano & Yosso, 2002). *(Ansari dissertation proposal, p. 63)*

In the excerpt above, Ansari first identifies three identity markers of her positionality (i.e., white, female, English-speaking) as well as professional aspects (i.e., scholar-practitioner, outsider in terms of the school community). The next sentence describes a potential pitfall: since she is making meaning mostly through dominant identities, there is the possibility of perpetuating deficit perspectives of MLLs as well as the monolingual status quo. She then offers strategies for addressing this potential issue—her own awareness, adopting a complex approach grounded in the voices and experiences of participants, and taking a critical perspective that explicitly calls out whiteness and questions the dominant narratives they produce.

The next excerpt comes from a completed dissertation, a participatory action research (PAR) project in which Dolid (2021) collaborated with a middle school English Language Arts teacher, Ms. Atsila. Read this excerpt twice. First, ask yourself: what elements of positionality and space-place-time are identified here? How does the description provided help us understand the situated dynamics of the project and Dolid and Ms. Atsila's relationship? On your second read, notice the differences in level of detail and verb tense between Ansari's proposal excerpt (above) and this one from a full dissertation.

> As an instructional coach within the Cutting Edge School district, my insider-status afforded me the opportunity to research the school district in which I work. However, my position as a coach and my perceived connections to district office administrators had the potential to create distance between me and Ms. Atsila. As I reflect on the study, the relationship and knowledge we developed through collaboration was unique to us; we developed an identity as a research team, and therefore the knowledge we developed [became] contextualized within the spaces, time and circumstances of the COVID-19 Pandemic, of teaching in a virtual setting, and of being a Mexican-American & Indigenous female teacher negotiating space with a White male euro-American instructional coach. These identities and contexts, in addition to the interacting forces of our students' identities and contexts, shaped the study. *(Dolid, 2021, pp. 69-70)*

Compared to Ansari's positionality proposal excerpt, Dolid's full dissertation example above features a higher level of concrete detail as well as describes everything in past tense. Additionally, while the proposal positionality chapter is speculative (what *might* happen), the full dissertation positionality section is reflective (what *actually happened* in the project). Accordingly, Dolid begins by describing elements of his professional identity and the ways they served as both enabling and (potentially) constraining: on the one hand, as a leader in the district in which his study took place, he had easy access to research sites. However, that same leadership position also "*had the potential to create distance between me and Ms. Atsila*" (which, for a PAR project involving a collaboration with one teacher, is a crucial insight). However, he goes on to explain that they *did* develop a unique relationship and knowledge, all shaped by several more elements encompassing not just positionality but also space and time: a white male and Indo-Latina negotiating in a virtual space during the COVID-19 pandemic, all of which shaped their relationship and knowledge.

As a final writing tip: if you include a substantial positionality statement, which indicates an onto-epistemological orientation that the researcher (and everything they bring and are connected to) matters to their research, make sure that you use *first-person voice.* Many doctoral programs still teach that using first-person voice is inappropriate for formal writing. This reflects a positivist perspective that research should be objective and neutral, and therefore, putting ourselves in our research taints the study. Programs often encourage students to use third person (e.g., referring to yourself as "*the researcher*"), position the study as the actor (e.g., "*this study draws on narrative inquiry*"), or use a passive voice that removes the researcher entirely (e.g., "*observations were conducted over a ten-week period*"). However, by making a deliberate choice to use first-person, you assume accountability for your decisions and actions by positioning yourself as an agentic actor: "*I conducted observations...*" "*I selected the case study approach because...*" Doing so also serves as a disruption of entrenched beliefs about research by reminding the reader that, in fact, you were present and influential in terms of planning and carrying out the study, interpreting data, and making choices regarding how to represent that data (which I describe in the next chapter).

ACTIVITY 21. THINKING THROUGH POTENTIAL IMPACT OF POSITIONALITY

Using Activity 20, select relevant positionality elements. Then, using the righthand column, think through ways that these positionality elements might be enabling or constraining, or might otherwise impact a facet of the study in some way. Be sure to think through whether that element might have implications for power relations between you and your participants.

Positionality Element	Potential Impact (on study framing, design, theoretical choices, site access, participant interactions, and/or analysis and interpretation)

ACTIVITY 22. DRAFTING THE INITIAL POSITIONALITY/REFLEXIVITY SECTION

Using the notes you generated from the two activities in this section, draft an initial positionality/reflexivity section that describes salient dimensions of your positionality (including contextual factors) and ways that those have or might impact the project facets noted in the last activity.

7.8 Writing Your Abstract (For Your Proposal)

As mentioned previously, your dissertation proposal consists of the first three chapters—the problem statement, literature review/theoretical framework (usually one chapter), and your methodology—plus an abstract, table of contents, and references. For your abstract, I recommend waiting until you have final approval from your chair. Up until then, things will likely be shifting and evolving, and you want to make sure that your abstract matches the rest of the proposal.

The abstract is an "at-a-glance" snapshot of your dissertation proposal. Typically, you will pose the problem, justify why your study is needed, and explain what you plan to do. The following guide offers one way to construct that snapshot.

ACTIVITY 23. DRAFTING THE ABSTRACT

Complete the sentence stems. Put the sentences into it paragraph form, edit out unnecessary language, and add transitions for flow.

The problem/issue is ______________________.

This is a problem/important because _________________.

Some researchers who have studied this problem have found _________________. Others have found _________________.

We still don't know ____.

Therefore, I am going to investigate __________________________________.

Using a conceptual/theoretical frame of _______________________________, I'm going to _____________________________ (design of study).

The central question (s) guiding this study is/are ____________________.

Conclusion

In this chapter, we worked through all the major elements of your methodology chapter (typically, chapter three in your dissertation). For your dissertation proposal, the central purpose in this chapter is to describe, in clear and detailed terms, the plan you will follow for conducting your study. After you conduct the study, you will go back to the methodology chapter and edit it to show what you actually did.

We discussed the following major elements of the methodology chapter:

1. The ***methodology description*** generally consists of two parts: 1) a discussion of the general research approach (i.e., quantitative, qualitative, mixed methods) and its theoretical underpinnings; and 2) the specific methodological approach (i.e., case study, action research, autoethnography, etc.) you will take.
2. For ***participants and contextual information***, you will first describe who exactly will take part in your study and how you selected them. That should be followed by a discussion of any necessary context, which may include the setting of a study and important background information your readers might need to understand your study's findings.
3. The ***data sources and collection procedures*** section describes, with as much specificity as possible, how you plan to actually carry out the methodological approach described at the beginning of the methodology chapter.
4. The ***analysis section*** describes the way you plan to systematically make meaning of your data In it, you need to 1) identify the analytic approach(es) selected; 2) define it/them and any connected ideas; 3) justify or provide a rationale showing alignment to the theoretical framework and/or how the analytic approach(es) support(s) the study goals; 4) describe the analysis step-by-step, in as much detail as possible; and 5) offer examples to illustrate the analytic process.
5. In the ***trustworthiness*** section, you show how you will ensure that your study is high quality (so the reader can trust your reported findings). To do this, you will offer a definition of your chosen trustworthiness approach or framework with a rationale, and then describe specific strategies that you will use to carry that out.
6. A key part of trustworthiness is practicing ***reflexivity***, or critical reflection regarding the ways your ***positionality*** (the constellation of identities you bring to your research) shapes the study and the knowledge produced from it.

Once you finish this chapter, you will need to actually conduct your study before moving on to the next one, which provides support for writing the findings section of your dissertation.

The Findings Chapter

Contents

Introduction

We are now moving beyond the dissertation proposal and focusing on the findings, which typically comprises chapter four of your full dissertation.

The findings refer to the big ideas/themes you constructed from your data analysis (the "what," i.e., what you "found"). Sometimes this dissertation chapter is referred to as the "data chapter" or the "results chapter."

Importantly, how you structure your findings will depend immensely on your orientations and values, goals of the study, methodology, and agenda as a researcher. In the following sections, I will offer an overview of some possible ways to structure and write your findings, but keep in mind that the ideas I present here in no way encompass *all* the approaches possible. Like in the last chapter, the approaches I will share have a qualitative orientation, although much of what follows can be applied to mixed methods and even quantitative studies as well. Ultimately, you need to work with your chair to determine your own approach to crafting your dissertation findings. This chapter offers ideas to help you do so.

Keep in mind that as a term, *findings* is somewhat of a misnomer, since there's nothing ready-made to "find" in your data. That would suggest that knowledge is pre-existing, and as such, positions the researcher as the objective discoverer of what is already there. I prefer to think of analysis as an active process of construction, which foregrounds researcher agency and accountability, and I encourage you to consider this idea as well.

8.1 Purposes of the Findings

WARM UP

Based on your analysis so far (just off the top of your head), what is your current thinking regarding how your emerging findings "answer" (or shed light on) your research question(s)?

As I noted above, the main goal of the findings chapter is to share *what* ideas emerge from your analyses processes. Figure 8.1 shows the main purposes to keep in mind as you begin to think about crafting your findings chapter. These include 1) communicating the big ideas constructed from your analysis; 2) showing how the ideas answer your research question and meet your study goals; 3) providing sufficient evidence that substantiates all the ideas you present in your findings; and 4) demonstrating that your findings are trustworthy. In the sections that follow, we will discuss each of these purposes in turn.

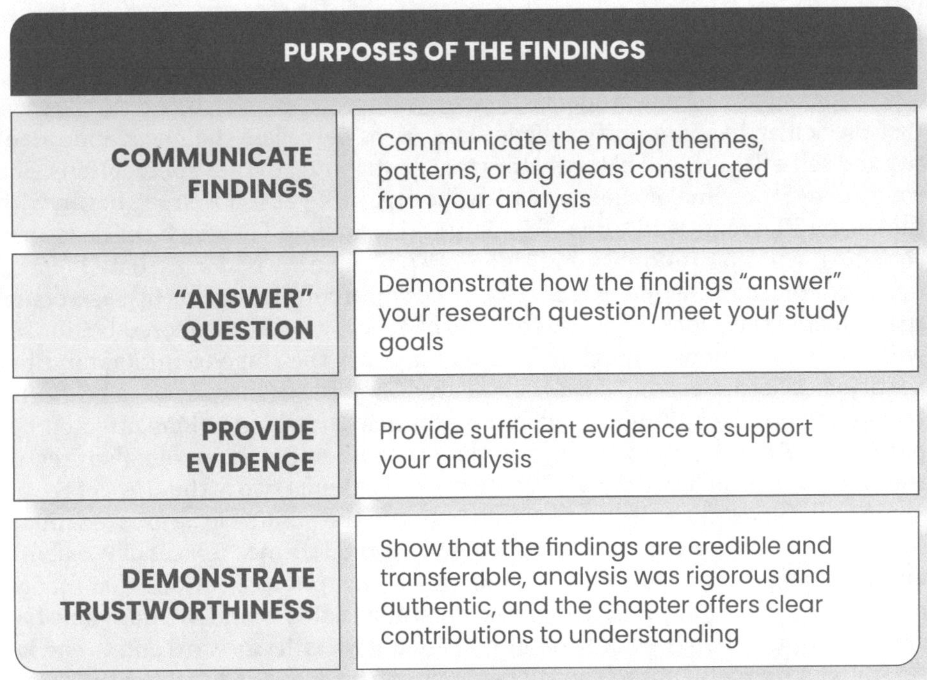

Figure 8.1: Purposes of the findings

ACTIVITY 1. ANALYZING A SAMPLE FINDINGS CHAPTER

Locate a dissertation in your topic area that uses a similar methodology as you used. Go to the findings chapter (usually chapter four). Create an outline that shows the organization and key findings. What do you notice about the organization? How would you describe it?

8.2 Communicating Findings

To articulate the big ideas of your analysis coherently, you will need to create an organizing schema (like the one discussed in chapter five for the literature review). The findings can be organized in different ways depending on the audience, the methodology, and the aims of the researcher/author. No single way to organize the findings is any better than another. What is important is to have a clear organizing schema that provides a cohesive, coherent research narrative.

Most of my students choose to create a ***thematic organizational schema.*** This means you organize your findings according to the themes (and subthemes) generated from your analysis. In a thematic organizational schema, when you land on themes or key ideas, these will usually become the headings of your finding sections. To tell a coherent story with these themes, you need to think about the connections between them and how they fit together to tell a coherent narrative.

For example, a former student (Crenshaw-Mayo, 2020) investigated a) the ways that Black men in community college classrooms perceived their academic identity and self-efficacy, and b) the factors that contributed to these perceptions. She constructed three major themes, which she organized as follows: she began with the theme "Current Conditions of Society and Schooling," in which she described the social and institutional conditions her participants had articulated (social inequity, educators' deficit perspectives, and white cultural norms in classrooms) that affected their identities and feelings of efficacy. She considered beginning with these conditions important because they set the stage to understand her participants' experiences. Second, she shared "Impacts of Inequities and Cultural Hegemony on Black Students," delving into *how* those conditions affected her participants' development of academic identity and self-efficacy, but also created trauma and mental health issues. In other words, theme two is the *effect* of theme one, which makes clear the relationship between the points of the organizational schema and creates coherence. Crenshaw-Mayo's final theme, "Spaces of Possibility and Belonging," articulated the campus spaces, people, and actions that made a positive impact on the participants. For my student, this would provide some balance to the other two themes to show there could be paths forward and to end her findings on a hopeful note. Overall, her logic can be described as follows: "This is what's wrong in community colleges, this is how it's harming Black men, and this is what might help us do better."

Let's consider another example of an organizational schema, which comes from my own work.

To articulate the different factors influencing classroom pedagogy, I often organize them into nested systems—the teacher system, the classroom system, the school system, the district system, and on. These start at the micro-level (the teacher system) and become more macro as they move outward (see Figure 8.2). Each of these systems represents a theme.

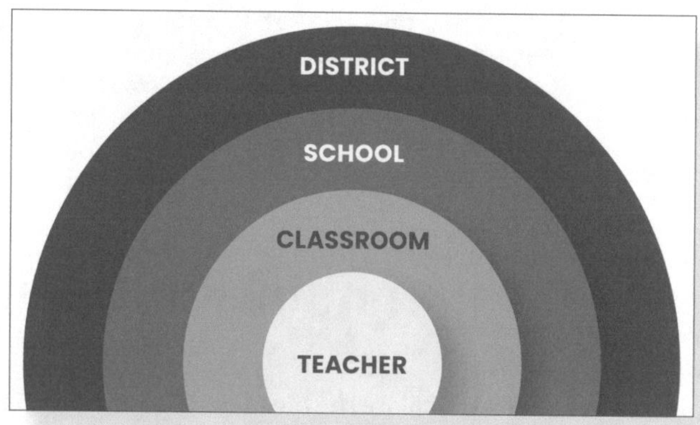

Figure 8.2: "Systems of First-Year Teaching" organizational schema

You may also be able to turn your themes into a framework of some kind.

For example, in my dissertation findings, I created a *typology*, or a classificatory system (i.e., types of something). From my examination of how three new teachers translated their preservice learning into practice, I clustered my findings into three themes, which I named "Processes of First-Year Teaching." These three major themes formed a typology that articulated three different kinds of processes first-year teachers might engage in. These processes are listed below:

- Process 1: Translating pre-professional learning into practice
- Process 2: Negotiating with students
- Process 3: Forming a teacher identity

I saw these processes across the three participants' data, but the particulars of how the processes played out were unique for each participant. Since I was using a case study methodology, this allowed me to use the same overarching structure for each case (the typology of first-year teaching processes), which would help the reader track ideas across each case. However, it also provided the flexibility to unpack those processes with different subthemes, which demonstrated the situated nature of constructing teaching practice.

Also remember that while you must explain and support your organizational structure, you also have some creative agency to frame your research story—and you want to do so in ways that make the most sense given your goals and orientations.

Take, for example, a recent dissertation candidate (Reese, 2023) who was investigating Black students' relational experiences with white teachers. From her data analysis, she quickly saw that she could create two themes: one reflecting characteristics and pedagogies of teachers with whom students described having positive relationships, on the one hand; and another describing characteristics and pedagogies of teachers with whom they did not have good relationships. However, she also noticed patterns that did not fit neatly into those categories. For example, students made remarks that gave the impression they did not think of relationships with their teachers as a natural part of school. Considering her goal to center student voice, she decided to create an organizing schema that divided her findings in two: "Hear My Words," which focused on students' explicitly described characteristics of teachers with whom they had positive and negative (or no) relationships; and "Feel My Words," which focused on teasing out the meaning behind students' articulated feelings and indirect statements.

Themes are not the only type of schemas that could be used. For instance, some findings chapters adopt a more narrative, story-like format. As an illustration, a former student investigating teacher autonomy in professional learning chronicled the journey of a professional learning community (PLC) from its chaotic beginnings to eventually becoming teacher-directed (Peugnet-Alan, 2018). Still other students choose to go the minimalist route and use their research questions as the overall schema. Personally, I don't think this is the most interesting way of structuring findings, but at the end of the day it's up to you to decide what best fits your needs. Whatever you decide to do, however, make sure that you create an outline and that you can articulate the logic flow. Always use headings and subheadings as scaffolds and sign-posts for your reader to identify, at a glance, what the key themes are.

Finally, a data display (a chart) or graphic may help you determine how to structure your findings.

Take, for example, the graphic below.

Figure 8.3 shows a relatively simple data display that can help me think through the logic of my findings and how I want to sequence the ideas. The story it tells is this: The teacher, students, and context all were involved in negotiations, and those negotiations 1) produced teacher identity in a particular way (which I've named "Becoming-teacher"), and 2) produced situated translations of the teachers' preservice learning into practice. To untangle this research narrative for my readers, I first need to describe the unique elements brought by students, teacher, and the context, with commentary on the specific ways they worked together (or their negotiations). Then, I'd need to discuss what was generated by these negotiations (teacher identity and pedagogical translations). So, I might create an organizational schema that looks like the example outline below.

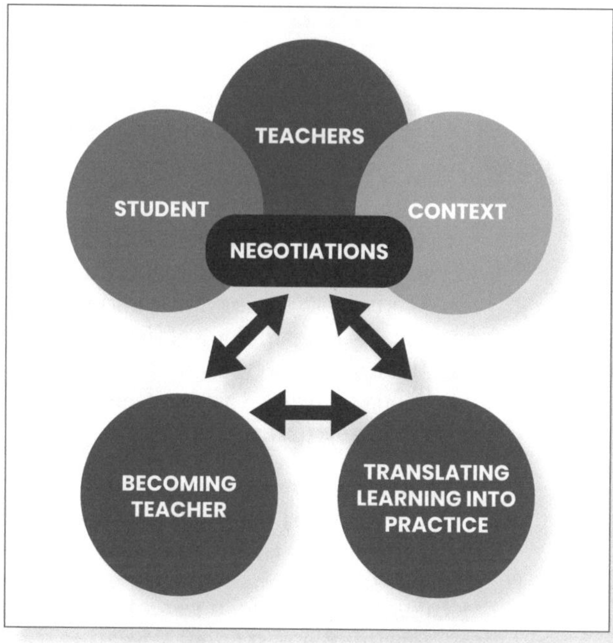

Figure 8.3: Sample findings graphic

I. Negotiating with Self, Students, and Context

a. Teacher Elements
b. Student Elements
c. Contextual Elements
d. Collective Negotiations

II. Productions of Collective Negotiations

a. Becoming-Teacher
b. Translating Learning into Practice

ACTIVITY 2. CREATING A SCHEMA

What are your current thoughts on how you might organize your findings? Is there a particular story that is emerging? Free-write or play with creating data displays to experiment with some possible schemas.

8.3 "Answering" the Research Question(s)

Your next task is to ensure that you offer an answer to your research questions.

By that, I do not mean that what you provide *the definitive answer.* You offer a situated response based on the big ideas communicated in your findings. In other words, the main points of chapter four (as indicated by the major headings of your organizational schema) should collectively represent your "answer" to the questions.

Let's return to the example from the previous section regarding processes of first-year teaching. In the chart below I think through ways that each first-year teaching process I generated from my data offers a response to my research question. Then, I add a summative statement at the bottom.

Question: Given their common experiences of preservice preparation in a hybrid urban teacher education program, how do three first-year teachers negotiate their preprofessional learning within their new environments as they construct their practice?	
Theme	**How It Connects/Responds to the Study Questions**
Process 1: Translating pre-professional learning into practice	This process directly responds to the question regarding negotiation of preprofessional learning with their new settings: it was a process of translation, not transference. The elements of their preservice learning were visible, but they were negotiated with the particular elements and conditions of their contexts, resulting in different enactments of practice.
Process 2: Negotiating with students	This process looks more closely at a major factor in the teachers' environments affecting their construction of practice: students. It looks at the ways that teachers worked together with students, how that connected to their enactments of practice, and how their preprofessional learning about student-teacher relationships and classroom dynamics factored in.
Process 3: Forming a teacher identity	This process looks at the role of teacher-self in constructing their first-year practice. It describes the relational work of ongoing identity formation, how that influenced their enactments of practice, and how that connected to their preservice learning.
Summary: Teachers constructed their practices through three main processes: translating their preservice learning into practice, a process of contextual negotiation that resulted in different enactments based on the setting; negotiating with students, or the processes by which teachers established relationships and classroom dynamics; and forming a teacher identity, a relational process of becoming-teacher.	

Let's take a pause so you can do the same activity to generate some thinking around the themes or main ideas you have identified so far.

ACTIVITY 3. CONNECTING THEMES TO STUDY QUESTIONS	
Record your themes or big ideas from your dissertation findings chapter in the lefthand column. Think through how that theme/idea connects back to or "answers" one or more of your study questions. Then, create a 1-2 sentence overall summary of how the big ideas answer your questions, using the text generated to help you.	
Theme/Big Idea	**How It Connects/Responds to the Study Questions**
Summary:	

Findings Assertions

Now that I have confirmed that my big ideas provide an "answer" to the research question I posed, I need to create accompanying assertions for them. An *assertion* (also known as a claim) is a declarative sentence that summarizes the main finding for that section. The findings section will usually have an overarching assertion or interpretive claim; and each theme will also have a main assertion (that may be unpacked into sub-themes with their own assertions). These assertions will then become the guiding statements for the section and topic sentences for the subsections, and you can build the paragraphs out from there to unpack the statement and provide evidence.

Let's look at an example of an overall assertion that summarizes the entire findings section (and keep in mind that because this assertion is about the findings as a whole, it will likely be more than one sentence). This overall assertion can also be considered the first part of the argument the researcher is making with the findings. Below I adapted my summary from the "addressing the question" activity above. As you can see, I edited my previous answers into four complete sentences for readability purposes (one long sentence may fatigue readers, making it difficult to follow my points).

Teachers constructed their practices through three main processes. First, they translated their preservice learning into practice, a process of contextual negotiation that resulted in different enactments based on the setting. They also negotiated with students, processes by which teachers established relationships and classroom dynamics. Finally, they engaged in identity-formation processes, which were constructed in relation to their students, contexts, and their emerging practices.

As the example above shows, I begin with a high-level summary sentence that scaffolds for the reader by cuing them that I am going to be talking about three processes. In the sentence, I also use signaling language that gestures toward my question—that is, I let the reader know I am answering how "teachers constructed their practices." However, I can't stop at that sentence, because there's no detail about *what* those processes entailed. It would be too vague. So, I then offer three sentences, each of which briefly define one of the three processes. As I offer more details about the processes, I further scaffold so the reader can follow along with my sequencing transitions: *first, also, finally.*

Next, you will need to create the major theme assertions (or assertions for the major sections of whatever organizational schema you have created). Let's continue with the same example. I now need to create an assertion for each of my findings, the three processes described above. Each of these sentences will introduce and offer a high-level summary of the finding. In fact, this summary is also the beginning of the argument I will make in this section (which I will have to build out to show my reasoning, or the analysis, and offer evidence to support it). You will also continue to develop smaller claims at the paragraph level, which I will address in the next section when I discuss analytic explanation.

Read the assertions below. Can you identify the summary and argument I'm making in each?

Theme 1 Assertion: Teachers translated their preprofessional learning into practice, negotiating this knowledge with the elements and conditions of their particular contexts. While elements of their preservice learning were visible, the contextual negotiations resulted in hybrid, situated enactments of practice across settings.

Theme 2 Assertion: Teachers engaged in negotiations with students to meet their needs and secure their participation, which created situated relational dynamics that enormously impacted their enactment of practice.

Theme 3 Assertion: Teachers, together with their contexts, negotiations with students, and practice translations, collectively and continuously constructed their teacher-identities. This relational process produced situated, fluid identities which could change from class to class and shaped their ongoing construction of practice.

Each assertion above provides both a summary of the claim, which is descriptive; and an argument, which communicates the interpretive analysis. I begin each of the three assertions with a descriptive statement of the process. This, by itself, is not sufficient—I also need to add an argument that shows my original meaning-making. In the first assertion, for example, my argument is that the teacher, students, and context interacted to produce situated translations of practice, which constituted *hybridities*. These hybridities did contain elements of teachers' preprofessional learning, but because they were actively negotiated between the teacher and other human and nonhuman factors, it was not in a "pure" form, but a mutated one. Then I argue that teachers' negotiations with students created class dynamics specific to each context, which in turn shaped their translation of preservice learning into practice. Finally, the argument of my third assertion is multifaceted: I claim that the identity-construction process is relational, and it produces teacher subjectivities which are specific to certain contexts, changeable, and influence their translations into practice.

Now it's your turn to create assertions for the developing themes or big ideas from your study.

ACTIVITY 4. THEME ASSERTIONS	
Record your themes or big ideas from your dissertation findings chapter in the lefthand column. Then, create an overall assertion followed by assertions for each of your themes (or the sections of your organizational schema). ▪ Use the research question activity as a scaffold to help you get started, but make sure to edit it into complete sentences. For assertions that are more than one sentence, don't forget to scaffold for your reader with signaling language and sequencing transitions.	
Overall Assertion (High Level Summary of All Findings)	
Theme/Big Idea	**Assertion**

8.4 Providing Evidence and Analytic Explanation

Each main assertion (i.e., what you came up with in Activity 4) should be broken down into smaller claims with their own subsections (i.e., chunk them out for your reader). Once you have this overall structure in place, it's time to begin fleshing the assertions/claims out into paragraphs, which will be constructed using evidence and analytic explanation.

Remember back in chapter three, when we discussed arguments and their three parts (claim, explanation, evidence)? Each assertion/claim that you make is essentially an argument; that means each should always be accompanied by sufficient evidence and analytic explanation to convince the reader of your work that the assertions/claims you made are trustworthy. Below I discuss these two language features of the findings chapter: sufficient evidence and analytic explanation.

Sufficient Evidence

To support the assertions signaling your key findings, you need to provide sufficient and compelling evidence from your data analysis that validates and illustrates those main ideas. Evidence could encompass quotes, photos, results of statistical analyses, summarized examples, vignettes, or other brief fragments of data that directly back up an assertion or smaller claim you have made.

I find it helpful to think about using evidence as a method of persuasion. You are trying to persuade your reader of multiple things in your dissertation: that a problem that needs to be addressed exists; that the phenomena need to be studied to generate knowledge to address that problem; and that your analysis includes key ideas that are important for understanding the phenomena/problem. To achieve the latter, a central theme in this chapter of this book, your findings need to be convincing. This requires compelling evidence that illustrates the claims.

At this stage in your writing, keep in mind the purpose of using evidence is *to support and illustrate.* The centerpiece of your findings is your assertions/claims and original interpretation. Your evidence is essential, because it serves to back up those assertions, claims, and interpretations, but it is in a supporting role. Early on in the writing process, one pattern I often see among doctoral students is that of offering multiple pieces of raw or unanalyzed data in a row (e.g., several quotes without accompanying explanation). This can fatigue the reader, who then would be more likely to miss your point. A more engaging and effective approach for each assertion/claim is to carefully review the supporting evidence and choose the most vivid excerpts that clearly illustrate your points.

Two common ways to use evidence are exemplars and vignettes.

Exemplars are powerful quotes or other data excerpts that demonstrate your big ideas. Typically, exemplars are identified through coding and memoing, and therefore come directly from your data.

Vignettes are constructed from raw data, but are pieced together and narrated by the researcher, rather than "found." Both strategies for using evidence illustrate and support your claims, and also provide rich description for your readers.

Let's examine at an exemplar taken from my own work.

> "We are just like, really dumbfounded by the fact that—you think you have made a good breakthrough, and not that it's for naught, because then you might have changed a couple students minds, but in the grand scheme of it, you feel like, it's a life size board game of like, Chutes and Ladders or something. Where like, you are never going to make it to a hundred, because there's a damn slide right there!" *(Mauro, Exit Interview, January 2013)*

This exemplar—a quote from an interview with one of my study participants—illustrates and supports previous claims I have made: 1) teaching is a co-construction between teacher and student, 2) students have agency in this interaction, and 3) teaching is not a linear process. It is also a compelling example—the participant's frustration jumps off the page, and he uses a metaphor of a board game familiar to many that paints a very vivid picture.

More often, however, you will construct examples through a blend of direct quotes and your own descriptive narration. For example, Ansari (2021) used transcripts of talk during an elementary science lesson, along with field notes she had taken during the observation, to construct the example shown below. Note that to illustrate how the teacher-participant translated an element of the professional development program into practice, the researcher wove together her own observations with a quote from the teacher-participant. In so doing, she captured some of the participant's voice while narrating and providing context (for example, noting that the groups got different materials and were given autonomy to decide what to do with them). Blending her own commentary with a quote also allowed the researcher to offer some foreshadowing for the analysis still to come (by, for example, referencing how the teacher's approach related to the practices learned in the PD program).

> Each group had different materials [and were] able to choose how they wanted to explore with them—a variation of the more structured [PD Program] approach where students' creation of their own investigations came after they had had the opportunity to build more collective knowledge through exploration with the same materials, followed by recording and sharing their data and ideas. She launched the students by saying, "Your group is going to be using the cradle. And they're going to be talking about how they could change the motion and the forces with the cradle...And I'm going to give some coins to the other tables who need coins...because they said maybe that would change the motion" (Lesson, Y1). After this, Patty provided little guidance, turning over all decision-making to the students as they set off to construct their understanding of force and motion. *(Ansari, 2021, p. 253-254)*

Below is a different example from my own research, which contains both researcher-narrated summary and raw data. Notice that although I narrate this story to fill in gaps and provide holistic understanding for the reader, my commentary remains descriptive (not interpretive—or at least not yet).

> June described attending an IEP meeting for Bobby, who had shared with her and his case manager his fervent desire to become a veterinarian. June told me that during the meeting, at which Bobby was present, the case manager implied he would not be capable of attending veterinary school and instead should set his sights on a related, but less rigorous path, such as a veterinary technician. She quoted the case manager as saying to the adults in attendance, "I explained [to Bobby] that there's going to be a lot of science, and so we were thinking about what kind of other technical areas he could go into." June was furious that the case manager and other adults were apparently in agreement that Bobby's dream was futile given his disability. She seethed, "[Bobby] looked so depressed! I was so angry! ...Are you really going to kill the one kid who wants to study science?...Shut the hell up!" June took Bobby aside after the meeting and assured him that he could, indeed, study biology in college and become a veterinarian if he set his mind to it and worked hard. She told him, "You can definitely be a biology major. Don't let anyone tell you (that) you can't do it. It's going to be hard, but you can do it." To assist Bobby in building a noteworthy resume for college applications, she helped him identify and apply for summer internships, wrote letters of recommendation for him, and connected him with a teacher in the school who worked for a summer science program at a local museum. *(Strom, 2014, pp. 256-257).*

This vignette illustrates and supports my finding that June, a participant in my study, built relationships with her students by advocating for them, actively demonstrating that she cared for and believed they were capable of success (which was part of my larger argument about why June was successful as a first-year teacher with a challenging student population). In addition to all of this, the raw data I incorporated that supports my researcher-generated summary also shows how June was an advocate for her students and cared deeply for them.

Evidence can also come in the form of an example completely summarized by the researcher. In these cases, the example originates from the data collected by the researcher, but instead of communicating it through direct quotes, the researcher provides a recap in their own words. You may use this strategy to describe evidence from observations that you have conducted, or the example might need to be summarized for brevity. Or, you may just want to vary the way you are presenting evidence so your writing doesn't begin to sound too repetitive.

Let's look at an example of researcher summary of evidence, which comes from another of my former advisees. Read the example below, which is followed by my interpretation.

> Charlie told us about an activity that she had led in her math class in which students create an individual budget and then tally up a month's "typical" expenses against the budget. Charlie was proud of the activity because it could be individualized to each student (they got to select what "packages" to "buy" for food and hygiene, for example) and as such was inclusive. However, during the class, a student of color pointed out to her that none of the hygiene "packages" had items for textured hair-care products. During this moment, Charlie experienced intense emotions, but took a breath and acknowledged that her student was correct, choosing to address the exclusivity of the activity with the whole class and apologized for her oversight. *(SchlaeGuada, 2022, p. 218)*

SchlaeGuada (2022) offered the summary above to demonstrate the ways one of their participants engaged in critical reflection "*in the moment*" (p. 217-218). In this case, the participant shared the story during a collaborative discussion with several other participants, who also chimed in to offer their thoughts. The transcribed comments would have been too lengthy to include, so the researcher made a practical decision to summarize the example in their own words.

ACTIVITY 5. ANALYZING FINDINGS CLAIMS AND EVIDENCE

Read the excerpt below (Strom, 2014, p. 239-240). What paragraph-level claims are made? What evidence is presented to support them?

As she indicated in her first interview and subsequent lesson debriefs, June believed that many of her students had internalized the label of "special needs" and lacked confidence in their academic abilities, which often resulted in "shutting down" or refusing to engage in particular academic tasks. I observed that such student response was particularly acute during summative or "high stakes" assessments. When a student "shut down," June simply tried to find other ways to help him or her, either by modifying the section of the exam with which the student was struggling, rephrasing her questions, or further scaffolding his or her work in some way. For example, when students were unable to complete a section of a formal assessment that asked for the definition of terms relating to the scientific method, June wrote the definitions on the paper and asked them to match the word to their definitions. On a portion of the previously described performance assessment, a student balked at writing a detailed answer to a prompt that asked for a description of how a media clip about euthanasia related to bioethics. In the lesson debrief following the interaction, June theorized that the student's refusal stemmed not from lack of knowledge but from lack of confidence in his ability to express himself in writing. To help the student, June asked him to explain the answer verbally while she wrote it down. Describing the interaction with the student, June shared,

> I said, 'Can you give me more...' And he was like, 'I can't.' And I was like, 'What if you tell me, and I write it?' And he's like, 'OK.' And this is word for word what he said, and I'm not even kidding: 'There is no

ACTIVITY 5. ANALYZING FINDINGS CLAIMS (CONT.)

cure. He can't move anything on his body. If he lives, he will suffer more. But if he dies he will be in peace with no pain. He should be allowed to die.' And I looked at him, and I was like... 'What you said was beautiful.' And he was like, 'Really?' And I was like, 'Yeah... 'We'll do this, but let's work on bits and pieces of getting you to be able to express your thoughts.' And he was like, 'OK,' and I saw emotion from him, like sincere emotion, for the first time.

Analytic Explanation

So far, we've examined use of evidence and *descriptive* commentary—that is, researcher narration focusing on articulating what is happening in the quote. However, descriptive commentary is not enough—your quotes or other supporting data fragments also need to be integrated into a larger discussion that frames and explains the evidence you present with your own original meaning-making. I refer to this as "analytic explanation."

Analytic explanation refers to explanations, interpretations, connections, and/or details that come from *your original analysis.* Analytic explanation typically accompanies smaller claims, like those at the section and paragraph level, rather than the main assertions that frame entire themes and their subsections.

When writing up findings, you will use analytic explanation in two main ways: unpacking claims to show your reasoning and interpreting/discussing evidence. I discuss these next.

Unpacking a Paragraph-Level Claim

Analytic explanation that unpacks a paragraph-level claim (i.e., a micro-level declarative statement) provides related, detailed discussion to show the reasoning that supports the claim.

For example, in her study of the ways science teachers enacted professional development (PD), Ansari (2021, p. 84-85) made a broad claim in her findings section that "teachers interpret their experiences in PD through their unique lens of background experiences, previous knowledge, and beliefs, and then make sense of their learning as they begin to translate that learning into practice within their specific school and classroom contexts." She went on to detail multiple ways the teachers in her study interpreted ideas and practices from a professional development program and translated them into their specific settings. For instance, one teacher, Heidi, demonstrated five different interpretations of learning from the PD program. For each of these interpretations, the researcher offered paragraph-level claims along with analytic explanation and evidence.

The excerpt below illustrates how Ansari presented one of those interpretations regarding vocabulary instruction.

> Although Heidi worked to align her practice with [program]'s goal of prioritizing students' development of conceptual understanding in their own words, instead of memorizing vocabulary, her practices demonstrated only a partial shift in this area. While she actively refrained from front-loading vocabulary, Heidi still identified student success in science learning as using academic vocabulary to define terms and express understanding. During the lesson, Heidi did not pre-teach vocabulary or provide specific definitions; nor did she prioritize vvocabulary over concepts during discussions, trying instead to draw out students' conceptual understanding of the phenomenon. As students described an academic concept or term in their own words, Heidi would casually share an academic term with the students, which demonstrates her interpretation of the "just-in-time" introduction of terms. While the PD facilitators generally introduced conceptual terms later in the flow of a unit, after students built an understanding of the concepts, Heidi instead used the opportunity to begin introducing academic terminology during the first lesson, thereby demonstrating a somewhat of a hybrid enactment of her PD learning. *(Ansari, 2021, p. 84-85)*

Above, Ansari (2021) makes a paragraph-level claim that, although Heidi showed some change in terms of her vocabulary-related instructional practices, she did not fully make the shift the program advocated for. Following this sentence, Ansari offers more specificity in terms of what that partial shift looked like: she had shifted one aspect of practice (refraining from not "*front-loading*" vocabulary) but had not shifted her mindset—she understood the end goal to be using academic vocabulary to define/discuss phenomena. She continues by offering evidence in the form of a researcher-summarized example from the lesson, describing how she moved toward conceptual understanding and use of one of the PD strategies she learned (providing terms "*just in time*," or the moment students need them). She then adds more analytic commentary to show how the shift was partial, describing the original practice and Heidi's interpretation, which Ansari suggests amounts to a hybridized version of the practice in question.

Read the next example, below, drawn from my own work. What is the paragraph-level claim, and how does the evidence support it? In what ways does the researcher add commentary and details that scaffolds the reader's understanding of the quote and its relevance for the claim?

> ...Many of Bruce's students showed enthusiasm, excitement, and curiosity about physics concepts. During demonstrations of phenomena, students clamored to be chosen as Bruce's assistant, literally jumping out of their seats to be able to shoot a Nerf gun alongside Bruce or otherwise help him create a visualization of a concept. Student enthusiasm for Bruce's physics class was also apparent from comments that often peppered lessons: "I love this class!" "I love physics!" or in response to an announcement about an upcoming lab, "Yay! I love labs!" *(Strom, 2014, p. 192)*

In the excerpt above, I make a paragraph-level claim about the eagerness of a group of students in relation to the instruction of Bruce, one of the participants in my study. I then provide researcher-summarized support for the claim by describing how the students leapt out of their seats to be Bruce's "*assistant*" (the "*leaping,*" in this case, is an indicator of students' excitement to participate). I follow this up with quotes from the students verbally expressing their enthusiasm. Notice here the language that I use to introduce the quote, and the ways that it scaffolds the quote for the reader: "*Student enthusiasm for Bruce's class was also apparent from comments that often peppered lessons...*" With this added commentary, I connect the claim (students were enthusiastic) to a brief explanation of the quote (things students often said in class). The first two quotes are about the class and subject itself, but I add a brief explanation prior to the last student quote both to make sure that the reader knows the context and to provide another example of excitement in connection to a particular activity (a lab) which was different from the one previously cited (Bruce's demonstrations), thereby showing the robustness of evidence for the paragraph-level claim at the beginning of the paragraph.

Interpreting Evidence

Another way you use analytic explanation is to interpret evidence. In the last section of chapter three, which describes how to use quotes, I discussed the importance of explaining each quote. Those principles apply to evidence as well. Quotes or other raw data do not stand on their own—they are almost never self-explanatory. You always need to introduce and interpret each piece of evidence for the reader, letting them know what is important about it, what it illustrates, or anything else that is significant. Bringing examples from data without accompanying explanation and connection to the claims being made puts the burden of interpretation on the reader—and that's *your* job!

Consider the following quote, which Dolid (2021) used to support a claim regarding tensions that arose from discussions of language during a middle school English Language Arts digital literacy project. What does it mean? How does it show tensions with language?

> Ms. Atsila shared, "And then thinking about you know, because language, what we use at home...can be a part of creating our sense of home. And even if you only speak English, at home, think about the way that you speak English at home, is it the same as at school? *(Dolid, 2021, p. 133)*

Now let's look at the quote accompanied by the researcher's interpretation. How does Dolid provide guidance and additional context for the reader to understand the purpose of his using that quote? Did it change or expand your understanding of the original quote?

> ...Ms. Atsila shared:
>
> > And then thinking about you know, because language, what we use at home...can be a part of creating our sense of home. And even if you only speak English, at home, think about the way that you speak English at home, is it the same as at school?

> In this framing to students, Ms. Atsila conceptualized language use as switching based on place, reinforcing the very familiar binary of home language and school language. At the same time, her perspective about home language use creating a sense of home was in alignment with situated, sociocultural notions of language use. At once, her statement reveals the competing forces simultaneously at work: we intended to make the classroom a place where language use was not restricted to school based forms, but at the same time recognized the realities that school and home language use might not match. *(Dolid, 2021, p. 133)*

As you can see in the revised paragraph, the added analysis offers a specific interpretation that a reader would probably not be able to make themselves (or at least not in that detail or depth).

Rather than leaving the reader to their own devices to determine the connection betwen the quote and tensions with language, Dolid actively guides the reader to build complex understanding of pedagogical change at work. He explains that, simultaneously, Ms. Atsila's statement reinforces a dualism (home/school language) while also signaling a constructivist view of languge. Not only is the added analysis supportive of helping the reader understand the main points, but it also brings out the researcher's voice and their original analysis (which, remember, is one of the key characteristics of high quality doctoral writing).

Let's examine another excerpt, drawn from Schlaeguada (2022). As you read, attend to the following: how would you describe the ways the researcher interprets the quotes for the reader?

> For example, Ellen discussed how her whiteness and queerness both evolve and impact each other, but also shared her uncertainty about wanting to further explore her identity by helping others in that process of coming into her identities: "The other place that I'm also in that stage in being gay... Where can I go with that? I'm out, I'm happy, I love my life, and I need to do something. I need to help more people" (interview, Ellen). Explaining the tension she feels with both of her identities, she continued, "I'm sort of... battling it with both places, like, being white and being gay... where am I going to do that?" In Ellen's understanding, being white and queer have been very separate in her mind and finding ways to work on/engage in both ways of learning about her identity have been difficult for her although she does want to develop both of her identities more. *(Schlaeguada, 2022, p. 206)*

In the first quote, the researcher foregrounds their interpretation of the participant's quote, making it clear to the reader that they are grappling with wanting to help others at the intersection of whiteness and queerness. Schlaeguada then adds more evidence to demonstrate this tension, making sure to introduce the evidence by directly stating the quote's relevance to their point ("explaining the tension she feels with both her identities...").

The researcher then concludes the paragraph by further interpretation, describing Ellen's binary understanding of whiteness and queerness and the participant's resulting struggles to reconcile the two identities.

At times, you may only need a brief introduction to drive home the point of the quote or other evidence, especially if it is part of a larger integrated discussion supporting the same claim. For instance, the example below from Ansari (2021) shows a quote with a brief description of the content to help guide the reader. As you read the sentence, consider the following: What information does the researcher include in the introduction? How does it provide guidance for the reader in terms of how to understand the quote?

> Early in the lesson, one student expressed her frustration, sharing, "I just don't know what's going to happen, what's supposed to happen". *(Ansari, 2021, p. 83)*

ACTIVITY 6: EVIDENCE AND ANALYTIC EXPLANATION

Read the example.

- **Can you identify the paragraph-level claims?**
- **What evidence is presented? How does the evidence support the claims made?**
- **What kinds of analytic explanation is included? In what ways does it help the reader to understand the evidence and/or interpret it?**

As June spent more time with her students, she began differentiating her negotiation strategies, learning that what worked with one student did not necessarily work with another. Some students responded consistently to a particular incentive or strategy, and thus she could rely on a specific tactic to work the majority of the time. By way of example, June explained, "[Student's name] responds really well to feeling successful. So if she feels that she's doing a great job, or that she's really smart, she'll keep pushing herself." When working with this student, June would continually remind her how well she was doing during class activities. She also maintained frequent contact with her mother, texting her often about the student's accomplishments. Other students were not as predictable, but she used her knowledge of them to determine a course of action. For example, she recognized that another student's needed to be in constant motion, and modified her instructional plans accordingly. During a class exploring the structure of water molecules, June named the student her assistant, directing him to draw accompanying visuals for the lesson and make appropriate notations on the board throughout the class. Explaining her thinking with regard to engaging the student in the learning activity, June articulated, "He can't help it, he needs to be moving…so who did I have at the board the entire time? [Student's name]. 'Can you write this, can you draw this? Can you do this?'" As June learned more about her students' needs and strengths, she was able to individualize her teaching strategies for them and achieved higher rates of participation in instruction, which in turn supported her enactment of practices that were learner-centered and involved cognitively challenging tasks, like scientific reasoning.
(Strom, 2014, 249-250)

ACTIVITY 7. BUILDING OUT PARAGRAPH-LEVEL CLAIMS, EVIDENCE, AND ANALYTIC EXPLANATION
Choose one subtheme or smaller section from your study to build out. ▪ Take one key idea from that subtheme/section and turn it into a paragraph-level claim. ▪ Bullet out your thoughts on what kind of unpacking needs to happen for your reader to understand the claim. ▪ Add evidence that supports the claim. ▪ Bullet out an interpretation of the evidence that shows how it supports the claim.
Sub-theme: **Paragraph-level claim:**
Analytic Explanation - Unpacking:
Evidence:
Analytic Explanation - Interpretation:

8.5 Demonstrating Trustworthiness

As mentioned in the beginning of the chapter, a final purpose of your findings chapter is to convince your reader that what you are reporting is credible, transferable, rigorous, authentic, and important—in other words, that your findings are trustworthy. To consider how we might do that, let's return to our trustworthiness chart from chapter seven (edited below to include only measures relevant to the findings) and examine how these might translate into writing strategies for the findings chapter.

Criterion	Measure(s) to Address Criterion	Trustworthiness Strategies for Findings
Credibility	Triangulating or crystallizing between multiple data sources	Referring to sources of data as you present the evidence; highlight instances of triangulation when possible
	Substantiating evidence that supports my claims	Ensuring that all claims are supported with robust, evidence
Transferability	Providing detailed descriptions of context and participants	Including any necessary contextual information (or perhaps a reminder)
	Reporting findings through thick description and explanation, including direct quotes from participants	Ensuring claims are accompanied by analytic explanation and data fragments with enough detail for the reader
Rigor	Providing in-depth examples and evidence to substantiate claims	Ensuring that all claims are supported with robust, detailed evidence and analytic explanation is specific, precise, detailed, and clearly connected to claims
Authenticity	Being transparent about goals, positionality	Using the "I" voice when possible
Contributing to Understanding	Scaffolding readers to follow and clearly understand major arguments and contributions through multiple linguistic strategies	During revisions, using signaling language to point out major ideas and other scaffolding moves to ensure that the reader can follow your line of thinking

For credibility purposes, triangulation across multiple data sources shows that what you are reporting is, indeed, a theme or pattern (and therefore your claim is credible). To emphasize points that have been triangulated across multiple data sources, refer explicitly to the data sources and the ways that the evidence was confirmed (or expanded, or problematized, and so on) through triangulation with additional sources.

For example, in an interview study with ten participants, you might add this statement to your claim: "*Eight out of the ten participants reported in their interviews that...*" Or, for a case study where you have triangulated a pattern of deficit thinking toward multilingual learners (MLLs) across different data sources, you might comment as part of your analytic interpretation: "*This deficit thinking was apparent in the participant's interactions and dialogue with MLLs during observations, and reinforced by statements he made in the two semi-structured interviews about the abilities of his MLL students.*"

In addition to triangulation, sufficient evidence supporting your claims is a credibility criterion, and overlaps as a measure of rigor. We have already discussed this in depth earlier in the chapter, so my discussion here will be brief. For these measures of trustworthiness, you need to present compelling evidence; show how it supports the claim; and, in revisions, examine your analytic explanation to ensure that it is specific, precise, and detailed. These latter features also overlap with measures of transferability—the reader needs to be able to judge what from the findings might be relevant for their own contexts, so there needs to be enough "thick description" for them to be able to determine that.

Regarding authenticity, you can find ways to refer to your role as a researcher in the project while writing the findings, which emphasizes accountability for the ways you and your perspectives have shaped the study and its outcomes. One subtle way to do this throughout the presentation of findings is to write from the first-person point of view ("I") when referring to any procedures, data sources, and so on. For example, *"20 classroom observations were conducted"* becomes *"I conducted 20 classroom observations."* (This also converts passive to active voice, which tends to strengthen writing generally). Writing from the "I" voice allows you to insert yourself as an agentic actor in the research process (rather than perpetuate the positivist idea that the researcher can ever be an objective, neutral entity who just "finds" the truth).

Finally, to emphasize the contributions to understanding that your findings make, use scaffolding moves to make your major arguments as clear as possible. Put the major takeaways from your findings in your introduction (the roadmap), with signaling language to point them out. You can also use this strategy as you introduce key ideas in the different sections of your findings. For example: *"In this section I argue two major points. First.... Then...."* Then, make sure that your headings refer to those big ideas for additional support as well as overall coherence.

Finally, use transitions to connect ideas and the broader flow of logic, which will help your reader grasp the relationship of the key ideas and follow your line of thinking overall. I take up these ideas in the next section in more detail.

8.6 Scaffolding Understanding for the Reader

Scaffolding to support your reader's understanding is important throughout the entire dissertation, but it is especially crucial for the findings chapter. You have been immersed in all the details of your participants; you have lived and breathed your data; you know your themes like the back of your hand. That creates a risk of unintentionally making short-cuts in your writing or using vague language. It will make perfect sense to you, because you have deep contextual and background knowledge of the study, but your reader does not, and can easily get lost.

To ensure that does not happen, you can use scaffolding strategies, such as road maps and topic sentences, signaling language, and transitions that communicate the relationships between ideas (see chapter two for a review of these, if needed).

In addition, you want to ensure that you are writing your findings in specific, precise, and detailed ways for optimal clarity (see chapter three for a review of the other "rules" of doctoral level writing).

Often this step will happen in the revision stages. Although of course it would be wonderful to write from the beginning with scaffolds in mind, often the first draft is about getting the ideas on paper and working through the logic flow. Give yourself permission to come back after you have the content and organization down and can then concentrate on embedding supports to help your reader follow along.

Let's take a behind-the-scenes look at revising a paragraph to better scaffold the integrated analytic explanation for readers.

Read the paragraph below, which comes from work by one of my former students (for the final product, see Dolid, 2021). Identify areas where scaffolds for the reader might be needed. Then, examine the revised excerpt that follows on the next page.

In a slightly different type of analytical thinking, all three students were able to discuss the relationship between modes and the relationship to the audience. They could all identify the strength and limitations of the linguistic versus the aural mode. For example, Jasmine Elf shared:

> Using books vs. movies as an example, books (or words) leave things up to the reader's imagination. The reader imagines what the characters look like, how they sound, how the setting appears. Movies (or sounds and pictures, but I'm mainly going for sound), however, give the viewer all of the information. The movies give the specifics to how these characters sound, how the setting is, and so forth. It is the same with the soundscape, since soundscapes were able to give more accurate and specific descriptions of the sounds, as opposed to words leaving it up to the reader.

Jasmine is able to take up the type of thinking we practiced during class sessions, examining the strengths and limitations of one mode versus another. In this case, she assesses how sound can leave less ambiguity, while alphabetic printed text might leave more to the audience's interpretation. This analytical and evaluative reflection demonstrates the application of an authorial decision making about what she would represent, how she might represent it, and how it might affect the meaning of the work.

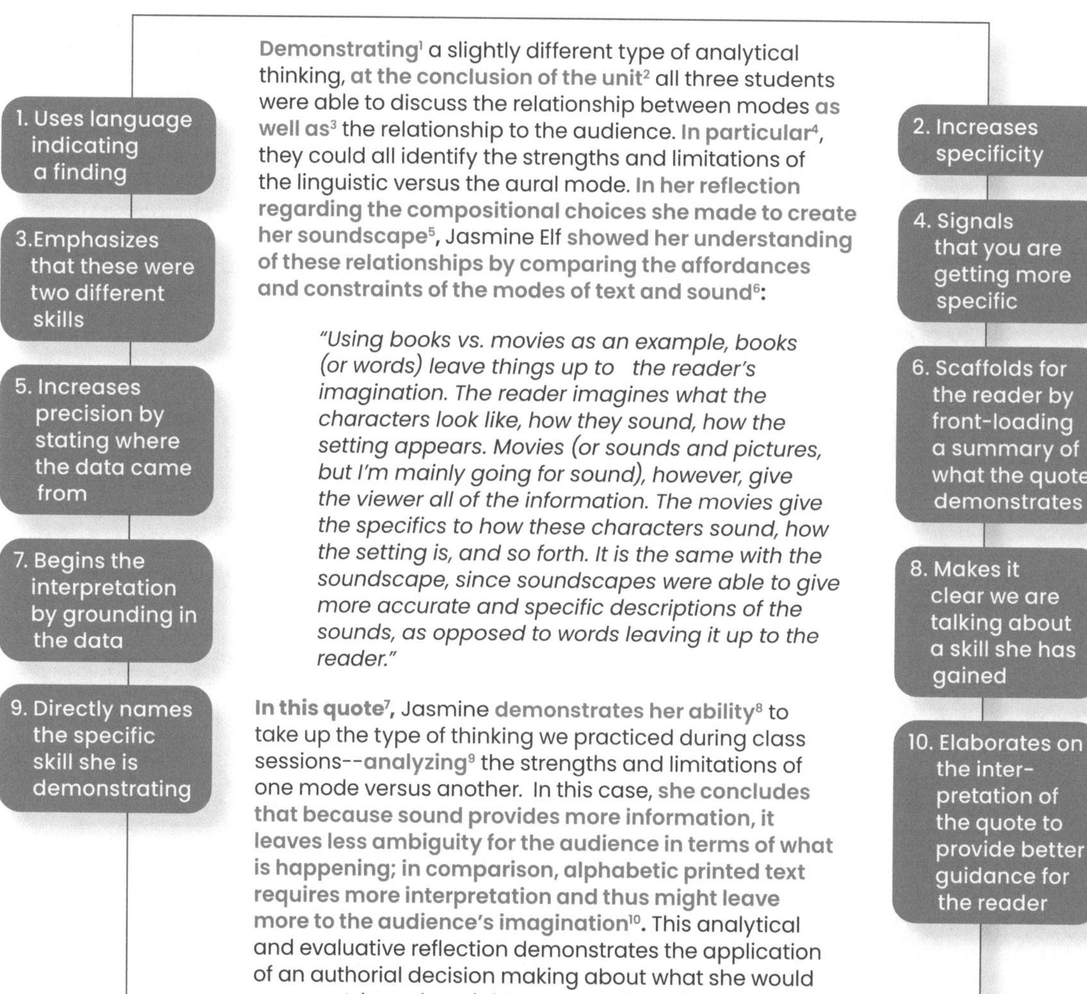

Figure 8.4: Annotated findings paragraph revision

In the revised paragraph (Figure 8.4), signaling language is used to clearly state that what is to follow will *demonstrate* something—that is, it backs up a claim—and the reader's understanding of the quote is scaffolded prior to presenting it. A transition is added to the sentence directly following the quote that both serves as signaling language ("Dear Reader, I am talking about the data I just presented!") and a bridge to keep the reader following your line of thinking. More specificity is added throughout (for example, clarifying when the activity took place and from which data source this student quote was drawn).

Finally, additional elaboration is added to the analytic explanation following the quote, thereby providing the reader with more details to ease the burden of meaning-making. Remember, you need to completely interpret the quote for the reader with enough detail to allow them to see what you see. Often, students provide high level summaries without enough elaboration for the reader to understand on the first pass. Without that support, the reader must carefully examine the quote multiple times and make inferences themselves about how the evidence provided demonstrates the claim being made about it. Instead, you need to directly point back to the quote with signaling language, and explicitly show the reader what it is about the pieces of the quote that support the claim you are making, with enough details that they can enter into it with you.

Let's look at a second example that revises a paragraph of findings to purposefully scaffold for the reader. In this example, I worked with my former student (see Nguyen, 2021 for final product) to bring out the claim as an organizational tool, and revise using it as a frame for the subsequent statements, along with increasing the specificity and details, and adding transitions.

Original text:

David's impressions of James Logan High School community is positive. He observed that students at the school are open to interactions with each other. David noted that his socialization with his peers to a certain extent have influenced his values, attitude, and behavior. According to David, adjusting to high school mainstream culture while interacting with students, faculty and staff at James Logan High School has helped him have a positive outlook about school and feel a sense of belonging. He is able to "talk to other students compared to others places where he's seen" limited willingness to be welcoming. David expressed that the faculty at the school have created a positive school community because they are intentional in establishing safe spaces for David and other students to check-in. As a result, the social effect has influenced David's resilience.

In the above paragraph, my former student begins with an overall claim about David's positive impressions of his school community. She then moves into a discussion of students, his interactions with them, and how those have affected him. The next sentence makes another claim about David's outlook and sense of belonging, this time including students as well as staff and faculty. She then adds a quote that provides evidence regarding his positive interactions with students. Following this illustration, she moves on to discuss the ways that faculty members have created a positive school community. She concludes the paragraph with sentence that connects this "social effect" to David's development of resilience.

The student and I worked to revise the paragraph into a logical sequence with a framing summative claim, adding other scaffolds along the way. As you read the paragraph below, examine the changes from the original, above. What scaffolding strategies do the changes draw on?

According to David, interacting with students, faculty, and staff at James Logan High School has helped him have a positive outlook about school and feel a sense of belonging as he adjusts to high school mainstream culture in the U.S.	*Overall claim for the paragraph cues the reader that the paragraph will discuss 1) students, staff, and faculty, and 2) how they influenced David*
His socialization with his peers has influenced his values, attitude, and behavior. He is able to "talk to other students, compared to other places where he's seen" limited willingness to be welcoming.	***Building out the first part of the claim (students), with supporting evidence***
In addition to other students, David expressed that the faculty at the school have created a positive school community because they are intentional in establishing safe spaces for David and other students to check-in. Teachers, counselors and administration purposefully conduct outreach to establish healthy forms of communication with David and other students to support them. In addition, David noted that "counselors and principals are not so strict to the point where students just do not want to be at school," which has helped to create a positive schooling experience for him.	*Building out the second part of the claim (faculty and staff), with supporting evidence*
The social interactions with his peers and the safe community established by school personnel seem to have increased David's resilience, which in turn helps with his mental wellness.	***Summary with connection to main research question to show that this is part of the "answer"***

Figure 8.5: Annotated revision of findings

ACTIVITY 8. BUILDING OUT A SECTION OF THE FINDINGS

Using the graphic organizer from the last section, edit your paragraph level claim, evidence provided, and analytic explanation given into paragraph form.

Once you have a draft, go back and identify places where you need more specificity, precision, details, and/or elaboration for the reader to be able to follow along. Then, examine the draft again to determine where you can add signaling language and transitions that make clear the relationships between ideas.

Writing the Introduction

A final way to scaffold for your reader is by providing an introduction with a road map that familiarizes the reader with the structure of the chapter and summarizes big ideas. Generally, the introduction to findings should include:

- A high-level summary of the key outcomes of your analysis; and
- A summary of the structure of the chapter that lets the reader know how the findings are organized.

There are also other elements that might be included depending on your study. For example, you may need to provide contextual information to help the reader make sense of your analysis. You might also want to include your research questions to remind your reader of them—or restate the objectives of your project. Whether you include these really depends on your chair, so be sure to consult with them.

Let's take a look at a sample introduction to the findings.

> To demonstrate the complexity of putting preservice learning into practice during first-year teaching, I present the case of Mauro, who taught eleventh and twelfth grade earth science and ninth grade environmental science in the same urban high school where he completed his NUTR residency year. The practices Mauro enacted in these classes were strikingly different. Within his earth science classes, Mauro was able to successfully enact key ideas from his preservice learning, including practices of problem posing and experiential, small-group activities. In contrast, his environmental science classes were more likely to be characterized by teacher-led, whole-class instruction, ideas that were contradictory of his pre-professional preparation. In developing the case, I first describe student-related factors operating in Mauro's two classes, detailing the ways he negotiated with his upperclassmen and freshmen to engage them in learner-centered instruction (a central emphasis of his teacher preparation curriculum) and how student responses to those negotiations influenced his teaching. I then turn to contextual factors in his two classes, examining how they constrained or enabled Mauro in constructing practices consistent with his pre-professional learning. *(Strom, 2015, p. 326)*

ACTIVITY 9.1. GENERATING TEXT FOR YOUR FINDINGS INTRODUCTION	
Use the organizer below to draft out your big ideas/aha's and a roadmap.	
Major Ideas/Aha's: Bullet out the major takeaways of your findings as a whole	
Road Map: Bullet out the headings of your findings schema, with brief explanations	

ACTIVITY 9.2. CRAFTING A COHESIVE FINDINGS INTRODUCTION
Edit your work from above organizer into a 1-2 paragraph introduction to your findings. Don't forget transitions!

Conclusion

In this chapter, we discussed how to build out the findings chapter (also known as the data or results chapter) of your dissertation. "The findings" refers to *what* you "found," or the big ideas/themes you constructed from your data analysis. We discussed the following major points:

1. To ***communicate your findings*** effectively, create an overarching schema to organize your chapter. Although most take a thematic approach, the findings can be organized in different ways depending on the audience, the methodology, and the aims of the researcher/author.

2. Your findings ***answer your research questions***. While not providing *the* definitive answer, your main ideas (themes) of your findings chapter should collectively represent your "answer" to the research questions.

3. For each finding, you need to generate an ***assertion*** or interpretive claim. Each theme will also have a main assertion (that may be unpacked into sub-themes with their own assertions). These assertions will then become the guiding statements for the section and topic sentences for the subsections.

4. As you build out your findings sections, you need to provide ***sufficient and compelling evidence*** from your data analysis that validates and illustrates the main ideas.

5. All claims and evidence must be accompanied by ***analytic explanation***, or reasoning, interpretations, connections, and/or details that come from your original analysis.

6. You also need to show that your findings are ***trustworthy***, which means showing how you put into practice the trustworthiness strategies you named in the methodology chapter.

7. You can use ***scaffolding strategies*** to support your reader to understand the main points of your findings. Use road maps and topic sentences, signaling language, and transitions that communicate the relationships between ideas; and ensure that you are writing your findings in specific, precise, and detailed ways for optimal clarity.

There is only one more significant part of your dissertation left to write now—you are almost there! Let's move on to chapter nine and close out your study with a strong, compelling discussion of your findings.

The Discussion

Contents

Introduction

This chapter addresses the final chapter of the dissertation (usually chapter five, although it may be different if you have multiple data or findings chapters). Although it is typically referred to as the "discussion chapter," this final portion of your dissertation has two parts—the *discussion* and the *recommendations*. If the findings are the "what" of your study outcomes, the discussion is the "so what" and the recommendations are the "what now." In other words, the discussion offers a conversation about what your findings mean in relation to the bigger picture. The discussion lays out the significance of your project (the *so what*) through major conclusions from your findings, connections to previous studies, and interpretation from your theoretical perspective. The recommendations extend the discussion by describing lessons drawn from the findings and conclusions that offer action steps to make change (the *what now*).

Just like the findings chapter, your discussion will be shaped by your orientations and values, goals of the study, methodology, and agenda as a researcher. This is where your voice can really shine!

While your discussion will be ultimately determined by you and the factors noted above, there *are* some common purposes and corresponding components in discussion chapters across the social sciences. I outline these in the next section.

9.1 Purposes of the Discussion

WARM UP

Imagine that you are presenting your study to a group of practitioners or professionals in your field who do not have a research background.

What points would you highlight in terms of 1) why the findings are important and 2) how findings can concretely inform their work? (Feel free to substitute another stakeholder group for practitioner/ professional.)

When I teach the discussion chapter to students, I often describe it as the "35,000-foot view" or the "aerial view" of the findings. That is, this final chapter entails *a macro-level interpretation* of your findings—what they mean in the larger context of your field/profession. Students often will find it helpful to distinguish between the findings and discussion chapters in this way: your chapter four—or findings chapter—is a description of the *particular* (what happened with your specific set of participants, context, and so on), with an *inward-facing* interpretation (i.e., discussing your analysis in terms of what it means for your participants). Your chapter five—or discussion chapter—is a *broader, outward-facing* interpretation (what your findings mean in the larger context of your field or profession).

As you offer that broader discussion, you will need to meet several objectives (see the figure below). First, you need to offer some conclusions based on your findings, which includes summarizing the "answer(s)" to your research question(s) and discussing the significance of your outcomes. Next, you need to discuss your findings in connection to other research (how does it compare with other studies that have been done in this area?). You also will discuss your findings through your theoretical lens (when I look at my findings from this perspective, what understandings does that yield?).

After that, you will articulate recommendations that flow from your findings (given what I found, what should we do now?). In this section, you will describe what the findings mean for particular milieus of your field (policy, practice, research) and/or groups of stakeholders connected to your topic. You'll also suggest actionable steps that specific groups can take to change things. The last part of the discussion chapter is your conclusion, which you will use to remind the reader of the most important ideas, outcomes, and contributions of your study.

PURPOSES OF THE DISCUSSION	
DRAW CONCLUSIONS	Explain the "so what" in terms of how your findings answer the research question(s) guiding your study and show how they are significant in relation to broader contexts.
CONNECT TO EXTANT RESEARCH	Discuss how the outcomes of the project support, extend, conflict with, or complexify previous research; articulate the empirical contributions of the study.
THEORIZE THE FINDINGS	Discuss the findings through the lens of your theoretical or conceptual framework; articulate conceptual contributions.
MAKE RECOMMENDATIONS	Contextualize the findings in terms of what lessons they provide for specific groups, with actionable steps to address the original problem driving the study.
CONCLUDE THE DISSERTATION	Highlight key ideas and important contributions of the study.

Figure 9.1: Purposes of the discussion chapter

ACTIVITY 1. DISCUSSION CHAPTER ANALYSIS
Analyze the discussion chapter (typically chapter five) of a selected dissertation to determine how the author addressed the following: ▪ The overall structure or organization of the chapter ▪ The interpretation of findings through the conceptual or theoretical perspective ▪ The discussion of how study findings compare to previous research in this area ▪ Implications or applications for policy, practice, and/or research ▪ Recommendations for action based on findings

9.2 Drawing Conclusions

The first element from Figure 9.1, "Drawing Conclusions," provides an overview of how the findings "answer" your research questions and describes the significance of your findings beyond just the participants in your study (in other words, what the findings mean in relation to broader contexts and issues). To get started, you might ask yourself: "when I think about my findings, what are the big a-has? What is important about them? What lessons do my findings provide that can inform my field?" Take a moment to complete the exercise below to generate thinking around these questions.

ACTIVITY 2. GENERATING IDEAS FOR CONCLUSIONS

List your major findings (i.e., your themes) in the lefthand column. Then, jot down your thoughts on 1) the big a-ha(s) from each finding and 2) what is important about that understanding (or what we can learn from it).

Don't forget that these should be outward facing (e.g., the a-has are relevant for the field, not just your participants).

Finding	What are the big aha's about this finding?	Why is it important? What can we learn?

Once you have drafted your major conclusions, you can develop each into its own discussion section. A good way to tackle this task is to memo or free-write on each conclusion to generate thinking around the big ideas. Once you have some ideas, add an appropriate heading, move the relevant ideas into an outline, and expand them into paragraphs (thereby forming that section of your discussion).

My suggestion is to approach each major conclusion as an argument about the importance of your research in relation to the larger field. That means you can go about drafting it the same way that you would any other argument: with a claim, an explanation, and evidence.

For example, one of my major conclusions from my own dissertation is that the relationship between teacher learning and practice is not a straight line, but rather, is complex and non-linear. This discussion point yielded two claims:

1. All three teachers engaged in three common meaning-making processes (making sense of learning about pedagogy in context, negotiating with students, and developing notions of teacher-self). However, those processes were co-constructed between themselves, students, and context; and as such the "translations" of pedagogical learning were situated and hybrid.
2. This suggests that the process of enacting practice is not one of "transfer" of learning, but rather "translation," where elements of the learning may be visible, but likely will be in morphed form.

Each of these claims would then be built out into paragraphs with appropriate explanation and evidence. However, there's an important caveat for the discussion regarding evidence: make sure that the evidence you provide really does support your conclusion. If you are conducting a smaller-scale study, be careful of overgeneralization (for example, the findings from an in-depth case study of one teacher cannot be applied to all teachers). Think transferability, not generalization, and avoid writing in absolutes. Instead, use more tentative language, with phrases like "*tend to*," "*may contribute to*," "*may partially explain*."

Let's look at an example from Dolid (2021) stemming from his action research project investigating digital literacies' affordances for teaching in culturally sustaining ways. I'm going to ask you to read it two times. The first time, read the excerpt for the structure and content of the argument: what is the claim? How does he explain and support the claim? How does he describe its importance? During your second read, look at the language choices. What do you notice about the way the claim is worded? What about the evidence?

Digital Multimodal Compositions have the potential to open up communicative pathways for students, which are essential for creating opportunities for success for students marginalized through restrictive pedagogical ELA practices. That is, compositions like those featured in

> this unit can help students capture and make meaning from their worlds in ways that might not be possible using print-based or solely linguistic modes. For example, in this study, Jasmine Elf was able to use features of multiple modes to coherently communicate her interest in gaming. She used a neon-green grid background evocative of computer technology in combination with a photo of two action figures from a game she plays, and placed white text on a solid black background to convey the large role that gaming plays in her life. This compositional technique, dubbed "modal matching" (Smith, 2018), brings into focus Jasmine's interest in a way that resonates not just with the mind, but also with the body. This integration and valuing of the mind and body is disruptive of traditional Eurocentric ways of meaning-making (Strom & Viesca, 2021), and indicative of alternative ways of making meaning outside of Whiteness. *(Dolid, 2021, pp. 202-203)*

In the paragraph above, Dolid begins with a claim that the assignment he and his partner teacher used in their co-planned unit, "Digital Multimodal Compositions," can help students, and especially minoritized groups, express themselves. He then offers explanation in the form of a restatement: activities like the one they used in his project expand the range of meaning-making and expression tools available to culturally and linguistically diverse students. To support his claim, Dolid provides an example showing how one student used her multimedia form to effectively communicate about her interests in a different way, one that blended body and mind.

In this paragraph, there are also two places where the significance of this finding is emphasized. First, Dolid stresses that opening up communicative pathways is important for marginalized student success in English language arts settings. Second, he notes that the multimodal media composition enabled his participant to make meaning in holistic ways that disrupted the status quo.

As an important side note, this is just a short excerpt from Dolid's conclusion section. In the full dissertation, the researcher provides additional examples for this claim beyond the one shown here. By itself, just the one example would not adequately support this conclusion.

Now, let's examine some of the linguistic choices made by the researcher.

First, notice Dolid's use of tentative language to avoid overgeneralization. First, he proposes that the tool "*has potential*" to improve student success. He avoids wording indicating that the compositions *will result* in positive academic change (his evidence would not back up such a statement). He also asserts that the compositions "*can help*" marginalized students express themselves "*in ways that might not be possible*" with more traditional formats. In this way, he is suggesting what the finding *might* mean for students, rather than positing a certain truth.

In a second important linguistic move, the researcher *summarizes* the example from chapter four without using direct quotes. No new data should be introduced in the discussion. When you provide evidence here that originates from your findings, that evidence should have already been discussed in your findings chapter, along with adequate illustration that integrates original data to support your meaning-making. For the purposes of your discussion, you should be merely *referring back* to an example you have already provided. Therefore, you do not need to repeat quotes or extensive details from your findings chapter—just what is necessary to explain and support your conclusion.

Now that we've looked at some examples of conclusions, it's your turn to put these ideas into practice.

In the activity below, take on one conclusion section and map it out. You might use your thinking in the previous activity to draft a conclusion, then use the organizer below to generate ideas following the argument structure we reviewed above (*claim, explanation, evidence*). The second part of the activity asks you to take these bullet points and edit them into cohesive paragraphs that will constitute one discussion section.

ACTIVITY 3.1. OUTLINING CONCLUSION PARAGRAPHS		
Use the organizer below to bullet out one conclusion section.		
Main Conclusion:		
Claim 1	Explanation	Evidence
Claim 2	Explanation	Evidence
Claim 3	Explanation	Evidence

ACTIVITY 3.2. OUTLINING CONCLUSION PARAGRAPHS

Draft the work above into one section of your discussion. Remember to use transitions, summarize and refer back to examples from your findings chapter, and avoid absolute language.

9.3 Connecting to Extant Research

ACTIVITY 4. QUICK WRITE

Off the top of your head, how do your findings compare to the major ideas in your literature review? What are the areas of similarity and difference? Are there any ideas that came up that are not included in your literature review?

Another purpose of your discussion is to show the reader how your study findings relate to previous research on the topic. Do your findings mainly align with previous evidence from literature in this area? Do they build on or extend main ideas from published research? Do they complexify or contextualize previous findings? Do they contradict what other researchers have found? Or is the relationship between your study outcomes and established literature mixed (i.e., some of your findings align with it, and others not so much)?

Read the following statements and think through which of them might accurately describe the connection between the extant literature and your findings (or elements of them). Beyond what is listed here, can you think of any other linkages that could explain how your study's outcomes relate to what other researchers have found on the topic?

- My findings *confirm or align with* evidence/outcomes from previous research on this topic.
- My findings *expand on or extend* evidence/outcomes from previous research on this topic.
- My findings *contradict or diverge from* evidence/outcomes from previous research on this topic.
- My findings *offer a more complex/situated perspective of* evidence/outcomes from previous research on this topic.

You might already have several ideas for articulating connections from your study findings to extant literature. But if you aren't sure how they relate, the following process is a good place to start:

1. Go back to the major components of your literature review and the empirical contributions you highlighted in chapter two of your dissertation.
2. Consider these points in light of your findings and the subsequent conclusions you have drawn from them. What kind of relationships do you see?

For example, in the literature review of my own dissertation, the studies I analyzed generally found that beginning teachers 1) struggled to enact the collaborative pedagogies learned in their preparation programs; and 2) tended to throw out this collaborative preservice learning and revert to transmission pedagogies (what some researchers have referred to as a "wash-out effect" with regard to their initial teacher education).

The findings from my study confirmed the evidence regarding pedagogical struggles. However, it did not match previous studies' findings in relation to the so-called "wash-out effect." Quite the opposite: I found that my participants *did* actively bring their learning from their preservice programs into their first-year classrooms. But moving that learning into practice involved many moving pieces: the teachers actively co-constructed their first-year practices with their students, contexts, and so on. Their preservice learning became part of that co-construction, and morphed in relation to their interactions with students, contextual constraints and affordances, and other conditions. So, my conclusion for this finding was that my participants' preservice learning did not disappear or "wash out"—it was enacted in a kind of hybrid form.

In my writing, I would not only articulate the above conclusion—I would also make a direct statement that connects the finding to previous literature. This speaks to yet another goal of your discussion: highlighting what your study is adding to the research literature, or in other words, what new knowledge you are providing the field with. In this case, the finding, and my analysis of it, provides *a more complex perspective* than what has been offered by previous research. That complex perspective is an expansion of our understanding, and as such, it is considered an empirical contribution.

Going back to the example: I also need to provide citations for at least a few of those studies about the "wash-out effect" to indicate which set of literature I'm talking about. If the body of literature is very large, simply pick a few exemplars and use "e.g." at the beginning of the parenthetical citation list to indicate to your reader that these are just a representative sample of a larger group of studies. See the sentence below for an example of how to make such a connection while citing relevant studies.

> Although a body of research exists demonstrating the often minimal impact of teacher education on beginning teachers' actual instruction (e.g., Cochran-Smith & Zeichner, 2005; Grossman, 2008; Zeichner & Tabachnik, 1981; Wideen, Mayer-Smith, & Moon, 1998), my data suggest that attending to the multiple meaning-making processes in which new teachers engage as they develop their early teaching practices can help the research community develop a more textured understanding of the complex relationship between preservice teacher learning and first-year teaching. *(Strom, 2014, p. 273)*

To write up these connections, you can consider two different structures. The simpler approach would be to create a separate section dedicated to examining the ways that your study finding and conclusions connect to the literature and elaborate on how these connections illustrate new empirical contributions. A more complex approach would be an integrated one: rather than a section just for articulating links to previous research, you structure your discussion by conclusion. Then, within each conclusion section, fold in references to show how your points relate to extant literature. I prefer this integrated approach because it feels more connected overall, but you can make that decision together with your chair.

Let's look at an example of a connection to previous literature to analyze the writing choices. As you read, ask yourself the following: what is my claim about the finding? How do I connect this claim to previously published research? How do I support my claim about the finding and its relationship to extant literature?

> In each of the three cases, contextual factors in the setting and the ways in which each teacher interacted with them had some influence on the teaching practices that were produced—a finding corroborated by many studies of first year practice (e.g., Allebone, 2006; Bianchini & Cazavos, 2007; Chubbock, et al., 2001; Fry, 2007; Scherff, 2008). The ways that Bruce related to and interacted with the contextual factors in his setting, for example, profoundly influenced his teaching in the classroom. Bruce began the year in an environment with factors known to hinder new teachers in their enactment of particular types of pedagogy—such as a lack of resources (Castro, Kelly, & Shih, 2010; Starkey, 2010; Tait, 2008), a mandated curriculum (Brashier & Norris, 2008; Ferguson-Patrick, 2011), a dysfunctional school organization (Scherff, 2008) and a lack of consistent and appropriate mentorship (Hargreaves & Jacka, 1995; Hebert & Worthy, 2001; Stanulis, Fallona, & Pearson, 2002). *(Strom, 2014, p. 283-284)*

In the example above, I begin with a claim—that all three teachers' practices were shaped by their contexts. I then state directly how this finding relates to the literature: "*—a finding corroborated by many studies of first year practice.*" I then cite multiple studies that have shown context as a factor influencing beginning teachers' pedagogy, using "e.g." to indicate that these are examples from a larger body of research. I then launch into support for my statements, using one of my participants, Bruce, as an example. I reiterate the claim I made at the beginning of the excerpt, phrased slightly differently and referencing Bruce only: "*The ways that Bruce related to and interacted with the contextual factors in his setting, for example, profoundly influenced his teaching in the classroom.*" In this sentence, notice that I also use a connector phrase ("*for example*") that pulls the idea from the previous sentence through and lets the reader know my intent (providing an example that will illustrate what I mean and support my claim).

In the following sentence, I get more specific with how Bruce's experiences align with previously conducted research, making an assertion that he was affected by "*factors known to hinder new teachers in their enactment of particular types of pedagogy.*" My phrase "*known to hinder...*" refers to a connection to previous literature, but if I stopped here, it would not sufficiently support my claim or fully show the connection to the literature I need to make. To provide concrete illustrations and link them to actual studies, I name several of these factors in turn, again using a connector ("*such as*") that communicates to the reader that these are examples. For each of the factors that I name (like a lack of resources and school dysfunction), I provide references to individual studies whose findings offer evidence showing how the corresponding factor influences new teachers' pedagogies.

As a final point: in the discussion, you want to provide enough elaboration to support your point, but not repeat what's already been said in your chapter four. Therefore, because I have already described these factors in detail in Bruce's section of my findings, I can just mention them to jog the reader's memory—I do not need to discuss them in detail again.

ACTIVITY 5.1. SURFACING FINDINGS–LITERATURE RELATIONSHIPS

Bullet out:

1. **The main ideas from your literature review**
2. **Your main findings**
3. **Your main discussion conclusions**

Looking across these columns, jot down some possible relationships.

Main Ideas from Literature Review	Main findings from Your Study	Your Conclusions	How Do These Compare or Connect?

ACTIVITY 5.2. ARTICULATING SPECIFIC LITERATURE CONNECTIONS

Using the previous activity, distill the specific findings/conclusions that you found connections for. Write brief summaries of your findings/conclusions and in the righthand column, draft out a description of the connection, with matching citations.

Findings/Conclusion	Description of Connection to Extant Literature with Citations

ACTIVITY 5.3. SURFACING EMPIRICAL CONTRIBUTIONS

Looking at the connections you have provided, what are the empirical contributions you can highlight (the new or different understandings your study offers connected to your original data analysis)?

9.4 Theorizing Findings

ACTIVITY 6. FREE-WRITE

What aha's have you had so far that relate to your theoretical framework? How has your theoretical framework, or related concepts, helped you understand your study findings or their significance?

A final task for the discussion portion of your fifth chapter is to theorize your findings. This means you will provide an interpretation of your findings/conclusions through your theoretical/conceptual framework and/or specific related concepts, and point out what this theorization (i.e., theoretical interpretation) adds to our understanding about your topic. You will also need to connect to the bigger picture, articulating how these insights help us think differently or in more nuanced ways about the phenomenon you studied and/or the original problem driving your study. I like to think of this task as "putting theory to work," which entails actively using your theoretical frame as tools for making sense of your findings and conclusions, and then sharing that sense-making.

You may already have ideas for your theoretical interpretations, but if you are not sure yet, a good place to start is to examine your findings and map out some possible theoretical connections (similar to activity 6, above). For example, consider the following. I collaborated with a colleague on a study examining assets-based pedagogies in science classrooms and how these teacher moves affect multilingual student participation (as a proxy for learning). The theoretical frame we used was positioning theory (Harre & Van Langenhove, 1999), which looks at social interactions as events in which people are "positioned" in ways that have consequences for what they are allowed to do and say, because these positions confer particular rights and responsibilities. One of the findings was that the teacher in the study explicitly encouraged students to use their cultural and linguistic resources as they made meaning of scientific phenomena. For example, she let them know they could write in whatever language they liked and could draw their observations if they preferred.

We used positioning theory to theorize this finding in the following way. We proposed that, by offering these multiple ways to engage in the activity and represent their understanding, the teacher legitimized students' resources in relation to science. This, in turn, positioned multilingual students as successful scientific meaning-makers. We then suggested that, as a possible consequence, this positioning could increase multilingual learners' access to meaningful participation in science learning as well as open the possibility of seeing themselves as a "science person" (which research shows is an identity multilingual learners and other youth of color are typically excluded from).

Let's take a pause so you can do some similar thinking.

ACTIVITY 7. THEORETICAL CONNECTIONS	
In the lefthand column, summarize your major findings/conclusions. In the righthand column, jot down how you might use your theoretical framework (or parts of it) to interpret each of them. If you are not sure, write down any connections between the finding and the theory/concept that you can think of.	
Findings/Conclusion	**Theoretical Interpretation**

Now, let's turn to how to formulate a theorization. Once again, I find it helpful to think of this task as that of making an argument. Therefore, one can construct a theorization with the same three-part structure (*claim, explanation, evidence*) as any argument. Figure 9.2, below, contextualizes the argument structure for an instance of theorization.

STRUCTURE OF A THEORIZATION	
INTRODUCE THEORY & CLAIM	Introduce the concept/theory/framework with the main gist of the theoretical interpretation (i.e., the theoretical claim)
PUT THEORY TO WORK	Provide an explanation of the theorization and why it is significant/how it contributes to new or nuanced understanding
ILLUSTRATE AND SUPPORT	Describe examples from the findings that illustrate the theorization and its significance or contribution

Figure 9.2: Sample structure of a theorization

Let's look a little deeper at the thinking behind this structure, using an example to illustrate.

Introduce the Theory and Claim: First, provide an introductory sentence or two that states the *theoretical claim*, as well as notes the theory, framework, or specific concept you are working with.

For example, in my own dissertation, I used the concept of *assemblage* (similar to a complex system) to theorize my findings. My main theoretical claim: I argued that this concept can help us understand teaching in more complex ways. When I came back to this concept while writing chapter five, it was the first time my reader had seen it since my theoretical framework, which was described in chapter two. Therefore, when I re-introduced the concept of assemblage, I also needed to remind my reader of its definition (a temporary grouping of humans, ideas, spaces, objects, and so on). Make sure to remember this for your own discussion: the first time you re-introduce a concept explained earlier in the dissertation, provide a brief reminder for your reader of what it means.

Put Theory to Work: Unpack the theoretical claim (i.e., show your reasoning) and provide adequate detail in the explanation so your reader can follow along.

Going back to the same example described above, I needed to explain further what I meant by my assemblage claim. So, I described how the concept of an assemblage helps us conceptualize the classroom as consisting of many moving parts, both human and nonhuman/material which, collectively, produce teaching. As such, this conceptual tool facilitates the analysis of teaching in ways that can account for its relational, co-constructed, and interrelated nature.

Illustrate and Support: Finally, provide summarized evidence from chapter four that illustrates the claim. Remember, at this point you are not introducing new data, you are merely referring back to evidence you have already presented and summarizing relevant pieces yourself.

To support my theorization of the classroom as an assemblage, I offered multiple examples from my teacher case studies that illustrated the relational work of teaching (for example, discussing examples showing how important teacher-student relationships are in shaping the pedagogies enacted) and described the influence of specific material elements (for instance, classroom space and time allotted for classes) on teachers' practices.

Now, let's take a closer look at a written theorization. In the excerpt below, can you identify the main theoretical claim, the explanation, and example? What kinds of scaffolds or supports for the reader do you notice?

> All three cases demonstrate the importance of attending to the *interrelational* aspects of the teaching assemblage. That is, highlighting the ways the components of a particular multiplicity interact and work together can inform our understanding of how first-year teachers construct their practice. For Mauro, June, and Bruce, some of the elements in their assemblages came into composition differently,

> resulting in developments that diverged from what might have been predicted from initial conditions. For instance, Mauro was teaching in the same school in which he spent his residency year, a condition that has been found to be supportive of first-year teaching (Hebert & Worthy, 2001; Luft & Roehrig, 2005). He was intimately familiar with his school setting, bypassing the common novice stressor of learning the norms of a new organization while starting a career (Sabar, 2004; Stanulis, Fallona, & Pearson, 2002). He also already knew his colleagues, was familiar with the general student population, and enjoyed the support of several other UTR graduates in the same school community. Despite these favorable circumstances, Mauro experienced extreme challenges with two of his ninth-grade classes. The way Mauro *interacted* with students in these two classes and the constraining contextual conditions present (e.g., large class size and mandated testing) combined to produce a teacher-centered instructional style and an authoritarian classroom persona. *(Strom, 2014, pp. 288-289)*

In the example above, my claim states that across my cases, attending to the interrelational aspects of the teaching assemblage was important. I then provide further explanation in the form of a restatement, emphasizing the significance of this theorization (it can better help us understand how first-year teachers construct their practices). I then add further explanation, highlighting the difference and unpredictability that emerged in the cases from the inter-relational aspects of teaching of teaching assemblage. In the next sentence, I launch into an illustration, describing how, despite some favorable circumstances, Mauro's pedagogy was tremendously impacted by interactions with students in his ninth-grade classes. Combined with some constraining conditions specific to that ninth-grade class, the assemblage together "produced" a style of teaching more traditional than in his other classes.

To help the reader understand my theorization, I embed several supports in the passage above. The restatement, signaled by the phrase "that is," offers the reader further detail and a second way of understanding what I mean by *interrelational* and *teaching assemblage.* I also use transitions throughout to smoothly link one sentence to another, which constructs a path to bring the reader along. These also signal to the reader the direction the sentence is going, cuing them as to what to expect: "*for instance*" (I am about to give you an illustration), "*he also*" (I'm adding on information to that example), "*despite these favorable circumstances*" (I am going to give you some information that might be different than expected). In the last line, I use the strategy of a parenthetical elaboration—I've previously discussed these constraining conditions, but the reader may not remember what they were. So, a quick reference to two of them will help jog the reader's memory and ensure that they understand my point.

Another important part of the theoretical dimension of your discussion is to explicitly point out the contribution you are making—how it helps us think differently, understand the phenomenon in more complex ways, and so on. The contribution is an important part of the "so what" of the discussion—what are you adding to the scholarly conversation on your topic?

Sometimes the contribution is added to a theorization as a conclusion to emphasize the "so what" of the interpretation. For example, I wrote the excerpt below as a conclusion to my argument regarding teaching as assemblage and the relational nature of teaching. Read the example and see if you can identify the contributions. What kind of language or sentence structures do I use to indicate that I am communicating a contribution?

> Adopting the relational view of teaching articulated above and using the connected construct of "assemblage" to discuss teaching practice is a shift away from a view of the teacher as autonomous actor or encapsulated individual that characterizes the positivist, process-product understanding of teacher development that prevails in the literature (Opfer & Pedder, 2011). From a rhizomatic perspective, the teacher is viewed as a multiplicity (a dynamic network that includes her beliefs, experiences, and personal qualities) *within* a multiplicity (a part of a larger system comprised of other actors in the school setting, features and conditions of the particular school context, educational policy mandates, among other elements). This notion might also be framed as a systems-level approach to teacher development (Bronfenbrenner, 1976; Davis & Sumara, 2006; Mason, 2008). From a systemic point of view, elements within the **teacher** herself (e.g., her beliefs, background experiences, preservice learning); the **classroom** (e.g., students, content, physical space); the **school** (e.g., school leadership, other teachers, particular school norms); and the **larger district/state/national contexts** (e.g., mandated curriculum, standardized tests, state and national standards) shape the development of teachers and teaching practice. Elements from each of these levels interact with the teacher to influence practice, thus becoming a part of the teaching-assemblage as well. Each assemblage is also an open system, continuously evolving into forms and generating productions that are new and qualitatively different. Because these influences are ongoing and constantly changing, such a rhizomatic view promotes a vibrant notion of teacher development as continuous transformation, rather than a static view of the teacher as "finished" once she completes her preservice preparation. *(Strom 2014, pp. 290-291; bold in original)*

I begin and end this example paragraph with statements of contribution. First, I state that the theorization I have just offered *differs* from what is typical according to the literature. The structure of the sentence is "[*my interpretation*] shifts away from [*status quo*]." Specifically, I am offering a systems-level understanding of teaching as a collective endeavor (the new interpretation resulting from my theorizing) rather than as something the teacher does by herself (the status quo understanding of teaching).

In the sentences that follow, I support my claim about this shift by unpacking how the conceptualization differs from "*a view of the teacher as autonomous actor or encapsulated individual that characterizes the positivist, process-product understanding of teacher development that prevails in the literature*" (i.e., the status quo). I describe how the teacher is a multiplicity that interacts with elements from other systems (e.g., classroom, school, district) to produce teaching. I end with a second contribution, which uses the following structure: "Because [*theoretical reasoning*], this theoretical perspective promotes [*new insight*] rather than [*status quo understanding*]." That is, I build on the theoretical explanation offered in the previous sentence (continuous evolution of assemblages) as a basis for arguing that this understanding helps us see teacher identity as "*continuous transformation*" (contribution), "*rather than a static view of the teacher as 'finished' once she completes her preservice preparation*" (status quo understanding).

Let's also break down some of the scaffolds in this paragraph. I use synonyms—for example, I use "*autonomous actor*" and then rephrase that as "*encapsulated individual*". This provides an additional opportunity for the reader to understand what you mean. Next, I use signaling language—"*from a rhizomatic perspective...*"—to let my reader know that I am about to share an interpretation from my theory. In the next several sentences, I use parenthetical elaborations to provide additional details or examples. For example, when I describe the teacher as a multiplicity, the reader might not know what I mean. However, if I provide more detail in parentheses (defining it as "*a dynamic network that includes her beliefs, experiences, and personal qualities*"), not only will my reader be more likely to concretely understand my point, but this move also provides further support, strengthening my interpretation.

ACTIVITY 8.1. IDENTIFYING CONTRIBUTIONS

Copy over the main gist of your theoretical interpretations from the previous activity. For each interpretation, articulate the contribution. What does this help us do or understand differently?

Theoretical Interpretation	Theoretical Contributions

ACTIVITY 8.2. PUTTING IT ALL TOGETHER
Draft one theoretical interpretation. Then, assess and edit as needed: 1) What is your claim? 2) What kind of explanation do you provide? 3) What examples from the findings do you refer back to as a way to illustrate your point? 4) What is the contribution offered by this theorization? 5) What are the supports that you have embedded for your reader?

OPTIONAL ACTIVITY: PLOTTING OUT YOUR DISCUSSION		
This organizer helps you organize your discussion into sections (each unpacking a major conclusion) and plot out the examples, connections to literature, and connections to theory (theorizations) for each. In addition, you can also think through your introduction.		
Intro	**Brief Summary of Findings ("answer" to research questions")**	
	Summary of Structure of Discussion	
Conclusion 1	**Main Conclusion**	
	Main Points to Make to Unpack this Conclusion	
	Examples to Support Conclusion	
	Connections to Literature	
	Connections to Theory	

OPTIONAL ACTIVITY: PLOTTING OUT YOUR DISCUSSION (CONT.)		
Conclusion 2	**Main Conclusion**	
	Main Points to Make to Unpack this Conclusion	
	Examples to Support Conclusion	
	Connections to Literature	
	Connections to Theory	
Conclusion 3	**Main Conclusion**	
	Main Points to Make to Unpack this Conclusion	
	Examples to Support Conclusion	
	Connections to Literature	
	Connections to Theory	

9.5 Making Recommendations

WARM UP

What groups of stakeholders are your findings relevant for? That is, who would benefit from learning about the lessons your findings provide? List as many as you can think of.

As you started your dissertation journey, you identified a problem or issue and articulated the importance and urgency of doing something about it. Then you designed a project that you argued would generate findings that could yield knowledge to help address that issue. Now, you are coming full circle, using the knowledge the study has generated to offer suggestions for specific groups to address the problem (or at least a dimension of it). This portion of chapter five is referred to as the *recommendations.*

I want to emphasize three important aspects of the recommendations section. First, the recommendations you make need *to clearly flow from your findings and/or conclusions*. All suggestions need to be traceable back to key ideas you have already discussed in chapter four and/or the previous sections of chapter five.

Second, your recommendations are *contextualized to specific groups or entities.* This means that you are speaking directly to a particular audience, such as practitioners, policymakers, leaders, community members, parents, and/or researchers (and so on); or you can address your recommendations to particular entities (e.g., school districts, teacher preparation programs, or nonprofit organizations).

Finally, the recommendations should contain *concrete and actionable* items or steps. They should make clear how the audience can translate the lesson(s) you learned from your study into action.

Let's look at an example based on a set of recommendations for teacher educators from my own research (which could also be addressed to initial teacher education programs). This recommendation flows from the finding that my study participants struggled to translate their preservice learning about inquiry-based teaching (a major focus of their teacher preparation program) into their new settings. Participants later described that they thought they spent too much time learning *about* inquiry-based learning, rather than practicing how to do it.

This finding yields two important lessons for teacher educators and/or teacher education programs:

1. Initial teacher preparation programs need to be careful to balance theoretical and methods instruction with practical application.
2. The complexity of translating teacher learning from theoretical and methods instruction into practice needs to be a central part of preservice teachers' learning experiences.

Below, I provide two sample recommendations connected to this finding. First, as you read the summaries, notice the way they are structured. How would you describe that structure? Second, examine the paragraph in terms of supports for the reader. What scaffolding strategies are used?

> Two recommendations flow from this insight. First, even before they set foot in a classroom, future teachers' learning should include analysis of the complexities of pedagogy in action. For example, teacher educators can include collaborative reading and discussions of scenarios that highlight the ways that the teaching methods they learn are enacted within settings with many barriers (or influencing elements). Second, teacher candidates not only need opportunities to practice early and often—they also need support to analyze those practices. One strategy is to create a lesson assessment protocol for teacher candidates to use after each practice opportunity that guides analysis of their translation of learning into practice. To start, they can summarize their intended activities, goals, and outcomes, followed by a guided reflection on how and why common elements may have affected their enactment of practice (e.g., themselves, student responses, or other classroom, school, and outside factors). Finally, they can reflect on their own responses to these influences and how else they might have responded in the moment.

You might have noticed that the recommendations in the example above are structured in two parts. First, I provide an *implication* based on the finding, which tends to be a general suggestion aimed at a specific audience. I find that my implications tend to take the form of a "should" statement: "Based on [specific finding], [specific audience] should..." In the second part of the recommendation structure, I describe a *concrete example* to translate that statement into action. For instance, the first suggestion I make is "*future teachers' learning should include analysis of the complexities of pedagogy in action.*" Then, I provide a specific action item with enough detail that it could be put into practice right away (group analysis/discussion of teaching scenarios that highlight the complexities of interaction that shape their practices).

I also use several different scaffolds to support the reader. I open with a topic sentence that both provides a transition ("*flows from this insight*") and contains signaling language letting the reader know that I am going to be talking about two different recommendations in this paragraph. Throughout, I also use transitions that help sequence the ideas and signal when I am moving from one idea to the next: *"First..." "Second..." "To start..."* and *"Finally"*. I also include transitions that help the reader understand my purpose for the sentence: I use *"For example"* to let them know I am going to give them a concrete action item, and "*one strategy is...*" which signals that I am providing another concrete item. I also use connectors to create a pathway for my reader from one sentence to the next: I use pronouns and synonyms (*"teacher candidates," "future teachers", "they"*) and words referring back to ideas from the previous sentence (for example, using "*these influences*" to refer back to elements that affect their practices). Finally, I also use parentheses to offer elaboration to help with understanding, such as offering examples of possible types of influences—"(*e.g., themselves, student responses, or other classroom, school, and outside factors*)".

ACTIVITY 9. PLOTTING RECOMMENDATIONS

Plot out one set of recommendations that flow from your findings for a specific stakeholder group. First, decide who the stakeholder will be. Next, add the finding/conclusion that the recommendation flows from. Then, sketch out the lesson(s) for that stakeholder group on the left, and a specific action they could take on the right.

Stakeholder Group	
Connected Finding	

Recommendation: Suggestion	Recommendation: Actionable Item

ACTIVITY 10. PUTTING IT ALL TOGETHER

Using the organizer above, move the set of recommendations into paragraph form. Once you have drafted the paragraphs, assess them for the following:

- Have you clearly labeled the stakeholder group in the heading and again in the topic sentence?
- How do you let the reader know what finding/conclusion this set of recommendations comes from?
- Does each individual recommendation in this set have a more general suggestion accompanied by a concrete, actionable item to put that suggestion into practice?
- What transitions do you use, and how do they build bridges for the reader to follow your points?
- What kinds of signaling language do you use to support your reader?
- What other scaffolds (elaborations, strategic repetition, etc.) do you use, and how do they support the reader's understanding?

9.6 Concluding the Dissertation

ACTIVITY 11. QUICK WRITE

You are standing in an elevator with a highly respected researcher from your field and introduce yourself. This scholar is very interested in learning about your study, but you only have until they get to the top floor to tell them about it!

Come up with a thirty-second soundbite highlighting the most important pieces of information from your dissertation to share.

Congratulations! We have reached the last section of the dissertation—the conclusion. The conclusion is your last opportunity to make your case about the importance of addressing the issue driving your study, highlight your study contributions, and explain how they can help address that original issue.

The following are common elements found in dissertation conclusions:

1. Summary of the project and its goals, plus any important findings you want to emphasize
2. Reiteration of the main argument regarding why we need to address the problem you posed at the beginning of your dissertation
3. Description of highlights from the findings and/or study contributions, pointing out how they can help address the problem
4. Uplifting statement or call to action

Let's look at some examples and the way they are structured around one or more of these elements. Read the excerpt below—which of the elements listed above do you see? What kind of signaling language do you notice?

In this study, I explored the way that secondary ELA teachers could use digital multimodal compositions to sustain languages and literacies of culturally diverse students. The major findings detail that when teachers engaged in a critical meaning-making process grafting concepts from research-based frameworks to disciplinary concepts, they could move within and beyond the traditional boundaries of an ELA classroom while engaging in transformative learning experiences using digital tools; and that students could agentically represent their lives. As educators and researchers continue to search for ways to disrupt the hegemonic and oppressive traditions of ELA classrooms, this study both provides a portrait of practice and a lens through which student lives can be centered and pathways to learning can be expanded. (*Dolid, 2021, pp. 340-341*)

In the excerpt above, Dolid (2021) focuses on the first two elements of the dissertation conclusion described earlier: he first summarizes what he did in his study, then moves into a high-level, interpretive summary of the findings. Rather than repeating what the key themes were from his chapter four, he focuses on what he wants the reader to take away: that the praxis-oriented process allowed teachers to adopt different, more expansive practices that better enabled students' authentic identity expressions. He ends by summarizing two of the major contributions of the study—it provides both a framework for and an in-depth example of culturally sustaining digital literacies pedagogy.

The next example is the final paragraph from Bravewomon's (2018, p. 169-170) participatory action research project in which she worked with elementary teachers to develop LGBTQ-inclusive curriculum to normalize a spectrum of sexuality and gender expressions. What elements does she use to structure this conclusion paragraph? How does this excerpt differ from Dolid's (above)?

> This study offers a window into not only the need to begin LGBTQ-inclusive instruction in elementary school, but also the feasibility to do so. The field of initial teacher credentialing programs and in-service [professional development] can offer teachers the preparation they need to build asset-based teaching practices. To do so, we need expansive and inclusive conceptual frameworks regarding sexual orientation and gender identity/expression for LGBTQ and non-LGBTQ students alike, such as the one offered in this chapter. This model of LGBTQ-inclusive leadership and teaching, a model for increasing LGBTQ-inclusive instruction enacted throughout a school culture, offers the promise of supporting pro-social behavior of all students in K-12 schools. Additionally, while a continued focus on LGBTQ youth in schools must be maintained, this model of an LGBTQ-inclusive leadership and teaching can also address needs of other student groups that are likely vulnerable to LGBTQ-targeted bullying, harassment, and invisibility. These include children of LGBTQ parents and guardians and non-LGBTQ youth targeted in bullying behavior for being perceived as LGBTQ. Given the comprehensive reporting of LGBTQ students' experience in K-12 schools and the growing body of research pointing to the need to understand how school culture can either sustain or interrupt social forces that create unsafe school conditions regarding sexual orientation and gender identity and expression, the use of frameworks such as the LGBTQ-inclusive leadership and teaching model offered here may help empower our teaching force to engage in effective practices that transform the daily experience of all students in K-12 schools.

Bravewomon begins this conclusion by reiterating her argument and stating that her study illustrates both need and feasibility for LGBTQ-inclusive curriculum. She then emphasizes and extends the feasibility claim, arguing that this work is something that teacher preparation programs and professional development initiatives *can do.* The researcher then restates a major contribution of her study (a framework for LGBTQ-inclusive pedagogy and leadership) and reiterates how this framework can help address the issue driving her study (bullying and lack of positive identity development experiences for LGBTQ youth). Finally, she ends with a hopeful statement, outlining the potential of such a model for empowering teachers to "*transform the daily experience of all students in K-12 schools*".

ACTIVITY 12. CONCLUSION TEXT GENERATION	
Think through the following prompts for your conclusion and bullet out your thoughts.	
Summarize your project and its goals.	
Are there any particularly powerful findings you want to emphasize?	
Restate your argument about the need to solve the problem you originally posed.	
List the most important contributions of the paper and how they will help mediate the problem.	
How does your study provide hope for the future? Or, what uplifting thought could you leave your reader with?	

ACTIVITY 13. PUTTING IT ALL TOGETHER
Using both activities from this section, write a draft of your conclusion. Once you have done so, go back and evaluate it for your use of the conclusion elements outlined above as well as the scaffolding strategies you are using to bring your reader across the finish line with you.

9.7 Updating Your Abstract

But wait! You aren't *quite* done yet. You need to update your abstract to reflect your study outcomes and contributions!

This part is easy. Just go back to your abstract and:

1. Check to make sure that your original abstract, up to your methods, accurately reflects what you actually did.
2. Add a summary of the key findings—just one sentence for each!
3. Close with what you see as the major contribution(s) of your project.

Conclusion

Congratulations—you have reached the end (of this book—but hopefully also can see the light at the end of the tunnel in your own dissertation process, too)!

In this chapter, we worked through the final part of your dissertation, the discussion chapter, which has two parts—the discussion (why your findings are significant) and the recommendations (what we should do with those findings). We learned about the following key ideas:

1. Your discussion should offer ***conclusions based on your findings***. Each conclusion should describe the significance of your findings beyond just the participants in your study (in other words, what the findings mean in relation to broader contexts and issues). Conclusions should not just repeat the themes of your findings—they should offer a broader interpretation of them and explain why they are important.
2. Your conclusions should also include discussion of your ***findings in relation to existing research***, showing how they support, contradict, expand, and/or complexify that literature. These connections help illuminate your study's empirical contribution.
3. Your discussion also should offer a ***theorization of your findings***, or an interpretation of your findings and conclusions through your theoretical/conceptual framework and/or specific related concepts. Point out what these theorizations add to our understanding about your topic and how they help us think differently as part of showing your theoretical contribution.
4. The second part of the discussion chapter is the ***recommendations***, which uses the knowledge the study has generated to offer suggestions to address the problem (or at least a dimension of it). The recommendations need to clearly flow from your findings, be contextualized to specific groups or entities, and contain concrete and actionable items or steps.
5. Finally, the ***dissertation conclusion*** offers a summary of the project and its goals. In addition, you can reinforce the main argument regarding the problem that originally drive your study; highlight important findings and/or study contributions that can help address that overall problem; and/or add a hopeful concluding thought or call to action.

A Beginning Note

I begin this note with several hopes:

I hope that this book has felt supportive to you.

I hope it has provided clarity about what doctoral level writing looks like and the major rules by which it operates.

I hope you took away the message that the doctoral writing process I present in this book is just one very pragmatic approach—that there are infinite possibilities, and none of them are "right" except the ones that work for you, with your specific worldviews, frameworks, research goals, and methodologies.

I hope that it provided opportunities to develop your voice—and confidence—as a writer.

I hope it helped you grow your writing practice, and offered some strategies and tools that will continue to support your scholarship in the years to come.

I purposely titled this note "A beginning." Often, my students view their dissertation as *the end*, because it is the culminating project of their doctoral studies. However, I invite you to consider your dissertation not as the last thing you do, but as the first—not the end, but the beginning of many years of continual growth as a writer and researcher.

Given that likelihood, try to keep a pragmatic frame of mind when it comes to your study. Know that most of the time, perfection is not possible. It's also not the point of this process. The point is to show that you have the know-how to carry out a trustworthy study and communicate about it effectively. For one, you may not be able to include everything you would like to in your dissertation. Sometimes you must make the decision to create a boundary—for time's sake, or perhaps at the request of your committee. But again, because this is just the *first* big research project you do, you can use any excluded ideas or material in any related writing in the future. Personally, there were several things that I wanted to include in my dissertation that I had to leave out—for example, I wanted to analyze my data with other theories, but I desperately needed to finish. So, I wrote down my ideas in a clearly labeled memo. Then I put those together with excess materials (like a set of interview transcript found poems I co-constructed with my participants that was nixed by my committee) and stored them in a folder for future projects. And, over the past several years, I have used these ideas and materials in other publications as well as in my courses as teaching tools.

So, rather than aiming for a perfectly polished product that contains *all the things*, work with your chair to determine when you've reached the point where you have achieved the criteria of a rigorous, trustworthy study that is effectively communicated. Because, to invoke that oft-repeated doctoral axiom, "the best dissertation is a done dissertation." And you have so many more things to do.

Finally, this book emerges from an alternative vision of academia as a place where affirmative support (rather than sink-or-swim approaches and nonconstructive critique) is the norm. It is a vision that is forward-looking and proleptic (a concept from Lev Vygotsky that entails believing that your students will be successful because they are capable and you will provide effective and appropriate supports—and communicating that explicitly to your students).

When I set out to write this book, I knew that many would dismiss it as "hand-holding" that could compromise students' ability to grow into an self-sufficient or independent thinker-researcher. But I propose we need to think carefully about that. If we understand that learning is relational, and knowledge is a product jointly constructed through dialogue and activity, then being a self-sufficient-scholar-independent-thinker contradicts what we know about learning (which is ultimately the point of a doctoral degree). Beyond being an outdated concept, it is also harmful to students from minoritized groups: as I explained way back in the first chapter of this book, expecting students to figure things out on their own (whether we are talking about writing or any other doctoral level practice) reproduces inequities. That's because those things they are figuring out were established by white, affluent men, and therefore will reflect and value Eurocentric, heteropatriarchal ways of knowing and being. It's just another version of the "pull yourself up by your own bootstraps" ideology that refuses to acknowledge that power relations exist, much less shape every facet of our daily existence—including (and maybe especially) what we do in our doctoral programs.

However, there *is* an alternative. We can understand that language isn't neutral—it's a mechanism of power. That the language we use in academia is not better or correct—it is imposed by the dominant culture. That without providing explicit support to learn doctoral level language use, we are complicit in reproducing inequitable patterns in the university and beyond. That there are highly supportive *and* highly rigorous strategies to provide that support (i.e., scaffolding). And, at the same time, we can continue to reinforce that there are many legitimate forms of language use—this is only one genre—and we can find creative ways to hybridize it.

I hope that you will carry forth the ethos of this book—relationality, explicit naming of the rules, and finding your own unique hybrid of what works for you—through the rest of your doctoral journey and into your professional or academic career (or wherever life leads you). I leave you with a found poem (originally published in Strom & Mills 2021) constructed from my favorite living theorist, Rosi Braidotti (2020), on the necessity of support and collaboration to survive academia:

Function in a group,
Function in a pack,
Function in a herd.
Run with the she-wolves.
Do not imagine
For a minute
You can take on
This system alone.

References

Acheson, K. & Gall, M. (1992). *Techniques in the clinical supervision of teachers (3rd ed.)*. Longman.

Adler, P.A., & Adler, P. (1998). *Membership roles in field research.* Sage.

Allebone, B. (2006). Who should I put in a circle group? Influences on the practice of beginning teachers: A small study. *Education 3-13, 34*(2), 131-141.

Allen, J. (2009). Valuing practice over theory: How beginning teachers reorient their practice in the transition from university to workplace. *Teaching & Teacher Education, 25*(5), 647-654.

Altheide, D., &Johnson, D. (2011). Reflections on interpretive adequacy in qualitative research. In N. Denzin & Y. Lincoln (Eds.), *The Sage handbook of qualitative research, 4th ed.* (pp. 581-594). Sage.

Anderson, G. L., Herr, K., & Nihlen, A. S. (Eds.). (2007). *Studying your own school: An educator's guide to practitioner action research.* Corwin Press.

Ansari, S. (2021). *Closing opportunity gaps for multilingual students through science professional development: How teachers translate learning into practice, and the ways ML students respond* (Doctoral dissertation, California State University, East Bay).

Bang, M., Warren, B., Rosebery, A. S., & Medin, D. (2012). Desettling expectations in science education. *Human Development, 55*(5-6), 302-318.

Barad, K. (2007). *Meeting the universe halfway.* Duke University Press.

Battram, A. (1998). *Navigating complexity.* The Industrial Society.

Beck, C., Kosnik, C., & Roswell, J. (2007). Preparation for the first year of teaching: Beginning teachers' views about their needs. *The New Educator, 3,* 51-73.

Bennett, J. (2009). *Vibrant matter: A political ecology of things.* Duke University Press.

Bergeron, B. (2008). Enacting a culturally responsive curriculum in a novice teacher's classroom: Encountering disequilibrium. *Urban Education, 43*(4), 4-28.

Bianchini, J., & Cazavos, L. (2007). Learning from students, inquiry into practice, and participation in professional communities: Beginning teachers' uneven progress toward equitable science teaching. *Journal of Research in Science Teaching, 44*(4), 586-612.

Birrell, J. (1995). Learning how the game is played: A beginning teacher's struggle to prepare black youth for a white world. *Teaching and Teacher Education, 11*(2), 137-147.

Bogdan, R.C., & Biklen, S.K. (1998). *Qualitative research for education: An introduction to theory and methods.* Ally & Bacon.

Bourdieu, P. (1973). *Knowledge, education, and cultural change.* Harper & Row Publishers.

Bowles, S. N. (2001). Deconstructing disability and (special) education: A rhizoanalysis. (Doctoral dissertation, University of Georgia, Athens).

Braidotti, R. (1994). *Nomadic subjects: Embodiment and sexual difference in contemporary feminist theory.* Columbia University Press.

Braidotti, R. (2013). *The posthuman.* Polity Press.

Braidotti, R. (2019). *Posthuman knowledge.* Polity Press.

Brashier, A., & Norris, E. (2008). Breaking down barriers for first year teachers: What teacher education preparation programs can do. *Journal of Early Childhood Teacher Education, 29*(1), 30-44.

Bravewomon, L. (2018). *It takes a team: A framework for LGBTQ-inclusive leadership and teaching* (Doctoral dissertation, California State University, East Bay).

Braun, V., & Clarke, V. (2006). Using thematic analysis in psychology. *Qualitative Research in Psychology, 3*(2), 77-101.

Britzman, D. (1991). *Practice makes practice: A critical study of learning to teach.* State University of New York Press.

Bronfenbrenner, U. (1976). The experimental ecology of education. *Educational Researcher, 5*(9), 5-15.

Butz, M.R. (1997). *Chaos and complexity: Implications for psychological theory and practice.* Taylor & Francis.

Byrne, D. (1998). *Complexity theory and the social sciences.* NY: Routledge.

Carver-Thomas, D., & Darling-Hammond, L. (2017). *Teacher turnover: Why it matters and what we can do about it.* Learning Policy Institute.

Castro, A., Kelly, J., & Shih, M. (2010). Resilience strategies for new teachers in high-needs areas. *Teaching and Teacher Education,* 26(1), 622-629.

Center for Research on Educational Outcomes (CREDO). (2009). *Multiple choice: Charter performance in 16 states.* Retrieved July 11, 2012 from https://credo.stanford.edu.

Center on Education Policy (CEP) (2006). *Ten big effects of the No Child Left Behind Act on public schools.* Retrieved on July 11, 2012 from http://www.cep-dc.org/.

Charmaz, K. (2006). *Constructing grounded theory: A practical guide yhrough qualitative analysis.* Sage.

Chirichello, M. (2010). The principal as educational leader: What makes the difference. *School Leadership-International Perspectives,* 79-100.

Chubbock, S. (2008). A novice teacher's beliefs about socially just teaching: Dialogue of many voices. *The New Educator, 4,* 309-329.

Chubbock, S., Clift, R., Allard, J., & Quinlan, J. (2001). Playing it safe as a novice teacher: Implications for programs for new teachers. *Journal of Teacher Education, 52*(5), 365-376.

Cilliers, P. (1998). *Complexity and postmodernism: Understanding complex systems.* Routledge.

Civil Rights Project. (2010). *Choice without equity: Charter school segregation and the need for civil rights standards.* Retrieved July 11, 2012 from http://civilrightsproject.ucla.edu/research/k-12-education/integration-and-diversity/choice-without-equity-2009-report/.

Clarke, A., & Collins, S. (2007). Complexity science and student teacher supervision. *Teaching and Teacher Education, 23,* 160–172.

Clarke, A. (2003). Situational analyses: Grounded theory mapping after the postmodern turn. *Symbolic Interaction, 26*(4), 553-576.

Cochran-Smith, M., & Zeichner, K. M. (Eds.). (2005). *Studying teacher education: The report of the AERA panel on research and teacher education.* Routledge.

Cochran-Smith, M., Ell, F., Ludlow, L., Grudnoff, L., & Aitken, G. (2014). The challenge and promise of complexity theory for teacher education research. *Teachers College Record, 116*(4), 1-38.

Coffey, H., & Farinde-Wu, A. (2016). Navigating the journey to culturally responsive teaching: Lessons from the success and struggles of one first-year, Black female teacher of Black students in an urban school. *Teaching and Teacher Education, 60,* 24-33.

Combahee River Collective. (1977). Combahee River Collective Statement. Retrieved July 24, 2024 from https://americanstudies.yale.edu/sites/default/files/files/Keyword%20Coalition_Readings.pdf

Crenshaw, K. (1989). Demarginalizing the intersection of race and sex: A Black feminist critique of antidiscrimination doctrine, feminist theory and antiracist politics. In *University of Chicago Legal Forum,* 1, 141-167.

Crenshaw-Mayo, C. A. (2020). *Let us breathe: White supremacist education and the experiences of Black males in community college* (Doctoral Dissertation, California State University, East Bay).

Damon, W. (2007). Dispositions and teacher assessment: The need for a more rigorous definition. *Journal of Teacher Education, 58*(5), 365-369.

Darling-Hammond, L. (2010). *The flat world and education: How America's commitment to equity will determine our future.* Teachers College Press.

Davis, B., & Sumara, D. (1997). Cognition, complexity, and teacher education. *Harvard Educational Review, 67*(1), 105-126.

Davis, B., & Sumara, D. (2006). *Complexity and education: Inquiries into learning, teaching and research.* Lawrence Erlbaum.

Davis, A. (1972). Reflections on the Black woman's role in the community of slaves. *The Massachusetts Review, 13*(1/2), 81-100.

DeFreitas, E. (2012). Classroom as rhizome: New strategies for diagramming knotted interactions. *Qualitative Inquiry, 18*(7), 557-570.

Deleuze, G., & Guattari, F. (1987). *Capitalism and schizophrenia: A thousand plateaus.* University of Minnesota Press.

Delpit, L. D. (1988). The silenced dialogue: Power and pedagogy in educating other people's children. *Harvard Educational Review, 58,* 280–298.

Delpit, L. (2006). *Other people's children: Cultural conflict in the classroom.* New Press.

Denzin, N. K., & Lincoln, Y. S. (1995). Transforming qualitative research methods: Is it a revolution?. *Journal of Contemporary Ethnography, 24*(3), 349-358.

Denzin, K. & Lincoln, Y.S. (2005). *The Sage handbook of qualitative research, 3rd Ed.* Sage.

Derewianka, B. (2012). Knowledge about language in the Australian curriculum: English. *The Australian Journal of Language and Literacy, 35*(2), 127-146.

Dolid, A. (2021). *Extensions of ourselves: Toward liberatory practices with digital technologies in literacy classrooms* (Doctoral dissertation, California State University, East Bay).

Ellingson, L. (2009). *Engaging in crystallization in qualitative research: An introduction.* Sage.

Ellsworth, E. (1989). Why doesn't this feel empowering? Working through repressive myths of critical pedagogy. *Harvard Educational Review, 59*(3), 297-324.

Emerson, R. M., Fretz, R. I., & Shaw, L. L. (1995). *Writing ethnographic fieldnotes.* The University of Chicago Press.

Esparo, L. J., & Rader, R. (2001). The leadership crisis: The shortage of qualified superintendents is not going away. *American School Board Journal, 188*(5), 46-48.

Fantilli, R., & McDougal, D. (2009). A study of novice teachers: Challenges and supports in the first years. *Teaching and Teacher Education, 25*(4), 814-825.

Feiman-Nemser, S., & Buchmann, M. (1989). Describing teacher education: A framework and illustrative findings from a longitudinal study of six students. *The Elementary School Journal, 89*(3), 365-377.

Ferguson-Patrick, K. (2011). Professional development of early career teachers: A pedagogical focus on collaborative learning. *Issues in Education, 21*(2), 109-129.

Foucault, M. (1976). *Discipline and punish: The birth of the prison.* Random House.

Freire, P. (1970). *Pedagogy of the oppressed.* Continuum.

Fry, S. (2007). First-year teachers and induction support: Ups, downs, and in-betweens. *The Qualitative Report, 12*(2), 216-237.

Giroux, H. A. (1992). Language, difference, and curriculum theory: Beyond the politics of clarity. *Theory into Practice, 31*(3), 219-227.

Giroux, H.A. (2009). Critical theory and educational practice. In A. Darder, M. Torres, & R. Baltodano, (eds.), *The critical pedagogy reader* (2nd ed) (pp. 364-383). Routledge.

Giroux, H. A., & Penna, A. N. (1979). Social education in the classroom: The dynamics of the hidden curriculum. *Theory & Research in Social Education, 7*(1), 21-42.

Glaser, B. & Strauss, A. (1967). *The discovery of grounded theory: Strategies for qualitative research.* Transaction.

Grossman, P., & Thompson, C. (2008). Learning from curriculum materials: Scaffolds for new teachers?. *Teaching and Teacher Education, 24*(8), 2014-2026.

Halford, J. (1998). Easing the way for new teachers. *Educational Leadership, 55*(5), 33-36.

Halliday, M.A.K. & Hasan, R. (1985). *Language, context, and text: Aspects of language in social-semiotic perspective.* Oxford University Press.

Haraway, D. J. (2004). *The Haraway reader.* Psychology Press.

Haraway, D. (1988). Situated knowledges: The science question in feminism and the privilege of partial perspective. *Feminist studies, 14*(3), 575-599.

Harding, S. (1980). The norms of social inquiry and masculine experience. In *PSA: Proceedings of the Biennial Meeting of the Philosophy of Science Association* (pp. 305-324). Cambridge University Press.

Hargreaves, A. & Jacka, N. (1995). Induction or seduction? Postmodern patterns of preparing to teach. *Peabody Journal of Education, 70*(3), 41-63.

He, Y. & Cooper, J. (2011). Struggles and strategies in teaching: Voices of five novice secondary teachers. *Teacher Education Quarterly, 38*(2), 97-116.

Hebert, E., & Worthy, T. (2001). Does the first year of teaching have to be a bad one? A case study of success. *Teaching and Teacher Education, 17*(8), 897-911.

Huberman, M. (1989). The professional life cycle of teachers. *Teacher's College Record, 91*(1), 31-81.

Ingersoll, R. (2003). Is there really a teacher shortage? *Consortium for Policy Research in Education (CPRE).* Retrieved on 6/13/2024 from https://www.education.uw.edu/ctp/sites/default/files/ctpmail/PDFs/Shortage-RI-09-2003.pdf.

Johnson, E. (2008). Ecological systems and complexity theory: Toward an alternative model of accountability in education. *Complicity, 5*(1), 1-10.

Karp, S. (2012). Challenging corporate reform, and ten hopeful signs of resistance. Retrieved 6/11/2024 from http://www.rethinkingschools.org.

Kayumova, S., & Strom, K. (2023, February 22). Ontology, epistemology, and critical theory in STEM education. *Oxford Research Encyclopedia of Education.* Retrieved 6/14/2024, from https://oxfordre.com/education/view/10.1093/acrefore/9780190264093.001.0001/acrefore-9780190264093-e-1508.

King, T. L. (2017). Humans involved: Lurking in the lines of posthumanist flight. *Critical Ethnic Studies, 3*(1), 162-185.

Ladson-Billings, G. (1999). Preparing teachers for diverse student populations: A critical race perspective. In A. Iran-Nejad & C. D. Pearson (Eds.), *Review of research in education* (pp. 211-248). American Educational Research Association.

Ladson-Billings, G. (2006). From the achievement gap to the education debt: Understanding achievement in US schools. *Educational Researcher, 35*(7), 3-12.

Lambson, D. (2010). Novice teachers learning through participation in a teacher study group. *Teaching and Teacher Education,* 26(8), 1660-1668.

Lather, P. (1986). Issues of validity in openly ideological research: Between a rock and a soft place. *Interchange, 17,* 63-84.

Lather, P. (1993). Fertile obsession: Validity after poststructuralism. *Sociological Quarterly, 34*(4), 673-693.

Lather, P. (1992). Critical frames in educational research: Feminist and poststructural perspectives. *Theory into Practice, 31*(2), 87-99.

Leavy, P. (2014). Introduction. In P. Leavy (Ed.), *The Oxford handbook of qualitative research* (pp. 1–14). Oxford University Press.

Leavy, P. (2017). *Research design: Quantitative, qualitative, mixed methods, arts-based, and community-based participatory research approaches.* Guilford.

Lillis, T., & Tuck, J. (2016). Academic literacies: A critical lens on writing and reading in the academy. In K. Hyland (Ed.), *The Routledge handbook of English for academic purposes* (pp. 30-43). Routledge.

Lincoln, Y.S. & Guba, E. (1985). *Naturalistic inquiry.* Sage.

Lucas, T. T., & Villegas, A. M. (2010). A framework for preparing linguistically responsive teachers. In T. Lucas, *Teacher preparation for linguistically diverse classrooms* (pp. 75-92). Routledge.

Luft, J., & Roehrig, G. (2005). Enthusiasm is not enough: Beginning secondary science teachers in primarily Hispanic settings. *School Science & Mathematics, 105*(3), 116-127.

Malone, B. G., & Caddell, T. A. (2000). A crisis in leadership: Where are tomorrow's principals?. *The Clearing House, 73*(3), 162-164.

Mason, M. (2008). Complexity theory and the philosophy of education. In M. Mason (Ed.), *Complexity theory and the philosophy of education* (pp. 46–61). Wiley-Blackwell.

Maxcy, S. J. (2002). *Ethical school leadership.* Rowman & Littlefield.

McDonald, M. A. (2005). The integration of social justice in teacher education dimensions of prospective teachers' opportunities to learn. *Journal of Teacher Education, 56*(5), 418-435.

McLaren, P. (2009). Critical pedagogy: A look at major concepts. In A. Darder, M. Torres, & R. Baltodano, (Eds.), *The critical pedagogy reader, 2nd ed* (pp. 61-83). Routledge.

Medin, D. L., & Bang, M. (2014). *Who's asking?: Native science, western science, and science education.* MIT Press.

Merriam, S. (1998). *Qualitative research and case study applications in education.* Jossey-Bass.

Merriam S. (2009). *Qualitative research: A guide to design and implementation* (3rd ed.). Jossey-Bass.

Miles, M. & Huberman, A. (1994). *Qualitative data analysis: An expanded sourcebook* (2nd ed.). Sage.

Morrison, K. (2008). Educational philosophy and the challenge of complexity theory. In M. Mason (Ed.), *Complexity theory and the philosophy of education* (pp. 46–61). Wiley-Blackwell.

National Council for Accreditation of Teacher Educators (NCATE). (2001). Standards for professional development schools. Retrieved on 6/12/2024 from http:www.ncate.org/documents/pdsstandards.pdf

National Center for Educational Statistics (2020). Characteristics of public and private elementary and secondary school teachers in the United States. Retrieved on 6/12/2024 from https://nces.ed.gov/pubs2020/2020142.pdf

National Center for Educational Statistics (2021). Racial/ethnic enrollment in public schools. Retrieved on 6/12/24 from https://nces.ed.gov/programs/coe/pdf/2021/cge_508c.pdf.

National Center for Educational Statistics (2019). Status and trends in the in the education of racial and ethnic groups 2018. Retrieved on 6/12/24 from https://nces.ed.gov/pubs2019/2019038.pdf.

Newman, E. (2010). 'I'm being measured as an NQT, that isn't who I am': An exploration of the experiences of career changer primary teachers in their first year of teaching. *Teachers and Teaching: Theory and Practice, 16*(4), 461-475.

Nguyễn, D. K. (2021). *Navigating cultures and myths: Case studies of Asian adolescent mental health* (Doctoral dissertation, California State University, East Bay).

Opfer, V., & Pedder, D. (2011). Conceptualizing teacher professional learning. *Review of Educational Research, 81*(3), 376-407.

Peugnet-Alan, T. (2018). *Examining coaching as a support for teacher professional learning and agency* (Doctoral dissertation, California State University, East Bay).

Piaget, J. (1952). *The origins of intelligence in children*. Norton.

Ravitch, D. (2010). *The life and death of the great American school system: How testing and school choice are undermining education*. Basic Books.

Reese, M. (2023). *To the heart of it: Relationships between white teachers and black students* (Doctoral dissertation, California State University, East Bay).

Richardson, A. (2019). *Illuminating student voices: The role of faculty and staff in retention and graduation* (Doctoral dissertation, California State University, East Bay).

Richardson, K. A., Cilliers, P., & Lissack, M. (2001). Complexity science: A "gray" science for the "stuff in between". *Emergence, 3*(2), 6–18.

Richardson, L. (1994). Writing: A method of inquiry. In N. Denzin & Y. Lincoln (Eds.), *Handbook of qualitative research* (pp. 516-529). Sage.

Rogoff, B. (1994). Developing understanding of the idea of communities of learners. *Mind, Culture, and Activity, 1*(4), 209-229.

Roulston, K. (2010). *Reflective interviewing: A guide to theory and practice*. Sage.

Sabar, N. (2004). From heaven to reality through crisis: Novice teachers as migrants. *Teaching and Teacher Education,* 20(1), 145-161.

Saka, y., Southerland, S., Brooks, J. (2009). Becoming a member of a school community while working toward science education reform: Teacher induction from a cultural historical activity theory (CHAT) perspective. *Science Education, 93*(6), 996-1025.

Saldaña, J. (2011). *Fundamentals of qualitative research*. Oxford University Press.

Saldaña, J. (2013). *The coding manual for qualitative researchers*. Sage.

Scherff, L. (2008). Disavowed: The stories of two novice teachers. *Teaching and Teacher Education,* 24(5), 1317-1332.

SchlaeGuada, B. (2022). *White & queer "holding up the mirror": Investigating the intersection of educator identities & impacts on critical antiracist pedagogical understandings, knowledge, and perceived practices* (Doctoral dissertation, California State University, East Bay).

Simon, N., & Johnson, S. M. (2015). Teacher turnover in high-poverty schools: What we know and can do. *Teachers College Record, 117*(3), 1-36.

Shields, C. M. (2010). Transformative leadership: Working for equity in diverse contexts. *Educational Administration Quarterly, 46*(4), 558-589.

Sleeter, C. (2008). Equity, democracy, and neoliberal assaults on teacher education. *Teaching and Teacher Education,* 54 (8), 1947-1957.

Smagorinsky, P., Gibson, N., Bickmore, S. T., Moore, C. P., & Cook, L. S. (2004). Praxis shock: Making the transition from a student-centered university program to the corporate climate of schools. *English Education, 36*(3), 214-245.

Solorzano, D. G., & Bernal, D. D. (2001). Examining transformational resistance through a critical race and LatCrit theory framework: Chicana and Chicano students in an urban context. *Urban Education, 36*(3), 308-342.

St. Pierre, Elizabeth Adams. (2011). Post-qualitatitive research: The critique and the coming after. In N. K. Denzin & Y. S. Lincoln (Eds.), *The Sage handbook of qualitative research* (4th ed., pp. 611-625). Sage.

St. Pierre, E. (2000). Poststructural feminism in education: An overview. *Qualitative Studies in Education, 13*(5), 477-515.

St. Pierre, E. (2004). Deleuzian concepts for education: The subject undone. *Educational Philosophy & Theory, 36*(3), 283-296.

Stake, R. (1995). *The art of case study research.* Sage.

Stanulis, R.A., Fallona, C.A., & Pearson, C.A. (2002). 'Am I doing what I am supposed to be doing?': mentoring novice teachers through the uncertainties and challenges of their first year of teaching. *Mentoring & Tutoring,* 10(1), 71-81.

Starkey, L. (2010). Supporting the digitally able beginning teacher. *Teaching and Teacher Education, 26* (7), 1429-1438.

Strom, K. J. (2014). *Becoming-teacher: The negotiation of teaching practice of first-year secondary science teachers prepared in a hybrid urban teacher education program* (Doctoral Dissertation, Montclair State University).

Strom, K. J. (2015). Teaching as assemblage: Negotiating learning and practice in the first year of teaching. *Journal of Teacher Education, 66*(4), 321-333.

Strom, K., Margolis, J., & Polat, N. (2019). Teacher professional dispositions: Much assemblage required. *Teachers College Record,* 121(11).

Strom, K., & Martin, A. (2017). *Becoming-teacher: A rhizomatic look at first-year teaching.* Sense.

Strom, K. & Martin, A. (2022). Toward a critical posthuman understanding of teacher development. *Teaching and Teacher Education.* Retrieved on 6/14/2024 from https://www.sciencedirect.com/science/article/pii/S0742051X22000592.

Strom, K., Martin, A., & Villegas, A. M. (2018). Clinging to the edge of chaos: The emergence of novice teacher practice. *Teachers College Record, 120*(7), 1-32.

Strom, K., Mills, T. & Abrams, L. (2021). Illuminating a continuum of complex perspectives in teacher development. *Professional Development in Education, 47*(2-3), 199-208.

Strom, K. & Viesca, K. (2021). Toward a complex conceptualization of teacher learning-practice. *Professional Development in Education, 47*(2-3), 209-224.

Tait, M. (2008). Resilience as a contributor to novice teacher success, commitment, and retention. *Teacher Education Quarterly, 35*(4), 57-75.

Tharp, R. G., & Gallimore, R. (1991). *Rousing minds to life: Teaching, learning, and schooling in social context.* Cambridge University Press.

Toulmin, S. E. (1958). *The uses of argument.* Cambridge University Press.

Towers, J. (2010). Learning to teach mathematics through inquiry: A focus on the relationship between describing and enacting inquiry-oriented teaching. *Journal of Mathematics Education, 13*(3), 243-263.

Tracy, S. J. (2010). Qualitative quality: Eight “big-tent” criteria for excellent qualitative research. *Qualitative inquiry, 16*(10), 837-851.

University of Manchester. (2023). AcademicPhrasebank. Retrieved 6/12/24 from https://www.phrasebank.manchester.ac.uk/.

Valencia, S., Martin, S., Place, N., & Grossman, P. (2009). Complex interactions in student teaching: Lost opportunities for learning. *Journal of Teacher Education, 60,* 304–322.

Van Langenhove, L., and Harré, R. (1999). Introducing positioning theory. In L. Van Langenhove and R. Harré (Eds.), *Positioning theory: Moral contexts of intentional action* (pp. 14-31). Blackwell.

Van Lier, L. (2004). *The ecology and semiotics of language learning.* Kluwer Academics.

Veenman, S. (1984). Perceived problems of beginning teachers. *Review of Educational Research, 54*(2), 143-178.

Villegas, A. M. (2007). Dispositions in teacher education: A look at social justice. *Journal of Teacher Education*, 58(5), 370-380.

Villegas, A. M., & Irvine, J. J. (2010). Diversifying the teaching force: An examination of major arguments. *The Urban Review, 42,* 175-192.

Villegas, A. M., Strom, K., & Lucas, T. (2012). Closing the racial/ethnic gap between students of color and their teachers: An elusive goal. *Equity & Excellence in Education, 45*(2), 283-301.

Vossoughi, S., & Gutiérrez, K. D. (2016). Critical pedagogy and sociocultural theory. In I. Inmonde & A. Booker (Eds.), *Power and privilege in the learning sciences* (pp. 157-179). Routledge.

Vygotsky, L.S. (1978). *Mind in society: The development of higher psychological processes.* Harvard University Press.

Waldrop, M. M. (1993). *Complexity: The emerging science at the edge of order and chaos.* Simon and Schuster.

Waterhouse, M. (2011). *Experiences of multiple literacies and peace: A rhizoanalysis of becoming in immigrant language classrooms* (Doctoral Dissertation, University of Ottawa).

Wideen, M., Mayer-Smith, J., & Moon, B. (1998). A critical analysis of the research on learning to teach: Making the case for an ecological perspective on inquiry. *Review of Educational Research, 68*(2), 130-178.

Wood, D., Bruner, J. S., & Ross, G. (1976). The role of tutoring in problem solving. *Journal of Child Psychology and Psychiatry, 17*(2), 89-100.

Zeichner, K. (2010). Rethinking the connections between campus courses and field experiences in college- and university-based teacher education. *Journal of Teacher Education, 61*(2), 89-99.

Zeichner, K. M., & Tabachnick, B. R. (1981). Are the effects of university teacher education 'washed out' by school experience?. *Journal of Teacher Education, 32*(3), 7-11.

-